London School of Economics
Monographs on Social Anthropology

Managing Editor: Peter Loizos

The Monographs on Social Anthropology were
established in 1940 and aim to publish results of
modern anthropological research of primary interest
to specialists.

The continuation of the series was made possible by
a grant in aid from the Wenner-Gren Foundation for
Anthropological Research, and more recently by a
further grant from the Governors of the London
School of Economics and Political Science. Income
from sales is returned to a revolving fund to assist
further publications.

The Monographs are under the direction of an
Editorial Board associated with the Department of
Anthropology of the London School of Economics
and Political Science.

London School of Economics
Monographs on Social Anthropology
No 64

Martin J D Hill

The Harambee Movement in Kenya:
Self-Help, Development and Education
among the Kamba of Kitui District

THE ATHLONE PRESS
London & Atlantic Highlands, NJ

First published 1991 by The Athlone Press Ltd
1 Park Drive, London NW11 7SG and
171 First Avenue, Atlantic Highlands, NJ 07716
© Martin J.D. Hill 1991

British Library Cataloguing in Publication Data
Hill, Martin J.D.
    The Harambee Movement in Kenya: self-help, development
    and education among the Kamba of Kitui district. – (LSE
    monographs on social anthropology, no. 64).
    1. Kenya. Akamba
    I. Title II. Series
    967.62
    ISBN 0-485-19564-X

Library of Congress Cataloging-in-Publication Data
    The Harambee movement in Kenya: self-help, development
    and education among the Kamba of Kitui district/Martin J.D.
    Hill.
    p.cm. – (Monographs on social anthropology; no. 64)
    Includes bibliographical references and index.
    ISBN 0-485-19564-X
    1. Community development – Kenya – Kitui (District)
    2. Kamba (African people) – Social conditions.
    I. Hill, Martin, J.D.
    II. Series.
    HN793.K58H37 1991
    307.1'4'0967624 – dc20

Typeset by Bookman Ltd, Bristol
Printed in Great Britain at the University Press, Cambridge

Contents

Preface

This is a study of the social organization of the 'Harambee' self-help movement in Kenya in the early 1970s, focusing on the Kamba (or Akamba) people of Kitui district in eastern Kenya. As a case study in the anthropology of development, it covers a wider field than has been conventional in social anthropology, but the collection and presentation of ethnographic data have been restricted to the main theme of the study. It is hoped that this approach will provide new insights into the Harambee movement in Kenya and also make a useful contribution to the ethnographic and historical study of Kitui Kamba culture and society.

Research was based on extended fieldwork in Kitui during 1973–4 while I was a postgraduate student in the Department of Anthropology at the London School of Economics. During seventeen months' fieldwork, I lived mostly in a village in Kitui. I was affiliated to the University of Nairobi as a research student in the Bureau of Educational Research of the Faculty of Education, which was later relocated at Kenyatta University. My subsequent work since 1976 for an international non-governmental organization did not give me the opportunity to visit Kitui again for more research. Professional responsibilities and family commitments resulted in a much-regretted interruption of several years in writing up this fieldwork material. This book is a revised version of my doctoral thesis, which was accepted by the University of London in 1990.

I gratefully acknowledge financial assistance from the Social Science Research Council (UK) for this research, and grants towards fieldwork expenses and tuition fees from the Central Research Fund of the University of London and the Radcliffe Brown Memorial Fund of the Association of Social Anthropologists.

I received valuable comments on papers given at seminars at

the University of Nairobi, the Institute of Development Studies in Nairobi, the London School of Economics, the African Studies Centre at Cambridge University, the African Studies Department at Sussex University, and the Institute of Education in London. I am particularly grateful for comments on the earlier stages of this work from Dr Stephen Morris and Professor Jean la Fontaine of the Department of Anthropology at the London School of Economics, and valuable advice and encouragement later on from Dr Peter Loizos of the same department.

Thanks are also due to Jane Pugh, chief cartographer in the LSE geography department, for re-drawing my maps, and to Karl Fulton for printing my photographs.

I owe a debt of gratitude to the family in Kamale village in Kitui with whom I lived in 1973–4. Samuel Muema wa Mutinda gave me much brotherly help, and his father, Mutinda wa Ndinga, gave me my Kamba name (Mutua wa Mutinda), my adoptive lineage (Mbaa Kanyaa), and paternal advice and protection. I particularly acknowledge the invaluable research assistance of Ngui wa Kitunguu, a secondary school graduate from the village.

The Chief of Nzambani location, Charles Musyoka wa Matuku, gave me permission to stay in the location and introduced me to Kamale village. He was always most helpful and friendly to me, over and above his official position, and I endeavoured to reciprocate by helping in a small way at the Harambee school in Nzambani then being planned, which was the main reason for my selecting that area for fieldwork. I wish also to record my deep appreciation to Dr Paul Ndilya wa Kavyu, currently head of the Department of Music at Kenyatta University, who was at the time conducting ethno-musicological research in his home district of Kitui, for his friendship and encouragement.

To the people of Kamale, I express my gratitude for their generous reception of me as an adopted stranger in their midst. They and countless other people in Kitui gave me friendly help with my research.

Finally, deepest thanks to my wife, Dawn Hill, who lightened the difficult time of fieldwork by visiting me twice at my temporary home in Kitui (where she was renamed Mwikali wa

Mutua), and who – with our children Carolyne and Andrew, born later in London – gave me support and encouragement in the equally difficult final writing stages.

Martin Hill
London, 1991

1 Introduction

Kenya has a pronounced history of self-help organization starting in the British colonial period but much more developed since Independence in 1963. The Kenyan self-help movement, known as the 'Harambee' movement, has been a marked feature of both rural and national society. It is perhaps the best-known self-help movement in an African or Third World country. Particularly during its first decade and under the first post-Independence government of President Jomo Kenyatta from 1963 to 1978, the Harambee movement was of major social and political importance to the new nation. It embraced a wide range of self-help structures from village to national level throughout the whole country, and performed many secondary political functions too.[1]

The period of fieldwork in 1973–4 on which this study is based was within this 'take-off' phase of the Harambee movement. Harambee was already by then evolving at different rates in different parts of Kenya – faster in more developed areas, slower in less developed areas – and virtually the whole nation was involved in it. Although some critical voices were being raised, it appeared to most participants and observers at the time as essentially positive in most respects. Since 1974 the Harambee movement has continued to expand, mostly in the directions already present then, but no further fieldwork has been undertaken by myself. This is therefore essentially a study of the first decade of the Harambee movement.

Most studies of the Harambee movement have been at national level without much empirical data on village self-help structures and activities.[2] This study adds to the literature on the Harambee movement by analysing its sociological and historical origins, and focusing on one particular village in one particular society and administrative district. On the basis of this analysis, certain conclusions are drawn regarding important features of Kenya's Harambee movement and community self-help organization in general.

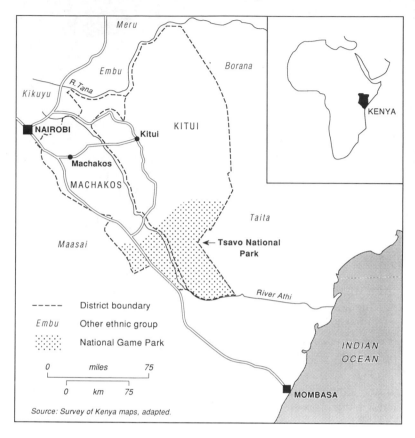

MAP 1 Kitui and Ukambani

Kitui (see Map 1), the area studied in 1973–4, is one of Kenya's less developed districts, and is part of what is informally known as Ukambani, the land of the Kamba (as they are conventionally called in English, although the plural prefixed 'Akamba' would be correct in the Kikamba language).

Kitui's population of about a third of a million (in the 1969 census) was sparse, averaging only eleven people per square kilometre over an area of just over 31,000 square kilometres (see Map 2). Kitui town, the district's administrative and commercial centre, 130 kilometres east of the Kenyan capital, Nairobi, had a population of only about 3,000 in 1969. There

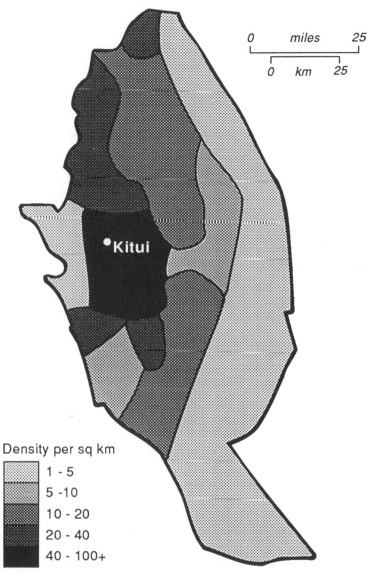

0   *miles*   25

0   *km*   25

●Kitui

Density per sq km

- 1 - 5
- 5 -10
- 10 - 20
- 20 - 40
- 40 - 100+

Source: Kitui District Development Plan, 1971

MAP 2   Kitui Population Density

were several smaller towns too, but the overwhelming majority of the population lived rurally.

Kitui is the eastern section of Ukambani, whose more developed section is the adjoining district of Machakos, bordering on Nairobi. The Kamba, a Bantu-speaking ethnic group whose language is Kikamba, numbered over one million in 1973 and constituted Kenya's fourth largest ethnic group. Most Kamba lived or had families in Ukambani, but there were also large and long-established settlements of Kamba outside Ukambani, the result of migration from more central areas – particularly in time of famine – and often along pre-colonial Kamba trade routes. The earliest settlements were in what is now Machakos district, to the west. Over the last three centuries, Kamba settlement had expanded from Machakos to Kitui. Significant minor linguistic and cultural variations had developed between the Kamba of Kitui and those of Machakos, and also to a lesser extent between different parts of Kitui itself. Compared to Machakos, Kitui was a larger, drier area, less densely populated, and less affected than Machakos by twentieth-century social and economic changes emanating particularly from the city of Nairobi, bordering on Machakos district.

Table 1   *Kenya Provincial Administration Structure*

Unit	Chief Officer	Example
Province	Provincial Commissioner	Eastern province
District	District Commissioner	Kitui, Machakos
Division	District Officer	Central, Mwingi
Location	Chief	Nzambani, Changwithya
Sublocation	Subchief	Maluma, Kyanika
Village	Local Leader [*mutui*]	Kamale, Mbaa Liu

The government administration in Kitui district (see Table 1) was headed by the District Commissioner (DC), who was responsible to the Provincial Commissioner (PC). The provincial administration in Kenya was under the authority of the Office of the President. The DC's office, as well as the offices of all other district departments (health, water, public works, police, and so on), was in Kitui town.

Kitui district, which was part of Kenya's Eastern Province,

Plate 1 Provincial Commissioner and Nzambani location chief

was divided administratively into five divisions, each headed by a District Officer (DO), and, below that level, twenty-eight locations, each headed by a Chief (see Plate 1). Locations were further divided into sublocations, headed by subchiefs, each containing between four and six villages in the sublocation. In terms of political representation, Kitui district in 1973 had six elected members of the Kenya National Assembly (parliament), of whom one was a Cabinet Minister and another an Assistant Minister, and in addition there was one nominated Member of Parliament. These administrative and political divisions of Kitui district are shown in Map 3.

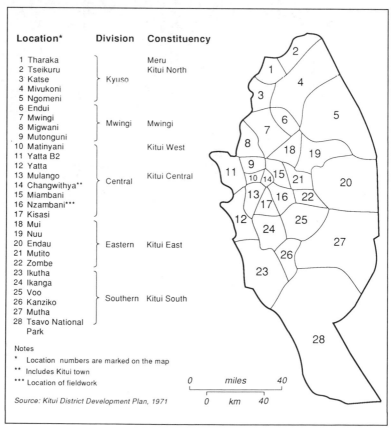

Location*	Division	Constituency
1 Tharaka		Meru
2 Tseikuru		Kitui North
3 Katse	Kyuso	
4 Mivukoni		
5 Ngomeni		
6 Endui		
7 Mwingi	Mwingi	Mwingi
8 Migwani		
9 Mutonguni		
10 Matinyani		Kitui West
11 Yatta B2		
12 Yatta		
13 Mulango	Central	Kitui Central
14 Changwithya**		
15 Miambani		
16 Nzambani***		
17 Kisasi		
18 Mui		
19 Nuu		
20 Endau	Eastern	Kitui East
21 Mutito		
22 Zombe		
23 Ikutha		
24 Ikanga		
25 Voo	Southern	Kitui South
26 Kanziko		
27 Mutha		
28 Tsavo National Park		

Notes
* Location numbers are marked on the map
** Includes Kitui town
*** Location of fieldwork

Source: Kitui District Development Plan, 1971

MAP 3 Kitui Administrative Boundaries and Parliamentary Constituencies

Plate 2 Homestead in Kamale

Fieldwork was carried out in Kamale village, thirteen kilometres southeast of Kitui town (Plate 2). Kamale shared the characteristic of Nzambani location, the administrative unit to which it belonged, of being resistant to many aspects of modernization and cultural change. Many Kamba cultural institutions described by Gerhard Lindblom,[3] a Swedish anthropologist who studied the Kamba for fourteen months in 1911–12, visiting Kitui for several months and attaining considerable fluency in Kikamba, were still apparent in Kamale in 1973. Kamale had also been part of colonial and post-colonial society in Kenya, with large numbers of its menfolk working outside the district. Its self-help history and organizational forms through the colonial period and after Independence were not remarkably dissimilar to those of the majority of other societies in Kenya, which had similar socioeconomic and political structures.

This study, which is located within the field of the anthropology of development,[4] focuses on the role of traditional social institutions in modern socioeconomic development. This is of particular interest to the issue in social anthropology concerning the extent to which traditional institutions are not intrinsically 'anti-developmental', as is sometimes assumed by development experts, but can and do play an important part in community development. Community self-help activity in Kitui was observed amidst the processes of change through which the society was proceeding through the prism of its own culture and history, and in the context of the development objectives which were present in the minds and activities of the members of the society. The focus of research was on development at the 'grass-roots' community level of the self-help movement.

Of particular interest are the social structural connections and continuities between the modern self-help organizational forms and traditional community institutions which were claimed as their basis. The historical and social structural changes underlying the integration between village-level self-help organization and the national self-help movement, which was so pronounced in government ideology and general opinion, are also studied in detail.

The literature on the Harambee movement[5] consists mainly of work by sociologists, political scientists and educationalists, with some contributions from economists and those concerned with development planning. By 1973, any fieldwork that had been done on Harambee had consisted mainly of short field visits coupled in some cases with the use of questionnaires. There was a notable lack of prolonged in-depth fieldwork studies carried out over a period of time in the same place or area. As the principal focus of my study was the link between traditional institutions of community co-operation and the modern self-help movement, research was based on the study of a single community, taking it as an example of what might be widely found elsewhere in the same cultural area.

The concluding chapter discusses, in relation to the Kitui material, the general issues concerning the Harambee movement which have been identified by previous researchers and are still vigorously debated.[6] They include the questions of whether the Harambee movement is a 'genuine' community development movement; how much it was merely a political phenomenon; and how 'developmental' it has actually been. An overall assessment of the Harambee movement in development terms is beyond the scope of this study. However, the presentation of this first-hand research data on the Harambee movement should be of use to those engaged in other studies of different kinds on the important and relatively little-understood phenomenon of self-help, or 'domestic development services' as it is known in United Nations literature.

Research Methods

The main research material, including ethnographic data on Kamba society and culture which was obtained using social anthropological methods of participant observation, was collected during seventeen months' residence in Kamale village. The available published ethnographic material on the Kamba was incomplete and uneven in quality. Valuable early work had been done by Lindblom[7] and Stanner,[8] who carried out extensive fieldwork in Kitui in 1911–12 and 1939 respectively. Other material included publications by colonial administrators,[9] Kamba scholars[10] and other researchers.[11] A survey of the ethnographic literature was compiled by Middleton and Kershaw in 1953 and revised in 1965, with a supplementary bibliography added in 1972.[12]

Plate 3   Harambee fund-raising in Mulango

Plate 4 Mwethya self-help group dancers in Nzambani

The aim of the research was not to reconstruct a picture of pre-colonial or 'traditional' Kamba society – 'traditional' being used here as a term of convenience only, which is not meant to carry any explanatory weight – but to understand the contemporary society, where many traditional ideas, values and practices were still current in 1973. The pace of social change in Kitui, and particularly the areas around Kamale, had not become so rapid that traditional ideas and institutions had disappeared, although this was becoming the case in the more developed central areas in Kitui such as Mulango, Changwithya, Matinyani and Mutonguni locations. Ethnographic material on Kitui society is included here to throw light on the organization of certain community institutions, workparties in particular, which were transformed into or mirrored in modern self-help organizational forms.[13]

An understanding of the historical background to the Kenyan self-help movement, particularly its colonial antecedents, is equally important, particularly the 'communal labour' (forced labour) system. Relevant historical material was collected on Kitui in colonial times from the Kenya National Archives in Nairobi, as well from interviews with older people in or from Kitui who were involved in events at the time, other government records that were available, and published historical research.[14]

Contemporary data was collected on the Harambee movement in Kitui in 1973–4 through continuous study and observation of the self-help group in Kamale;[15] participant observation of the development of Nzambani Harambee School;[16] attendance at numerous self-help events in the area and also throughout Kitui district, including many Harambee fund-raising activities (Plates 3 and 4); interviews and regular contacts with government and church officials in Kitui associated with self-help activities; visits to all the twenty-five secondary schools in Kitui, which included government and mission schools, eleven Harambee schools and eight former Harambee schools, with surveys of Harambee students and interviews with teachers and school committee members;[17] press articles on Harambee in the Kenyan news media, such as *The Nation* and *The Weekly Review*, published in Nairobi; and numerous interviews and discussions with people in Kamale village and Nzambani location.

2 From Forced Labour to Harambee

This chapter locates the Kenyan self-help movement in its historical context, with particular reference to Kitui. The antecedents of the Harambee movement lie in a common feature of colonial rule in Africa and elsewhere – forced labour, one aspect of which was 'communal labour'. This was the term used in Kenya (and other British colonies too) for obligatory unpaid community work on public projects. In French colonies it was termed *corvée*. Important symbolic aspects of the Harambee movement were its political representation as a creation of national independence as against colonial rule, and its social structural representation as embodying African communal tradition as against foreign imposition.

Communal labour is first examined in the first half-century of colonial rule in Kenya, and then in its modifications in the last decade of colonial rule in the 1950s. This is followed by a description and analysis of the post-Independence Harambee movement and changes in community development ideology and practice.

Colonial Rule and Communal Labour in Kitui

The British East Africa Protectorate was declared in 1895, following the Berlin Conference of 1885 and the establishment in 1888 of the Imperial British East Africa Company (IBEAC).[1] The IBEAC was an agency established by the British government with a mandate to replace the slave trade by legitimate commerce. In western Ukambani the IBEAC established a small fort in 1889 on land said to have been 'given' to it by Masaku, a Kamba trader – hence the name 'Masaku's', later Machakos. The Protectorate subcommissioner for Ukambani, John Ainsworth, visited Kitui in 1896 to extend British rule there. He returned the next year and obtained land at what is now Kitui town from a Kamba trader called Mwiilu, at a place called Nengia. A small camp was built there in 1898. This became known as Kitui, although the name Nengia was also used for some years.

The beginning of colonial rule in Kitui coincided with the devastating famine of 1897–8 called *Ngomanisye* ('covering everywhere'). It was accompanied by a rinderpest epidemic. A quarter of Kitui's population died in it.[2]

Colonial rule in Kitui brought new political and jural institutions operating through a heirarchy of paid and unpaid Kamba officials which was subordinate to a separate hierarchy of European (white British) officials linked to the colonial and metropolitan centres of power in Nairobi and London. Effective colonial control gradually spread into the surrounding areas over the next decade to form the new administrative district of Kitui. The district was bounded by the Athi river to the west and the Tana river to the north, and by the limits of Kamba settlement *vis-à-vis* other ethnic groups to the south (Maasai) and east (Borana, also known as Galla – a pejorative term now replaced by Oromo in Ethiopian ethnography, and Taita).

Kitui had inspired no significant commercial or strategic interest on the part of earlier European travellers, due to its poverty of natural resources, the sporadic fighting between Kamba and Maasai or Borana, inter-clan raiding and feuding, and its people's unwelcoming attitude to outsiders. There was considerable conflict between Kamba, Swahili and Indian traders on the coast–inland caravan routes. The German traveller Ludwig Krapf had visited the area twice in the mid-nineteenth century, first in 1849 when he was seeking the source of the Nile and secondly in 1851 when he was sent by the Church Missionary Society to help open a mission station in Ukambani on the caravan route. At Rabai on the coast, prior to his first visit, he had met Kivoi (or Kivui) wa Mwendwa, a Kamba caravan leader and ivory trader, who encouraged him (for his own motives) to visit his home in Kitui. Krapf was nearly killed in a raid by 'bandits' in which Kivoi lost his life. His published account of his somewhat unpleasant experiences[3] probably deterred other potential visitors.

A small mission station was established by the German

Evangelical Lutheran Mission (also known as the Leipziger Mission) in southern Kitui in 1891. The Mission later opened other stations in Kitui – in Mulango in central Kitui in 1899 and in nearby Miambani in 1903 – but an attempt to open one in Mivukoni in the north failed. Its links with the British colonial administration were minimal. In addition to proselytization efforts, which were largely unsuccessful, the Mission did some famine relief work, in Ikutha in particular during the 1897–8 famine.

Communications to areas off the main Mombasa–Nairobi and Kitui–Machakos caravan routes (and later the Mombasa–Nairobi railway, begun in 1895) were difficult and colonial rule extended only slowly from central Kitui to its peripheries. There was some small-scale initial resistance to colonial rule, including attacks on government parties and trade caravans, which led to reprisals by the authorities – the burning of villages and crops and confiscation of livestock.

The most immediately felt and particularly disliked changes brought by colonial rule in Kitui were taxation and forced labour of various kinds. These interacted with the economic changes set off by the introduction of a colonial coinage and the growth of the market economy, particularly through Asian commercial networks, which grew up in the new town (officially gazetted in 1909) at the administrative centre of the district. The previously well-established Kitui Kamba trade networks, involving long-distance trading of game trophies (mostly ivory – Kamba were famed as hunters, using bows and arrows), cloth, ironwork and bead jewellery, snuff, arrow-poison, food, livestock, hides, and sometimes slaves, between the coast and inland parts of Kenya (even into Tanganyika and Uganda) did not survive long in the new economic and political climate.[4]

Taxation raised revenue to support the colonial administration and its institutions.[5] The first tax in Kitui was levied in the vicinity of the government centre in 1902 at the rate of 1 rupee a year. This 'hut tax' was paid by married men according to the number of their wives. It was payable in cash or livestock equivalent. In 1910 it was extended to unmarried adult men with the purpose of driving them into the labour market in order to earn money to pay the tax. The Governor of Kenya stated in 1913:

> We consider that the only natural and automatic method of securing a constant labour-supply is to ensure that there shall be competition among labourers for hire and not among employers for labourers; such competition can only be brought about by a rise in the cost of living for the native, and this can only be produced by an increase in tax.[6]

Hut tax was steadily increased until by 1917 it was 5 rupees. The amount of hut tax was kept approximately equivalent to a labourer's monthly wage. A major colonial problem throughout this period was how to obtain African labour for white settlers' estates. Many Africans, Kitui Kamba in particular, refused to work on these estates because they were treated badly and wages were poor, and in Kitui people were usually able to pay their tax with the livestock they had.

Labour recruitment for government service and settler farms was not left solely to economic pressures created by taxation. District Commissioners were also instructed to recruit workers by force, by setting labour quotas for location chiefs to fulfil. In addition, the military manpower needs of the colonial government during the First World War led to the introduction of conscription for African males as well as European males. The former were conscripted into the unarmed Carrier Corps. There was considerable fighting between the British forces in Kenya and Uganda and the German forces in Tanganyika. Up to 75 per cent of the able-bodied men in Kitui were conscripted. As many as a quarter of them died, mostly as a result of the appalling conditions to which they were subjected rather than from actual fighting.[7]

In 1918 the District Commissioner of Kitui wrote candidly in his Annual Report: 'There is no such thing as voluntary labour here.'[8] He opposed the prospective ban on private labour recruitment through the administration. The ban, however, became law in 1919, but the practice often continued – for example in a special recruitment in Kitui in 1924 of workers for the East African Railway. But the high rate of evasion and desertion, despite the penalties for such offences, made forced labour recruitment more and more unworkable and unenforceable. By the early 1920s many people were also leaving Kitui voluntarily to look for work on their own initiative as their need for cash for consumer goods, school fees and other new items increased after the war.

As well as the extraction of forced paid labour for government, settlers and private government-supported employers, there was also forced unpaid labour for all non-employed adult males in the 'Reserves' (rural areas reserved for African habitation). Under the Native Administration Ordinance of 1912, all males aged eighteen to forty-five who were not in education or employment were required to work unpaid on certain rural public works projects for up to twenty-four days a year. This was called 'communal labour'. It was administered by chiefs supported by 'tribal' (or administrative) police. There were penalties of fines (with the eventual sanction of imprisonment) for evaders. Communal labour took place mostly in the dry season – the agricultural slack season. There was continual small-scale resistance and evasion, rather than any organized opposition.

The 1920s and 1930s were times of extreme and deliberate underdevelopment throughout Kenya.[9] African tax revenue was used largely for the development of the urban and European-reserved areas, with almost no development in the Reserves beyond what was done by communal labour. Communal labour, which included the building of roads, made colonial administration and communications more practicable and assisted in the spread of commerce and labour recruitment. Over half of Kenya's revenue in the 1920s and up to a third in the 1930s came from taxation of Africans, with a large part of the rest coming from import duties on African-purchased goods. The colony was geared to giving every possible incentive to white settlers, including freedom from income tax, government provision of infrastructure facilities, protection of settler agriculture from peasant competition, and the provision of cheap labour through government-administered forced recruitment and laws which kept wages low and protected 'masters' rather than 'servants'. The Reserves were systematically starved of development funds, and few government services were provided. In Kitui, for example, there were no agricultural or veterinary services until the 1930s.

The Kitui District Commissioners frequently complained about this lack of government development expenditure in their Annual Reports:[10]

> There seems to be no fair reason why a district should pay four times as much [tax] as is devoted to its upkeep, especially when that district is badly in need of increased revenue for its better administration. (1912)

> The revenue has always largely exceeded expenditure but none is spent in the district with the specific object of directly benefiting the natives and what has been done is due to the individual efforts of the officers. (1915)

> It is regretted that government has found itself able to spend so little money on the district and that this year only about £20 has been available for the upkeep of the local hospital for natives, who have paid over £25,000 in direct taxation. (1925)

> I am very strongly of the opinion that the Akamba do not obtain government services commensurate with their contribution to revenue and I have made efforts to obtain more services. (1932)

At the end of the 1930s the anthropologist Stanner, who was conducting research into colonial administration in Kitui, wrote:

> The main patterns of colonial activity in Kenya so far have been almost wholly European privilege and profit. The acceptance of the obligation of colonial stewardship is still little more than a façade.[11]

Stanner noted that Kitui had paid over £1/2m in tax over the previous fifteen years with virtually no government expenditure on development. Moreover, of money spent in Kitui, three-quarters was spent on salaries for administrators, most of the rest on government transport, and virtually nothing on development.

An administrative change in 1924 led to the formation of partly elected Native District Councils. These Councils were given the responsibility of implementing communal labour, which was thereby represented by the authorities as being done at the people's choice. Kitui Kamba, on the other hand, called it *wia wa muzungu* ('white man's work').[12] Stanner commented that communal labour was 'the most cordially hated public duties to which the Kamba have been called'. Communal labour was imposed through the Council being presented each year with a Standard Form Resolution to which it was expected to give automatic assent. The Council contained elected representatives, but chiefs and members nominated by the District Commissioner formed a majority of its members. The Kitui Council generally rubber-stamped the District Commissioner's resolutions, but so hated was communal labour that in 1934 the Council voted to abolish it. However, the roads reached such a bad state, since the Council had little money to pay workers to clear them from the encroaching bush, that it was obliged to reinstate unpaid communal labour for local road-building the following year.

In 1924 the Councils were also given powers to levy additional taxes for local development and certain limited areas of responsibility in the development field, notably in primary school education and primary health care. Hitherto education and health had been almost totally left by government to the responsibility of Christian missions. In 1909, the government built a small primary school in Kitui town – one of the first government schools in Kenya. It was intended to train chiefs' sons to be the next generation of chiefs, but this failed and hereditary chiefships never became established – Kamba society had no chiefs, in any case.[13]

With the exception of the government primary school in Kitui town, primary schools were all mission-managed and built by local people, usually the 'Christian few'.[14] The Africa Inland Mission (AIM), an American Baptist mission organization founded in 1895 and already established in Machakos and other parts of Kenya, became the main mission in Kitui when the German Protestant mission was expelled in 1914 on the outbreak of war between Britain and Germany. The schools were fee-paying and those outside the mission station, known as 'out-schools' or 'bush schools', were staffed by

African catechists with only loose support from the mission centre. From 1924 the Native Council set up in each district took over the management of primary schools, although the links with the Mission were maintained. Intermediate schools, leading on to secondary school entrance, started to be built by the Native Council. Gradually educational demand began to outstrip mission resources and a few schools were opened without mission management. One Kitui chief started his own school in Mutha location in 1915 when the AIM was unable to send a teacher. In the early 1920s the desire for schools was still increasing relatively slowly in Kitui, even in areas influenced by other socioeconomic changes.

From the outset, education was dependent on local community contributions. Mission contributions were limited to provision and payment of a teacher and a small amount of funds for the running of the school. Land had to be found for the school site – for example, on bush land or pasture which was not under particularized ownership or use, or on land donated for the purpose. Buildings were erected through local labour, either through a workparty of parents interested in educating their children, or through communal labour administered by the chief or subchief.

The pattern of mixed community and external financing and management continued after the Native Council took on primary school management and staffing. The Council also part-funded mission-managed schools. But despite this recognition of local development aspirations through the responsibilities given to the Council in the field of education (as well as health – Kitui District Hospital was built in 1928), it had insufficient funds for the tasks before it. Some funds which might have been used for development purposes were tied up in a 'Famine Fund' reserve, from which, even during a major famine in Kitui in 1929, only a maximum of 5 per cent was permitted to be disbursed.

From 1930 the Kitui District Commissioners' reports mention increasing interest in education and the building of more schools. But the early 1930s were marked in Kitui by recession, a fall in employment and livestock prices, extensive crop damage from swarms of locusts, and severe drought and famine over a number of years. As the local economy began to pick up in the late 1930s, war broke out again between the colonial powers of Britain and Germany, and development in the district was again at a standstill. There was renewed conscription of men and, following the earlier popularity in Kitui of employment in the colonial army and police, Kitui Kamba willingly joined up in large numbers and Kamba became the dominant ethnic group in these forces.

The post-war period introduced two important new factors into the situation. Large numbers of Kitui Kamba troops who fought in the Second World War returned home afterwards with new socioeconomic and political aspirations. These aspirations were not satisfied by the slow pace of post-war development provision by the colonial government. The British Colonial Development and Welfare Act (1940) allocated only a total of £5m a year for development in all Britain's colonies for the next five years. At the same time, nationalist aspirations were on the rise in Kenya, as throughout the British Empire. The colonial authorities were forced to regard development as essential from both economic and political points of view. With little funding provided by the government, the onus was laid on the people themselves to develop their own areas. Failure to respond to government propaganda to that effect led to people being blamed for their own lack of development. Thus the Kitui District Commissioner wrote in 1945 of the 'very inert lump of Kamba opinion which is not responsive to progressive ideas from external sources'. He noted, possibly with some exaggeration, 'Education has barely touched the fringes of the tribe.' Another District Commissioner shortly afterwards chose instead to blame the Africa Inland Mission in Kitui for not bringing more development to the district.

In 1946, partially elective Location Councils started to be formed as a second tier of African political representation in addition to the district-level Native Councils. They were given responsibilities in each location for primary schools, soil conservation, agricultural development, livestock care, sanitation, water supplies and hygiene. In education, the same relation between council, mission and local community remained in force, with many schools being built by communal labour.

Despite Britain's signing of the International Forced Labour Agreement of 1930, there was still forced labour in many community projects. Forced labour recruitment was abolished by law in Kenya, but communal labour (which was forced and unpaid) was exempted from this ban and remained in effect.

Communal labour was, however, a matter of continuing conflict between nationalists and the colonial authorities. There was also some disagreement about communal labour between the Colonial Office in London, the Colonial Governor in Nairobi and some District Commissioners – over whether or not it should be declared illegal under the 1930 Agreement. The matter was not tested in the courts. The Governor declared in 1947 that while certain minor communal services were legal, unpaid work on major projects, such as dams and soil conservation, could be carried out by communal labour only under special circumstances and under a special order signed by himself. Whether any such orders were signed is unclear. No special order was signed for Kitui and communal labour continued to be unpaid for dams, schools and some soil conservation work.[15]

Communal labour thus continued in Kitui as before. District Commissioners in their Annual Reports described it as 'voluntary', on the grounds that it had the assent of District and Location Councils. No other funds were available for district development in the event that communal labour might have been abolished. In the post-World War II period of rapid socioeconomic changes and increasing demand for development, there was no alternative to communal labour as the principal means of building schools and health facilities and improving local roads. However, the actual or purported development purpose of some communal labour tasks was little understood or appreciated. Soil conservation, a common colonial theme of the 1930s,[16] was one of the most irksome tasks. Terracing, bush clearing and the clearing of cattle paths were unpopular in Kitui and often seen as of little benefit. The construction of dams was more debatable, as these would clearly benefit the communities building them – especially in a dry area such as Kitui, which had unreliable rainfall and periodic drought and famine – but the dams were not always successfully built.

By the late 1940s it was evident that there was an urgent political need for the colonial authorities to reform communal labour in order to utilize its central features to create a local development infrastructure, which the colonial government did not intend to finance. This coincided with the introduction of Community Development into colonial administration policy. The Community Development policy was designed in part to meet criticism of colonial rule by liberal lobbies in the colonial centre, but without putting colonial interests in jeopardy; in part it was also intended to defuse opposition by nationalist groups in the colonies which were calling for political independence.

Colonial Community Development

The first official use of the term 'Community Development'and its elevation into a key feature of British colonial administration appeared in the 'Despatch on Community Development to British Colonial Territories' dated 10 November 1948 from the British Colonial Secretary, Arthur Creech Jones. The 'Creech Jones circular', as it became known, represented a reinterpretation of colonial indirect rule (rule through a native administration) as a 'dynamic' rather than static policy, responding to change and the demand for development in the colonies. It was located within the overall stated objective of guiding colonies to eventual 'self-government'.[17]

The new policy based on these general notions, which was set out further in an article published by Creech Jones in 1949,[18] was initially called 'Mass Education', but the alternative term 'Community Development' eventually stuck, in preference also to 'Social Development'.[19] Together with the growth of local government, this was to be 'placed in the forefront of our development policy in Africa....Mass Education is to be regarded as one of the central features of the African policy of His Majesty's Government'.[20] The same policy was extended to other British colonies too.

By 'Mass Education' was meant:

a movement to secure the active co-operation of the people of each community in programmes designed to raise standards of living and to promote development in all its forms. It is no new movement but the intensification of past plans for development by means of new techniques; its main novel feature lies in the great emphasis which it places on the stimulation of popular initiative.

The concept and policy were later defined more succinctly as follows:

We understand the term 'mass education' to mean a movement designed to promote better living for the whole community, with the active participation and, if possible, on the initiative of the community, but if this initiative is not forthcoming, by the use of techniques for arousing and stimulating it in order to secure the active and enthusiastic response to the movement.[21]

The Creech Jones circular noted that African opposition to this concept of Mass Education could be expected; it would be seen as an inferior substitute for the demanded rapid acceleration of formal education for Africans; and, like 'relevant' or 'vocational' education, it would be criticized for seeking to deny Africans the opportunity to obtain the academic education more readily provided for other racial groups.

The new policy was based on reports from bodies such as the Phelps-Stokes Commission and the Advisory Commission on Education (which had produced a report in 1944 entitled 'Mass Education in African Society') and also on the recommendations of colonial administrators at the regular Colonial Office Summer Conferences in Britain, which started in 1947 and often led to important new legislation for the colonies. The recommendations of the 1948 Summer Conference at Cambridge on 'The Encouragement of Initiative in African Society' had led directly to the Creech Jones circular later that year.[22]

The Creech Jones circular admitted that development in the colonies had hitherto been 'static', but in the wake of the 1940 Colonial Development and Welfare Act, a new phase was envisaged. The Act allocated £5m per year for development projects and a further £1/2m for research in the colonies for the next five years, over and above 'normal' development carried out by different government departments. The 1940 Act was preceded by the 1929 Colonial Welfare and Development Act, under which only £8.8m had been spent for this purpose over the whole of the previous eleven-year period. The amount that would be actually available to any single district in the British Empire under the 1940 Act was, nevertheless, very small. 'Normal' government development activity – financed from colonial tax revenues – also remained starved of funds. In these circumstances, if any serious development efforts were to be made without the injection of substantial extra funds, alternative forms of financing and resource mobilization had to be found.

Mass Education was intended to satisfy African educational aspirations as well as fulfil imperial responsibilities. It was linked to the officially stated policy from 1945 onwards to prepare colonies for eventual 'self-government' (which did not necessarily mean full territorial independence) – although this had no timetable and there was a general belief that there was unlimited time ahead to achieve this in a manner satisfactory to the colonial authorities. It set out to offer 'the improvement of the life of the community' through 'training of the community as a whole'.

The generally accepted view of African societies by colonial administrators of the time was that they were organic wholes that had been subjected to disruptive socioeconomic changes.[23] It was believed that in certain respects they should be protected from this disruption; in other respects, their resistance to change and 'inertia' should be overcome to enable them to develop according to colonial objectives. Special techniques for stimulating 'initiative' in African communities were to be developed through research and training by a new Clearing House for Social Development at the University of London's Institute of Education (which would publish relevant material in the new *Journal of African Administration*) and through use of the experience of colonial administrators in the field. Training centres would be set up in the colonies and trained British and African staff would co-ordinate development activity on a community basis to improve agricultural techniques, water supplies, soil conservation, livestock management, home care and childcare, as well as to continue educational development activities for which the demand was growing fast.

The Creech Jones circular was supposed to end the debate about development in the colonies and begin the action. Its implementation, however, was slow and undramatic. In Kenya, the responsibility for Community Development was added to the tasks of District Officers until District Community Development Officers (all of whom were initially British colonial officers) were appointed. In some districts in Kenya, Africans were appointed Assistant Administrative Officers for this purpose – the most senior post to which Africans were admitted in the colonial administration. Their salaries were paid by District Councils rather than central government. A few pilot projects were tried out in 1949–52, but with the declaration of a State of Emergency in 1952, these either collapsed or were suspended; all resources were devoted to security issues and most of the few Community Development posts that had been created were axed.

The language of Community Development entered into District Commissioners' reports from the early 1950s, when the term 'self-help' first became popular within the colonial administration.[24] Yet the so-called 'self-help projects' appear to have been largely communal labour under a new name. They were unpaid, organized by chiefs, approved and sometimes contributed to by District or Location Councils. The work centred on building primary schools, earth dams (water reservoirs) and water catchments, maintaining or extending local roads, and soil conservation work. Several of the projects were probably inefficient in their use of manpower owing to poor organization, lack of co-ordination and deficiencies of technical support.

Despite its social value, communal labour continued to attract the hostility of those opposing the continuation of colonial rule. As Independence came nearer, District Councils were empowered to reduce the list of tasks for which communal labour was obligatory, and what was left tended to be branded by nationalist politicians as 'colonial slavery'. The reality of much community development which was praised by certain visiting foreigners and others as 'the new colonialism'[25] – a phrase supposed to mean acceptably reformed colonial rule – was far from the notion of self-help as being based on voluntarism, popular participation and local decision-making. Community Development philosophy in the colonial world of the 1950s appeared to allow under this rubric any development activity involving the community as a whole which was judged by the authorities to be to its benefit.[26]

Community Development in Kitui, 1948–63

In the years following the Creech Jones circular of 1948, new community development ideas were implemented in Kitui through the existing administrative system. A Community Development Officer organized some women's clubs, ex-servicemen's associations, sports and government information film shows. The same (British) officer was given the responsibility of selecting projects for communal labour.

After 1945, the pace of educational expansion was already quickening with a rapidly widening acceptance of education for secular modern purposes. There were twenty-one elementary schools in Kitui in 1947, and the first Kitui pupils entered secondary school outside the district (some at Makerere College in Uganda) in 1948. In Kitui the level of educational provision and the prominence of education as a new differentiating factor in society proceeded slowly. Kitui Government African School reached secondary school certificate (twelfth grade) only in 1960 – the first in the district. A few Kitui people received secondary and higher education outside the district, but in the field of education Kitui as a whole lagged behind most other districts in Kenya.

From 1948 to 1952 a new and energetic District Commissioner, Paul Kelly, was instrumental in organizing Location Councils and increasing communal labour work on schools, soil conservation, dams and health dispensaries. He wrote 'As voluntary labour is required, these dams are built at the option of the local people'.[27] In this case he evidently meant that they were approved by Location Councils, which contained a majority of *ex officio* and nominated members. Kelly formed a District Development Team of department heads to establish a district development strategy – an early attempt at comprehensive integrated local planning, as developed after Independence. His team adopted a plan for each location to build an elementary school and a dispensary, and set a target of fifty dams a year to be built in the district. This was a heavy schedule of hard work, compulsorily involving all non-employed men and women and also older boys and girls who were not in school. The targets were largely achieved. In 1950 there were forty-three elementary schools, educating 3,770 boys and 665 girls. The main opposition came from nationalist politicians from the Kenya African Union (KAU) who demanded that the work should be paid. Financial contributions – for building materials, for example – were made by the District Council, partly through funds originating from the Colonial Development and Welfare Act allocation, at the rate of £50 per small dam and £100 per large dam. Some of these funds were allocated to providing food for the youths and girls who had to work for long periods at the dam site, away from their homes, but not to paying them (the funds would not have been sufficient in any case).

A political motive linking the encouragement of local development activity and the control of political opposition is made clear from the District Commissioner's confidential handing-over report to his successor when going on leave in 1949: 'The Kitui Akamba are at present too busy with building, terracing, clearing bush and dams, to leave much time for politics'.[28] The programme appeared to continue relatively smoothly in Kitui, and in 1952 the District Commissioner wrote:

> Community spirit and rivalry of a healthy nature continued to flourish and is and must be the basis on which the district progresses. No compulsion has had to be brought to bear on any of the development projects carried out, on which steady propaganda has been made with regard to dam construction, grazing schemes and soil conservation, although there are always opponents of any such schemes.

Regarding educational development he wrote, somewhat defensively:

> It is safe to say that education is available for any child whose parents wish it, up to the 8th grade of schooling. The demand

for education appears on the surface to be increasing rapidly but attendance at some schools here clearly shows that to many parents at least the herding of stock is of greater importance than education. That the demand is on the increase is largely a platform of the 'politicians'.

Handing over to his successor, Mr Browning, in 1952, Kelly wrote: 'We must not lose sight of good government in material progress, especially as the Kamba provide so large a proportion of the forces of law and order in East Africa.' He recommended his successor to 'preserve the discipline of semi-communal work linked with dancing'.

The reference to dancing highlighted one feature of communal labour – the encouragement of workparty songs during village work and of traditional dancing by youths and girls after their work at the dams. Traditional dances [*wathi*] had been actively discouraged by AIM missionaries in Kitui (and sometimes banned by Christian chiefs) on the grounds that they were 'pagan' and immoral, and church members were prohibited from participating in them. The District Commissioner opposed this view and saw the advantage of encouraging traditional dances to alleviate the days and nights spent at the work site. This was evidently successful with many youths and girls, and fitted into Kamba custom. It appears that while the authorities permitted traditional dances on communal labour work, they often stopped them in the villages. This policy emphasized a growing division among young people in Kitui between on the one hand those who went to school and church (probably mostly the children of Christians), were not allowed to dance, and were excused communal labour; and on the other hand those who worked at dams, were allowed to dance, and did not want to go to school.[29]

In 1954 the same District Commissioner wrote: 'The spirit of self-help has continued to flourish and has been fostered by all government departments.' The next year (1955) he expanded:

> The policy of the district has remained on a basis of self-help and this is undoubtedly paying dividends as the people are beginning to think for themselves as to how to improve their own country and as to where the money to pay for it has to come from. Almost

every project carried out has an element of self-help in that either finance or labour or some other contribution is given by the location concerned.

In 1956 the District Commissioner wrote:

> The political and agrarian awakening of the district started in Kelly's time [1948–1952] and it was, I think, his creed that 'God helps those who help themselves' that set the path of development followed today.[30]

During the State of Emergency declared in Kenya in 1952 (in force until 1960) a number of Kenya African Union members in Kitui were detained under emergency regulations on suspicion of links with the nationalist 'Mau Mau' organization (the Land and Freedom Army). The district records state that twenty-five were detained in 1956, most of them members of the African Brotherhood Church, a Machakos-based independent church which had seceded from the AIM and established itself in Kitui in 1946. A larger number of people in Kitui were made subject to orders restricting their movements – for example, 138 such orders were made in 1956.[31] Any form of dissent or nationalist expression was deemed subversive. Unpaid 'Home Guards' and 'screening committees' were set up in all locations in Kitui to handle security matters, identify 'subversives', report them to the authorities – who would decide whether to detain or restrict them or order them to be ritually cleansed with a traditional oath – and pre-empt any interest in Mau Mau. The main issue on which KAU politicians tried to mobilize people against the colonial authorities was communal labour. In comparison, dissatisfaction with the level of taxation was of much less importance because taxation levels in Kitui had remained relatively unchanged from 1917 to 1950, due to the poverty of the district and chronic drought and famine.

Development initiatives outside the administrative framework were closely monitored for political motivation. An attempt was made in the early 1950s by the Akamba Association, a mainly urban-based voluntary welfare association which was encouraged by the colonial authorities, to open an independent primary and secondary school in Kitui. This attempt failed, and no such school actually opened, due to the declaration of the Emergency and the administration's obstruction of any activities which appeared to represent political opposition to it. The authorities evidently feared that an independent school in Kitui might become a focus of nationalism, as the independent schools movement among the Kikuyu was.[32]

In the years that followed the Creech Jones circular (1948), some efforts were made to reduce the coercive elements in communal labour in line with the growing propaganda of self-help. The Creech Jones circular had stressed the need for 'the stimulation of popular initiative' but it made no mention of utilizing indigenous institutions of community co-operation which were used for several agricultural and building tasks. These institutions were, naturally enough, well known to local chiefs who were in charge of communal labour and to those working on communal labour. It is perhaps surprising that more effort was not made by colonial administrators until the early 1950s to capitalize on these traditional community institutions to gain support for community projects such as building schools.

The adaptation of indigenous institutions to rural community development was the subject of research in 1949 by Philip Mayer, an anthropologist in the employment of the Kenya colonial administration. It is not clear to what extent his research was conducted on his own initiative rather than as a result of governmental interest. He wrote up his findings in a paper entitled 'Agricultural co-operation by neighbourhood groups among the Gusii in South Nyanza',[33] which was based on a short period of field research among the Gusii in western Kenya. This was published in mimeographed form in 1951 with an introduction stating that 'native authorities are much concerned with the question how far traditional institutions and methods can be made to serve the needs of modern development'.[34]

Mayer's findings were accompanied by recommendations to the South Nyanza District Administration, which advised that instead of compulsion or even demonstration techniques, much village improvement, and especially agricultural modernization, could be undertaken by utilizing traditional workparty institutions. He described these in some detail and wrote that a pilot scheme was set up in one Gusii location with the approval and interest of the District Commissioner. The result of the project, however, was not reported by Mayer and the outcome of his recommendations has not been described in any of his further published material. It is likely that Mayer, as a 'government sociologist', had in mind the broad proposals of the Creech Jones circular as well as changing anthropological perspectives on traditional institutions, which were coming to value them for their modernizing potential. His fieldwork conclusions and the above-mentioned paper might have been familiar to Kenyan administrators concerned with introducing Community Development to Kenya, in particular the staff teaching at the Jeanes School at Kabete, which was the centre in Kenya for teaching techniques of community development and mass education.

In 1953, two years after Mayer's article and one year after the declaration of the State of Emergency, the Kamba of Machakos district were selected for an experimental project in community development. The Machakos project was headed by John Malinda, himself from Machakos. He held the newly created post of African Administrative Officer, the highest administrative post open to Africans – he was possibly the first holder of this post – and he carried out the project largely on his own responsibility.[35] Malinda's project involved using customary Kamba workparties for modern tasks in the field of community development work. He had not read Mayer's paper, nor is there any evidence that any other official involved with the project was familiar with it. Indeed, publications by the Kenya Community Development Commissioner in 1958 and 1960, which refer to Malinda and the Machakos project, make no mention of Mayer's work.[36] However, Malinda did attend a course at the Jeanes School and it is possible that Mayer's recommendations were passed on to students there.

Malinda's aim was to encourage new village development work and at the same time remove the aspects of the communal labour system which were most disliked in Machakos, as well as in Kitui and probably all other rural areas of Kenya. Communal labour was hated less for the actual work involved (which had positive benefits for the participants in many cases) than for the degree of coercion exercised by chiefs, who had powers to arrest, fine or jail evaders. Whereas District Commissioners gave a favourable picture of communal labour in their annual reports – which were not themselves published but were used by the Colonial Office to compile published reports for each colony – its day-to-day administration was in the hands of location chiefs. These latter were open to corruption and abuse of office, both of which were apparently common. Stories abounded in Kitui of chiefs' relatives being excused work, their enemies being victimized, friends favoured, and bribes demanded for permission to be absent. Migrant workers returning home on leave were often forced to participate in communal labour, and in Kitui youths and unmarried girls had to work continuously on remote sites – for example building a road or a dam – without being allowed home for weeks. Although such stories as were reported to me in the early 1970s may have become slightly exaggerated, it is likely that they had a considerable factual basis.

Malinda based the new community development groups on traditional Kamba workparties – the neighbourhood *mwethya*. He called them by the same name. Communal labour tasks were still done in the previous manner, but the locally elected committees of the new *myethya* (plural of *mwethya*) took the decisions on what projects to undertake and how to undertake them. A committee was allowed to employ its own methods of ensuring compliance, although the sanctions of communal labour remained in force. The committees chose their projects from among tasks which they saw to be of direct benefit to the villagers. In addition to building schools, they undertook soil conservation tasks (particularly terracing – Plate 5 – which was very successful in Machakos), made boundaries for land newly registered with individual title deeds, constructed dams and other water supplies for domestic and livestock needs, cleared local roads and footpaths, and built new houses. In the late 1950s, during the Emergency, Machakos received visitors from other parts of Kenya and abroad to see this showpiece of 'the new colonialism'.[37] The Machakos *mwethya* workparty model of community development appears to have been subsequently adopted by district administration officials in many other parts of

Plate 5   Terracing in Machakos district

Kenya, including Kitui. The evident enthusiasm of participants and their achievements clearly impressed people.

Whether the work was genuinely voluntary is doubtful – District Commissioners' reports can hardly be taken as independent evidence. The District Commissioner's handing-over report in Kangundo in western Machakos in November 1955 states that communal labour remained for two days a week, as there was no other possibility, and that the communal labour tasks were transferred to neighbourhood groups wherever possible. This does not necessarily imply that there was no difference between communal labour and the new community *mwethya* groups, but it does mean that a transitional situation had evolved where new community development ideas were having an impact on colonial administration activity.

The choice of Machakos district for the project was significant. Machakos was seriously eroded, and the forceful methods of reducing the livestock population in 1938 – linked to the development of a British-owned meat factory which would purchase the slaughtered meat at reduced prices – had not only totally failed but had also generated long-lasting resentment and a readiness to protest vigorously, even violently, against any such schemes.[38] In 1952 Kamba were the majority ethnic group in the security forces and though they were regarded as generally loyal during the Emergency, there was a risk that they might join the rebellion led by their Kikuyu 'affines'[39] in neighbouring districts, either for nationalist reasons or simply because they felt economically deprived by colonial policies. Kamba economic aspirations had therefore to be met in some definite ways. The choice of John Malinda to commence the project in his home district thus suited several political and other purposes. Interviewed in 1974, Malinda said that the use of *myethya* for community development tasks had been his own idea and that his intention had been to bring development to the Kamba in a way that was acceptable to them and met their aspirations, and that this was successful enough for the colonial authorities to give their assent to it.

The success of Malinda's work rested on several factors. Principal among these was probably its implementation by a Kamba official with far better knowledge of local social organization, ideas and language than any European colonial administrator. The project was, furthermore, phrased as a reform of communal labour in the direction of local organization and decision-making, in place of the issuing of orders and punishments by chiefs and tribal police. The demand for development in a rapidly changing society ensured that the tasks undertaken were consistent with people's aspirations. The Kamba felt 'underdeveloped' but had not channelled their frustrations into political protest or rebellion on any significant scale – unlike their Kikuyu neighbours, who were experiencing much greater problems of land shortage originating in the alienation of land to white settlers, as well as much greater racial discrimination.

In Kitui during the second half of the 1950s there was an enormous increase in the demand for educational expansion. This was met initially through communal labour work in building elementary schools, together with increased involvement by the Africa Inland Mission and the Roman Catholic Mission, and the grants and the payment of teachers' salaries by the District Council.

In 1957 Kitui received its first African Administrative Officer, Titus Mbathi, who was from Mulango location in central Kitui. Educated in India – but not in any community development-related course – he was responsible for community development in the district. He started in Kitui the same village development system based on neighbourhood workparties [*myethya*] which had been pioneered in Machakos district by John Malinda. Beginning with villages near his home close to the Africa Inland Mission headquarters in Mulango, Mbathi organized new *mwethya* neighbourhood groups throughout Kitui district. The new *mwethya* groups in Kitui appeared to be more closely under the control of the district administration than they had been in Machakos, probably because the lesser impact of social change in Kitui had led to a correspondingly lesser popular demand for development. Mbathi, interviewed in 1974, said he accepted this view and the necessity for it, in the interests of the people and the projects that would benefit them.[40]

The similarity in terms of government control and coercion between the new *myethya* and communal labour in Kitui was borne out by a statement from informants in 1974 that 'there was no difference between those *myethya* and "white man's work" [i.e. communal labour]'. This was also corroborated by a letter from Mbathi in the Kenya National Archives, addressed to the District Commissioner, forwarding people's complaints about the lack of difference between the two institutions. The letter received the reply that *myethya* were voluntary while communal labour was compulsory.[41] But the evidence is that *myethya* were also compulsory and that they also performed communal labour work. The colonial records show that in parts of north Kitui in the late 1950s people had to work one day a week on communal labour and one day a week on *myethya*. In Kyuso division in the far north, people had to work two days a week on communal labour and three days a week on *myethya* during the dry season.

The colonial reports of the period also contain references to complaints about the *mwethya* system in southern Kitui, which resembled common complaints about chiefs – that corruption and abuse of power had led to chiefs benefiting personally from the work, for example, by having the groups build their own houses; that much effort was wasted through badly planned or useless projects; and that illegal *myethya* 'courts' were punishing evaders with fines of money or livestock which the officials or committees appropriated for themselves. However, much depended on local officials, and a District Commissioner's comment that *myethya* in one area interfered with the two days' work required for communal labour indicates that there at least, *myethya* were proceeding enthusiastically, whereas communal labour was not – a major difference evidently existing between them, in terms at least of people's motivation and willing participation.

Political changes on the eve of Independence led to the District Commissioner allowing the District Council to delete dams and bush-clearing from the list of compulsory communal labour tasks. Some of these tasks had previously been transferred to the *mwethya* system. However, with the compulsion and penalty system removed, these tasks were very rarely undertaken again on a genuinely voluntary basis.

Myethya too came under political attack. In 1960 the District Commissioner wrote:

Community Development work was concentrated on fostering group work by *myethya*. This system which in recent years has achieved a great deal in improving agricultural and domestic life throughout the district now, thanks to destructive political activity, survives with any strength only in the remoter parts of the district [i.e. the least politically conscious in nationalist terms].[42]

In 1962 the last British District Officer in Kitui, compiling the annual district report on behalf of the first African District Commissioner, wrote:

Low-grade political agitators poisoned the minds of the citizens against self-help schemes and the Native Authority. The district's main wealth lies in its vast reservoir of unskilled labour. If this could be tapped in *myethya* self-help endeavour, then real and lasting progress will result. It cannot be tapped at the moment because such action is denounced as colonial slavery, but it may well be that when *uhuru* [Independence] is achieved there will be such an upsurge of nationalist pride that everyone will work unpaid for the new Kenya.[43]

He added that 'the demand for [educational] facilities, especially in central division and Mutonguni/Migwani locations, was out of all proportion to the funds and teaching staff available.' Plans for thirty new intermediate schools were not realized because of lack of local government funding.

In Kitui, perhaps even more than in Machakos, the spirit of self-help and community development had been subordinated to the relations of colonialism. The persistence of communal labour regulations and the weak application of local initiative and decision-making in the new village development structures had made the system called 'self-help' vulnerable to the charges levelled at it by nationalist politicians that it was 'colonial slavery'. The District Officer's speculation on the eve of Independence that a new and vigorous self-help movement could arise from the achievement of political independence was strikingly accurate but displayed little understanding of why the existing system had been rejected, or why and under what conditions self-help might revive and flourish after Independence.

Independence and the Harambee Movement

'Harambee' was the new national slogan used, although not coined, by Jomo Kenyatta, the leader of the Kenya African National Union (KANU) and the first Prime Minister, later President, of the independent nation born in 1963. He formally introduced the slogan when he was sworn in as the elected Prime Minister in June 1963 to lead the country to full independence from Britain on 12 December the same year (named *Jamhuri*, or Republic Day). Since then, Harambee has been the motto on the national crest and the customary rally-cry at mass rallies – for example on Jamhuri Day each year and at rallies held by government officials or politicians at other time.[44]

'Harambee' derived from a Kiswahili work-gang cry – *'Aaaaaa – mbee!'*, which may be translated as 'Ready – push!'. In Kenya its normal translation into English was 'Let's pull together!' and its equivalent in other Kenyan languages is the term for 'community co-operation' – for example, *ngwatano* in Kikamba. *Ngwatano* is a reciprocal term (through the suffix *-ano*, or *-ana* in the verbal form *kukwatana*) meaning 'helping each other', as distinct from *ngwatio*, 'help', which was also sometimes used as a synonym. The term 'Harambee' had been used before Independence by some politicians, but it did not acquire national currency until Kenyatta's dramatic use of it at Independence. After that time, it became firmly associated with the post-Independence self-help movement.

The central message of the 'Harambee' slogan was Self-Reliance. This was expressed most concretely in the rural self-help movement, but the slogan underlay wider social, political and economic policies of independent Kenya which were propagated as representing 'the spirit of Harambee'. In the first decade of Independence it was often linked to other slogans or catchwords of the politicians of the new nation who preached 'Independence and Hard Work' (*uhuru na kazi* in Kiswahili), 'No manna from heaven', and 'No free things'.[45] Slogans specifically linked Harambee to Kenyatta himself.

The Harambee movement is appropriately called a 'movement', in the sense that it developed rapidly throughout Kenya in response to people's actions and aspirations rather than simply as a creation of the government. Its origins lay in the previous government-directed 'communal labour' system, which had been partially modified, as described above, in the last few years of colonial rule. However, the ideology as well as the actual practice of Harambee stressed firmly the people-directed nature of the new self-help organization. In ideas, values and practice, it developed as a politically deliberate contrast to colonial community development organization, and became central to the ideology of political independence and nationhood.

Table 2   *Kenya Primary School Pupils, 1938–73*

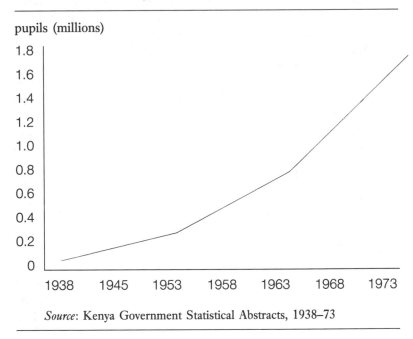

pupils (millions)

Source: Kenya Government Statistical Abstracts, 1938–73

Throughout Kenya in 1973–4 the Harambee slogan was prominent at government and political rallies, and Harambee events were featured in the news media almost daily. 'Harambee' conveyed positive meanings in government evocation no less than in popular expression.

Since Independence, thousands more primary schools had been built 'by Harambee' (see Table 2 and Plate 6). Hundreds of secondary schools were built (Table 3) with substantial contributions of money and labour from local communities and were called 'Harambee Schools'.

Table 3 *Kenya Secondary Students, 1938–73*

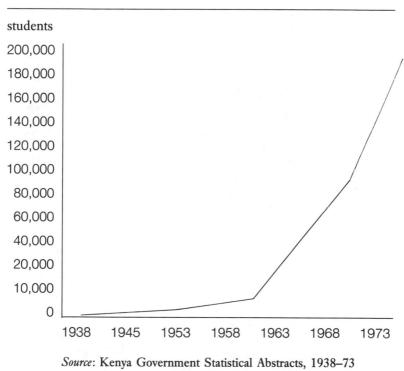

Source: Kenya Government Statistical Abstracts, 1938–73

The Ministry of Community Development and Social Services attempted to keep records of all self-help projects throughout the country to arrive at an estimated value of Harambee development.[46] The total value of Harambee contributions in just over a decade of Independence (1963–73) was estimated by the Community Development Department at £20m. This included thousands of village nursery schools and primary schools, wells and cattle-dips; over 250 rural health centres: over 700 secondary schools; and various piped-water projects, the biggest valued at £1/2m. In addition, seventeen post-secondary

Plate 6   Primary school in Nzambani

Institutes of Technology were being planned, each budgeted at over £1m.[47] The actual total value of Harambee contributions in cash and labour during this ten-year period was possibly twice the official estimate, perhaps as much as £40m. Although compared to government development expenditure over the period this figure was relatively small, it was achieved with minimal government assistance or resources. The quality of the projects varied from those that were successful and efficient, where there was no significant difference between the project created by Harambee rather than by government, to those that failed and wasted the resources put into them. Some projects – particularly the bigger ones – were only minimally participative in the community development sense. But by and large, it was evident that the Harambee movement was the product of 'felt needs' and embodied the aspirations of a development-minded population.

Harambee projects in Kitui ranged from the regular activities of the village self-help groups active in every village in the district, to the Ukamba Agricultural Institute (UKAI – an acronym also meaning 'come' in Kikamba) projected on an ethnic basis for the Kamba, alongside similar Institutes of Technology being proposed at the time by each other major ethnic group in the country. UKAI, planned mainly by Kamba educationalists in Nairobi working with Kamba politicians, may have been remote from the wishes and conceptions of most Kamba. But for villagers throughout Kitui, and also for most Kitui Kamba living or working outside Kitui, most of whom retained important social and economic ties with their district and village of origin, the village self-help group was a major institution in which they had a permanent involvement for themselves and their descendants.

The tie-up between the Harambee movement and the village self-help group was further strengthened by the overt and functional derivation of both from an important traditional form of community co-operation – the neighbourhood workparty [*mwethya*], which is described in detail in Chapter 4. As explained earlier in this chapter, the workparty model had already been introduced into Kitui and most of the rest of Kenya in the late 1950s. Its fuller realization after Independence represented a substantial social and political reformulation of the concept, as is described in Chapter 5. 'Harambee' evoked the workparty spirit, and indeed the village self-help group was itself a kind of permanent workparty.

If most newly independent African nations placed high value on self-help and self-reliance at the time of Independence, Kenya developed in the Harambee movement what was the most extensive self-help system of them all. 'Harambee' was a symbol of Independence. Though hardly a coherent political ideology, it contained an emotionally powerful and politically important appeal to unity, development, nationalism and the preservation of traditional cultural values. It became a vital part of the developing national culture despite the remarkably small input from government in terms of financial contribution.

Harambee in Kitui, 1963–74

In Kitui, the revival of *myethya* after Independence was rapid. With new African administrators (not usually of the same ethnic group as the local people) and a new political spirit, the most immediate and concrete representations of Independence were new self-help projects especially in the field of education.[48] New government-financed development projects often took time to be realized. Educational projects, particularly primary schools (Plates 7 and 8) and new self-help secondary schools, were started quickly and were popular. Unpopular communal labour tasks such as soil conservation and dam-building were not revived – indeed, the new administrators were particularly careful to make a clear distinction between pre-Independence and post-Independence community development work. In interviews, government officials always stressed their determination 'not to spoil the spirit of Harambee'. There were no longer any administration-imposed fines, beatings or jail sentences for absentees from self-help work. Sanctions and penalties were present, but they were instituted and imposed by the groups themselves. Perhaps even more important than the emotive appeal to nationalistic endeavour was the grounding of self-help in existing social structures and cultural traditions. Urban migrants, who retained extensive ties and relationships to

Plate 7 Mwethya making bricks for a primary school in Nzambani

Plate 8   Primary school choir singing for a Nzambani mwethya group

Plate 9 Mwethya groups working on Maluma cattle-dip

their village homes, also saw self-help development as directly benefiting their families and themselves.

The major popular demand in Kenya at Independence was for African advancement in education and employment. Education was seen as the main means of social mobility and occupational advancement and the main avenue through which African Kenyans could enjoy the 'fruits of *Uhuru* [Independence]'.

Education, at both primary and secondary levels was severely underdeveloped in colonial Kenya, and there was a massive spurt in educational development, particularly at the secondary level, immediately after Independence, through both government and self-help efforts (see Tables 2 and 3 above).[49] The majority of self-help projects after Independence were in the area of education. Only after educational needs were regarded by local communities as having been met – primary schools, secondary schools and pre-school nurseries – did they move their priorities into other areas of self-help community action, such as cattle-dips (Plate 9).

In Kenya, as has been described above, African education had owed little to government funding or organization until shortly before Independence. The onus for educational development had been laid first on the Christian missions and then on the Native District Councils. Thus there had long been a special link between education and community involvement in the development and financing of education.

Shortly after Independence, the self-help drive in the field of primary education was channelled into a new institutional relationship between government and local communities. In 1965 the Ministry of Education assumed responsibility for primary schools throughout the country, with the exception of mission schools and private schools. The government henceforward maintained, staffed and equipped primary schools, while local communities had to build and furnish them, also providing the land. This was achieved by local communities in Kitui through the self-help system based on *myethya* in their new form, as described in Chapter 5.

3 Kamale Village

The Village and its Neighbourhoods

Kamale village, where fieldwork was carried out, is in Nzambani administrative location, thirteen kilometres south-east of Kitui town, the district headquarters (see Map 4). Leaving the town on the main murrum (unpaved) road leading south to join the Nairobi–Mombasa highway at Kibwezi, one passed the office ('camp') of the Nzambani location chief at Chuluni, seven kilometres away. Just beyond Kwa Kinyai market, a road branched off east and at Nzewani market a narrow dirt road going south ended at Kamale village school. A fairly typical Kitui Kamba village, Kamale was densely populated in the central areas on both sides of the road; in its eastern and southern extensions the population thinned out towards more remote areas of pasture and bush.[1]

Nzambani, though near the district centre and containing in its northern parts some relatively good agricultural land, was known as a somewhat backward and change-resistant area. Its eponymous landmark, Nzambani rock, which could be seen from the Kitui–Mombasa road (Plate 10), had some fame due to the legend, probably never empirically tested, that those who walked round it seven times would change sex. In several respects Nzambani had retained many traditional institutions and beliefs which, in the more developed central locations in the district, existed only in the memory of elders.

In 1973 Kamale had a population of about 800.[2] Its boundaries were formally set and recognized by the district administration (Map 5). In the more densely populated central area, homesteads of between two and five dwellings and store-houses lay adjacent to one another, separated only by eucalyptus hedges or small cultivated areas (Plate 11). Paths led off the main village road in different directions; the habitations became sparser as one walked further out and one passed fields of maize, cow-peas and

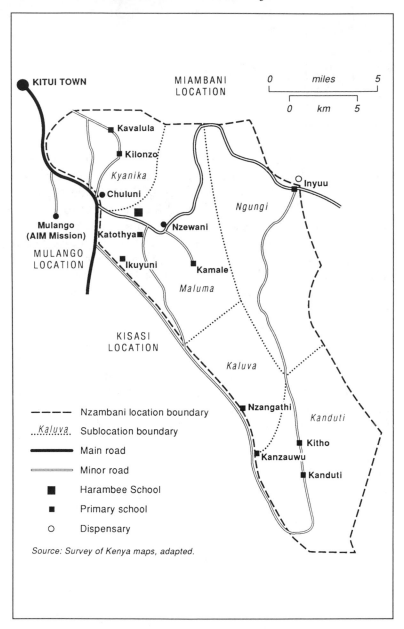

MAP 4 Nzambani Location

Plate 10   Nzambani rock

pigeon-peas, occasional riverine plots of bananas or sugar-cane, and a few small gardens of tomatoes and onions. Beyond was pasture for cattle, and uncultivated bush. A seasonal river formed the village boundary on three sides, separating Kamale from adjacent villages.

The village had a primary school, which was opened in early 1973 with one classroom completed and another unfinished, built with mud-bricks and iron-sheet roofing. A pre-school nursery near it was a more temporary construction. Nearby there was a small shop owned by a young trader from the village, stocked with little more than a dozen basic items such as tea, salt, cooking-fat, snuff, cigarettes, matches and sugar. Two other small modern enterprises were a brick-kiln for firing mud-bricks and a sugar-grinder for grinding sugar-cane to make beer. There was no electricity or piped water. Villagers obtained water from three communal wells and a few small privately owned wells, and a communal earth dam (water-reservoir) was used for watering cattle.

The majority of houses were circular, built with fired or sun-dried mud-bricks and either thatch or iron-sheet roofs. Only a small number of families with urban migrant workers had four-room rectangular houses – one of them also had painted walls and glass windows (Plate 12). A few people in the village had bicycles, but there were no motor vehicles. Motorized transport to Kitui town was available from Nzewani, when people needed to visit government offices, the hospital, court or market, but this often involved a long wait for a bus or Land Rover, and most people usually walked.

Kamale had its own self-help village development group, comprising all adults in the village. The Kamale self-help group, called the Kamale *mwethya*, worked regularly on self-help projects in the village and also combined with other similar groups from neighbouring villages on joint projects from whose facilities Kamale people would also benefit. Over the previous decade the self-help group had built the village road and some wells, but its major task was the construction and maintenance of the village primary school. In 1973 the major projects outside the village, to which villagers contributed with money or labour, included a projected self-help secondary school for the whole

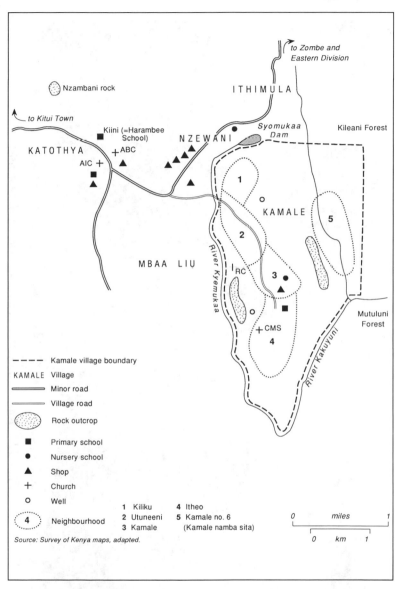

Nzambani rock

ITHIMULA

to Zombe and Eastern Division

to Kitui Town

Kiini (=Harambee School)

NZEWANI

Syomukaa Dam

Kileani Forest

KATOTHYA

+ABC

AIC +

KAMALE

5

1

2

MBAA LIU

River Kyemukaa

RC

3

Mutuluni Forest

+CMS

4

River Kakuyuni

- - - - Kamale village boundary

KAMALE　Village

====== Minor road

======= Village road

Rock outcrop

■　Primary school

●　Nursery school

▲　Shop

+　Church

○　Well

4　Neighbourhood

1	Kiliku	4	Itheo
2	Utuneeni	5	Kamale no. 6
3	Kamale		(Kamale namba sita)

Source: Survey of Kenya maps, adapted.

0　　　　miles　　　　1

0　　km　　1

MAP 5 Kamale Village

Plate 11   Kamale homestead with traditional beehive house

Plate 12   Modern house in Kamale

location (Nzambani Harambee School), a cattle-dip and a projected agricultural college (Ukamba Agricultural Institute, UKAI) which was then being planned for Kamba students generally, forty kilometres away in Yatta on the northern borders of Kitui and Machakos districts, the two sections of the Kamba people.

'Kamale' was the name given to the village at some point in its history, probably in the late nineteenth century.[3] The name derived from the verb *kumala*, 'to plaster' – for example, 'to plaster a threshing-floor with dung' – and was said to refer to the relatively high density of settlement and cultivation in the area. The area had probably been settled in the nineteenth century, with the central parts settled first, followed by expansion into outlying areas by new immigrants or new generations of older settlers. By the 1950s, land shortage in the central areas and the occupation of most of the cultivable land had brought new settlement to an end, although local expansion still continued at a slow pace, converting pasture or bush into arable land.

As the population expanded during the twentieth century, different settlement areas had become recognized as separate 'neighbourhoods'. Kamale in 1973 had five distinct and named sections or 'neighbourhoods' (*utui*, plural *motui*, deriving from the verb *kutua*, to reside). The term for 'village', *ndua*, was a different derivative of the same verb. The village's constituent neighbourhoods were geographically distinct areas of settlement, surrounded by cultivated fields, pasture and bush land. The five neighbourhoods were: Kamale, Kiliku, Utuneeni, Kamale Itheo ('Lower Kamale') and Kamale Number 6 (see Map 5). Two of the neighbourhoods had informally named geographical sections, one named after a natural feature and the other after a lineage ancestor, which might eventually become new neighbourhoods themselves. The three central neighbourhoods contained between twenty-six and thirty-one households or domestic groups each, with between 137 and 162 people in each neighbourhood. Table 4 gives demographic data from my household survey. In line with Kenya's population as a whole, about half the village population was of children and youths.

Table 4 *Kamale Households*

Neighbourhood	Homesteads	Households	0–9		10–19		20–39		40–59		60+		Total		
			m	f	m	f	m	f	m	f	m	f	m	f	all
Kamale	30	46	15	23	18	19	23	24	13	13	10	4	79	83	162
Utuneeni	31	46	16	22	23	16	12	21	10	16	9	6	70	81	151
Kiliku	26	37	22	20	11	14	20	18	8	13	8	3	69	68	137
TOTAL	87	129	53	65	52	49	55	63	31	42	27	13	218	232	450

= 118   = 101   = 118   = 73   = 40

(children 219)   (adults 231)

Notes

The three neighbourhoods surveyed contained about 56% of the village's population, approximately 800 people. The other two neighbourhoods, Itheo and Number 6, had 50 and 11 homesteads respectively. The average number of people per household was approximately 3.5.

Descent and Marriage

The traditional organization of descent-groups was of fundamental importance to social organization in Kamale, as throughout Kitui. Among the Kamba there were twenty-five patrilineal clans, dispersed throughout Machakos and Kitui districts as well as other smaller areas of Kamba settlement outside Ukambani. Some were named after or associated with a mythical totemic animal or bird ancestor. Others had special features – for example, one was associated by other clans with the evil eye [*kyeni*]; another was characterized by joking stories about it; members of another were prohibited from making pottery.[4]

Each clan [*mbai*] was segmented into lineages at varying levels of patrilineal descent, which were also themselves segmented on the same principle. Descent-groups at all levels of segmentation were called *mbai* and all were in theory exogamous, although in practice the level of exogamy varied and was linked to a local descent-group. Lineages were generally identified by the name of their founding ancestor – for example Mbaa Kanyaa, Kanyaa's lineage. Each clan or lineage had a rallying-cry [*kwiyava*] whereby any member hearing the cry was bound to help another who shouted it. Thus Kitondo clan members would shout '*ava Mbuli!*', 'sons of Mbuli!', to summon help. There were special markings for arrows, cattle brands, beehives (Plate 13), and pottery belonging to or made by members of the descent-group. Members of the same descent-group were called *mbaitu*, as against members of other descent-groups, who were called *awanda*.

Kamale had members of eight patrilineal descent-groups, of which four (Ngwenze, Kitondo, Kitulu and Ngo) had substantially more members than the others (see Table 5). Although four of these lineages were from the same clan, the village did not have a single dominant descent-group, unlike two of the nearby villages, Mbaa Liu and Mbaa Kataa, which were named after the large local lineages of Liu and Kataa.

Settlements containing more than one clan or lineage were commonly named after some natural feature of the area or on the basis of some other characteristic not associated with a descent-group, thus asserting the non-lineage basis of the

Plate 13   Beehive with Kitondo clan marking

community. The latter was the case with Kamale, as well as the adjacent village of Ithimula.

Table 5   *Descent-Groups in Kamale*

Descent-Group	Clan*	Households in each neighbourhood				
		Kamale	Utuneeni	Kiliku	Itheo	TOTAL
Ngwenze	Kanyaa/Nziu	8	27	1	2	38
Kitondo	(Kitondo)	21	3	10	12	46
Nziu	(Nziu)	–	–	4	2	6
Kitulu	Awini	–	1	4	17	22
Mutei	Awini	–	–	1	1	2
Muta	Ausini	–	–	1	–	1
Kiluu	Awini	–	–	5	–	5
Ngo	Awini	1	–	–	16	17
TOTAL		30	31	26	50	137

* Where the descent-group is a minimal lineage, the maximal lineage and then clan is given in this column. In other cases, the descent-group as stated is the clan itself (in brackets).

Although no neighbourhood in Kamale was based exclusively on one descent-group, Table 5 shows that there were concentrated clusterings of members of one or two descent-groups in each neighbourhood. This was particularly true in Utuneeni neighbourhood, where all the homesteads but four were of Ngwenze lineage. The other neighbourhoods were more mixed in lineage terms, but even so households of the same descent-group were mostly adjacent to each other as a result of previous expansion of younger generations of families on to nearby land.[5]

People addressed each other by kinship terms – there was no term of address for 'neighbour'. Everyone could trace their kinship relationship to each other through putative common descent or through non-descent ties created by marriage and affinity. However, both fellow lineage members and others were expected to follow norms of social behaviour and action which depended on a situational selection of social relationships based on descent or affinity, gender, age-status or generation. There were reciprocal terms of address for members of the same generation – *mwa* – and of higher or lower generation – *avai*. These social norms were combined with the rights and duties arising from co-residence in the same neighbourhood.

Local descent-groups rather than neighbourhoods were the basic land-holding corporations and units of dispute-settlement. The social importance of neighbourhoods rested partly on the informal social relationships of neighbourhood co-residence, which could be personalized into friendship ties, but more importantly on the central institutional expression of the neighbourhood – the neighbourhood workparty [*mwethya*]. This was the major form of labour co-operation, which is described in detail in Chapter 4.

The local patrilineal descent-group – whether named as a clan (such as Kitondo) or a maximal or minimal lineage of a clan (such as Ngwenze, a lineage of Kanyaa lineage, itself a lineage of Nziu clan) – was a jural and land-holding corporation. Disputes between members of the same or different descent-groups were generally settled by descent-group elders. The descent-group regulated inheritance of land within the group, for all land was in theory vested in the descent-group. Descent-group elders also sought to control sale and purchase of land to people outside the decent-group.

Men obtained access to land as a result of their membership of a descent-group through patrifiliation. They were buried on this land. Occasionally in the past, new members were incorporated into a descent-group through a special ritual – for example in the case of a 'dependant' [*mbooswa*] who had come to live with a family, such as a famine refugee or a captured enemy. Land could also be purchased – the buyers in the village being almost entirely wealthier local farmers or urban migrants. Land sales were expected to be more frequent in the future, as land registration and the issuing of individual title deeds were just starting in the village. The preference was to sell land within the descent-group. In 1974 there was much local resistance to the proposed purchase of some land in the village by a Swahili trader who had a shop in the nearby small market of

Nzewani, and the descent-group controlling the land was trying to prevent this.

Women gained land rights through marriage to a descent-group member. At marriage, a new wife received land from her husband, which she cultivated to feed her family. This was divided on her death among her sons in equal shares. Any land a man himself owned – that is, land pioneered or bought – was divided among his sons and along equal lines of matri-segmentation if he had more than one wife. The eldest brother, or the eldest male of each matri-segment, had jural authority over his younger brothers' land. Despite the rules, however, disputes over land were common.

The clan, rather than the lineage, was traditionally the level of descent-group organization at which bloodwealth compensation [*mambo*] was paid in the event of a murder. Bloodwealth took the form of livestock gathered by the murderer's agnatic kin to be paid to the agnatic kin of the murder victim. The amount was traditionally 14 cows, or in modern times the monetary equivalent reckoned at 120 shs per cow (an equivalence fixed at some time in the past and preserved despite inflation more than doubling the monetary value of a cow). In the past two decades the collection of bloodwealth had been controlled by officially recognized clan associations and confined to clan members in nearby locations rather than throughout the whole of Ukambani or the whole of Kitui. (Murder by an agnatic relative, however, was believed to be automatically punished by spiritual affliction of the murderer, and no bloodwealth was paid.) Payment of bloodwealth was not quite a defunct institution in 1973, and notionally existed alongside the impersonal modern police and judicial processes. A village murder would probably have led to the traditional reconciliation processes if murderer and victim were of different clans, and bloodwealth payments would probably have been demanded. Nziu clan members in Kamale had paid bloodwealth seven years previously.

Of the eight descent-groups in Kamale (Table 5), some were localized minimal lineages, such as Mbaa Ngwenze (Ngwenze's lineage), which was named after a focal ancestor (Ngwenze); the maximal lineage (Mbaa Kanyaa) was not usually referred to, and the clan (Mbaa Nziu) was hardly ever mentioned.

Other descent-groups were named after the clan (for example Mbaa Kitondo) but were in effect local lineages of the clan, with the point of segmentation marked only when relevant by reference to a particular ancestor. The difference between the stress on the lineage as against the clan probably pointed to different strategies of migration and local settlement. The former represented a more 'closed' strategy where known descent was the basis of incorporation into a new settlement; the latter reflected a more 'open' strategy of recruitment of even distant agnatic kin to form a new local descent-group.

Marriage was regulated by descent-groups and established relations of affinity between two exogamous descent-groups. The preferred marriage was that of a man to a woman of the same descent-group as his father's father's wife – that is to say, a classificatory second matrilateral cross-cousin (father's mother's brother's son's daughter). Marriage with a first matrilateral cross-cousin (mother's brother's daughter) was strictly prohibited. These marriage rules made possible a cycle of affinal relations between descent-groups linked in pairs over alternate generations. However, because the number of clans was large (twenty-five in all) and because descent-group exogamy was variable, the range of affinal ties possible through the two marriage rules – the positive preference and the negative proscription – was not closely restricted.

Marriage was recognized by payment of bridewealth by the husband's descent-group to the wife's descent-group. The customary bridewealth payment in Kamale in 1973 was 2 bulls, 8 cows and 46 goats, paid by instalments. After an inital negotiated payment of some of the goats, a bull and one or two of the cows, followed by other gifts and exchanges, the new bride [*kiveti*] was ritually taken to her husband's home. The marriage became firm on the birth of children, particularly a son, and on further payment of instalments of the bridewealth. Payments might not be finished even in a husband's lifetime, thus creating debts in the next generation.

There was no specific institution of divorce *per se*, only separation or remarriage. If the marriage broke down and the wife moved back to her parental home, the husband would seek to retrieve the bridewealth already paid from her agnatic kin or from her new husband – that is, the next man who started paying bridewealth to her agnatic kin and thus established that she was his wife. It was customary for a widow to be remarried to (that is, inherited by) a close agnatic relative of her deceased husband (particularly her husband's elder brother). The new husband continued the bridewealth payments not completed by her former husband (to which the new husband might in fact already have contributed).

In addition, there were three further forms of marriage, which were similarly regulated by descent-groups and marked by the commencement of marriage payments:

– an infant girl could be betrothed to an adult male, or a mature woman to a male child;

– a girl could be 'married' to the name of the deceased unmarried son of a woman who had no other son, so as to obtain an heir for the deceased son and, by extension, an heir for the deceased son's mother too;

– a woman without a son could pay bridewealth to obtain a 'wife' for the son she had not had, so that she would have a 'daughter-in-law' and a 'grandson' could be born to inherit her property.

In both the latter two cases, it was expected that the 'wife' would live in the homestead of the payer of the bridewealth and would choose a sexual partner either freely or within the range of kin who had rights of licensed sexual access.[6]

The function of these supplementary marriage institutions was evidently to ensure that no man or woman was 'childless' – that lines of descent and inheritance for both men and women were kept continuous and unbroken as far as possible. Even if an individual was biologically childless through infertility, everyone could be a parent in the more important social sense. In this sense, these additional marital institutions ensured overall equality of marital status where biological or individual factors might have made some less equal than others.

Polygyny was permitted under the same conditions as described above. In a first marriage, a man in his twenties usually married a woman in the first few years after her puberty. A wealthier and older man could marry a second or further wife among girls of that same age. In Kamale in 1973, only seventeen men had more than one wife – fifteen had two wives and two had three: some of these were wealthier than the average, but it seemed – though research data was incomplete – that most polygynous marriages were contracted either through widow-inheritance or in order to have a second chance at producing a male heir when the first marriage had not done so.

Even when younger Christians in Kamale had a church wedding ceremony according to the marriage rituals and conventions of their particular sect, this still followed the prior establishment of the marriage through bridewealth payments and in accordance with traditional marriage rules. Some traditional rituals connected with marriage might be wholly or partially ignored or rejected, but no Christian sect sought to ban bridewealth, though some were opposed to polygyny.

Households

In Kamale, the basic unit of residence was the homestead. Traditionally the homestead was called *muvya* – 'gate' – in reference to the narrow entrance to the thick thorn fence which used to surround it and protect it from enemy and beast Homesteads used to be quite far apart from each other and were called 'the gate of so-and-so', being named after the head of the homestead, its most senior lineage member. The average homestead consisted of an unfenced compound close to its neighbour, containing one, two or three round mud-walled thatched houses, livestock huts, and one or two small grain-stores in a central cleared open area (Plate 14). Homesteads in the outlying areas were still fenced though, like others in the central areas, they were smaller than in the past (Plate 15). There were also some fenced cattle enclosures in the pasture areas far away from the residential areas.

Two-thirds of homesteads in Kamale comprised a single-family domestic group or household, typically of a man, his wife and their dependent children.[7] The term for household was *musyi* – 'house'. A particular household was called 'the house of so-and-so', after the household head, who was called

Plate 14   Widow's homestead in Kamale

Plate 15   Fenced homestead in Kamale bush area

'the owner of the house' [*mwene wa musyi*], and was the potential founder of a new lineage. Of the other one-third of homesteads in Kamale, which contained more than one household, most contained two households, and only a very few contained three. In the past, homesteads were generally larger and contained more households. In 1973 the term *muvya* was rarely used to describe a person's home because few homesteads were still fenced and most were of one household only – hence they were usually called *musyi*.

The household was physically centred on the house [*musyi*] of the wife of the jural household head. The house was traditionally built for a bride when she moved from her parental home to her marital home. It was sited on her new husband's lineage land, and the house was built by a special workparty, *mwethya wa uthoni*, 'the workparty of affinity'.[8]

Both the old thatched 'beehive' house – *kikuli*, of which few examples were still found in 1973 (see Plate 11 above) – and the round mud-walled thatched house which had become the standard architectural form since the 1950s usually contained separate areas for sleeping, cooking and storage. The focal point of the house was the hearth of three cooking stones next to the centre pole supporting the roof, where the wife cooked the household meals. In the two previous decades many people had built separate kitchens and separate livestock huts, of the same construction type but smaller. There were twenty-two modern rectangular houses in the village – the vast majority of dwellings were traditional rondavel houses, with walls mud-smeared or constructed of sun-dried mud-bricks, and with a roof of thatch or iron (zinc) sheeting.

The development of new housing forms and layouts, with a store, kitchen and livestock pen separate from the sleeping or domestic area, did not in itself alter the activities or social functions of the domestic unit, or its development cycle. The wife organized the house: it was 'hers' and her husband was, as it were, only a permanent visitor. Her younger children of both sexes and older unmarried daughters also slept there, while older boys usually slept in granaries or shelters in the fields or pastures. In a polygynous family, a man's second wife would have the house built in the same homestead as the first wife and would eventually establish a separate household there. In modern times, second wives and their children tended to live in a separate homestead near their own fields. In Kamale there were examples of both joint and separate households of a polygynous marriage.

In the development cycle of the wife-centred household, the new household was first dependent on the husband's natal household (for example, of his mother and his unmarried siblings) but after the new wife had given birth to one or two children, her own economic and domestic activities attained greater independence, until she cooked eventually for her husband and children only. The development towards further household economic independence continued until the domestic group migrated to form a new and independent homestead on lineage land nearby or on newly cleared bush land. The new homestead thus became the focal point of a new local lineage. In the past, the cycle of domestic group development from marriage to migration took much longer, and many homesteads used to contain a four-generation descent-group composed of brothers' and their sons' families. In 1973 such large homesteads were very few, and some new homesteads were being established by much younger families than would have been permitted in the past.

In 1973 many households in Kamale were headed by women, either because their husbands were absent working outside the village or outside Kitui altogether, or because the husband had one or more other wives, and had based himself at the house of the latest-married wife. He was still expected to visit, eat and sleep at each wife's house, treating them all the same, although the senior wife had a higher degree of respect. While the husband was away working, the 'acting' jural head of the household was the next most senior close agnatic male relative – for example, the husband's brother.

Kinship

Ties of kinship rested on relations founded on institutions of descent and marriage. Kinship was a fundamental principle of social organization in many institutional spheres.[9] Understanding kinship was essential for understanding the society and functioning effectively in it. Material collected in Kamale about kinship is presented here in order to complete the picture of Kamale society with relation to the issue being studied, and for the ethnographic record, where previous treatments of the subject have been inadequate. It is not claimed, however, that this is a definitive or complete account of kinship among the Kamba of Kitui.

Two contrasted types of kinship relationship were constantly stressed – *kikio*(verb – *kwiia*), meaning 'respect/avoidance', and *kuthauka* (a verb without a noun equivalent), meaning 'to joke or make fun'. Both were special terms without other referents and were associated with kinship relations of authority on the one hand, and familiarity and prescribed playfulness on the other.

Broadly speaking, *kikio* was required behaviour between patrilateral and matrilateral kin of the same and adjacent generations, and it applied particularly between a man and his mother's brother's daughter, with whom marriage was strongly prohibited, although there was no *kikio* with the other cross-cousins. *Kikio* was also the required relationship of affinity, *uthoni*, except for two particular affines [*athoni*, sing – *muthonua*] – wife's brother and sister's husband.

Kikio varied in intensity: it was strongest between father and son, mother and son, father and daughter, mother and daughter, husband and wife, brother and sister, and mother's brother and sister's son. *Kikio* between spouses and between siblings was less strong. Beyond the immediate family, the respect/avoidance of the relationship gradually diminished with genealogical distance, although it was always present in the relevant classificatory kinship relationship.

Kikio was a similar feature of the relationship of affinity where it also varied in intensity. It was most intense with the 'real' affine (*muthonua* – wife's mother and husband's mother); less intense with other close affines, such as spouse's elder siblings, husband's elder brother and sister's daughter's husband; and least intense, though always notionally present, with more distant affines.

Kikio, from the side of the junior partner in the relationship, was traditionally marked by name avoidance (periphrasis) – substituting 'son of . . . ' or 'daughter of . . . ' for the person's own name; the obligation to comply with requests or orders; and the observance of avoidance rules, such as not passing close to someone, not having physical contact with them, not making any reference to sexual matters or pregnancy in their presence. (These traditional avoidances, however, were little observed in 1973.) The ultimate sanction on the preservation of *kikio*, still much feared, was the power of the superordinate person in the relationship to curse [*kumanya*] the offending subordinate. I heard of no case in 1973–4 of a curse being formally laid on anyone or anyone dying from being cursed, and it still remained an ultimate threat based on the belief in the efficacy of the curse, even if it was not a punishment actually used.

Kuthauka was a prescribed relationship of joking, making fun or playfulness, which operated in social areas where there were no important authority or property/inheritance relationships. It was the obverse of *kikio* and applied to relationships where there was no *kikio*, such as between kin of alternate generations, with spouse's younger siblings, with classificatory wives ('wives of the descent-group'), and with the cross-cousins except for mother's brother's daughter (who was termed differently and aligned to mother). In the *kuthauka* relationship joking was obligatory, and consisted of such 'fresh' behaviour as making sexual references, making fantasy requests, discussing intimate or embarrassing issues, gossiping and, between potential sexual partners, having licensed sexual access – but not marriage. Like *kikio*, it varied in intensity according to the structural closeness or distance of the relationship.

Table 6 indicates the range of relationships reflecting these two modes of socially prescribed behaviour of *kikio* and *kuthauka*, and the kin terms associated with them.

Kinship was also organized according to the principles of the unity of the descent-group [*mbai*] – with the corresponding co-identity of affines [*athoni*] – and the unity of the generation [*nziawa*]. But there were other categorizations too. For example, generational 'skewing' corrected the dogmatic application of generational unity so as to protect important principles of kinship and marriage, by merging mother's brother's daughter (with

Table 6   *Kamba Kinship Terms*

Term	−+	Referent	Details
nau	−	F, FZH	1st person only, 2nd *au*, 3rd *ithe*. *Tata* = informal term for F.
mwaitu	−	M, FBW	= ours; 1st person only, 2nd *nyukwe*, 3rd *mwenyu*. Females use *inya* for M.
mwendw'au	−	FB, FZ, MZH, MBDH	= beloved father [*mwendwa au*]. = *mwendwasa*.
naimiwa	−	MB	= *inya ume wakwa* (my male mother). Reference only: address term is *mama* (tone _ −, contrasts to tone − _ = mother in Kiswahili), reciprocal in address.
mwivawa	−	ZS, ZD	also *mwiw'a*.
umau	+	FF, FM, WFF, WMF, FZS, FZD, MBS	Reciprocal in address.
susu	+	MM, FM, WFM, WMF	Reciprocal in address.
kiveti	+	W, BW, ½BW, FBSW	= term for wife/married woman; obsolete address term = *kiwandu*.
muimiwa	+	H	=*mume wakwa* (my man).
muthonua	−	WM, MBW, WsrZ, WF, WBW, ZSW, ZDH	= affine; address – *muthoni*.
mwendya	−	MZ, MBD	= beloved mother [*mwendwa inya*]. Reciprocal in address; generational skewing assimilates MZ to MBD.
mwanaaya	−	B, ZH, WB, FZDH	=*mwana wa inya* (mother's son); also *mwanaamwaitu*.
mwanaasa	−	½B, FBS	= *mwana wa asa* (father's son);
mwiitwaya	−	Z, ZHZ	= *mwiitu wa inya* (mother's daughter); also *mwiitwaitu*.
mwiitwaasa	−	½Z, FBD	= *mwiitu wa asa* (father's daughter).
mukuwa	−	elder sibling	=*mukuu wakwa* (my elder).
mwinawa	+	younger sibling	= *munini wakwa* (my small one).
mwanaakwa	−	S, BS, WBS	= *mwana wakwa* (my boy).
mwiitwakwa	−	D, BD, WBD	= *mwiitu wakwa* (my girl).
musukuwa	+	SS/D	
nzukulu	+	SSS/D	*nzukuku* may be same, or SSSS/D.
muamua	+	WjrZ	Reciprocal in address.
mwanaa-mwendya	−	MZS	= son of *mwendya*; also *wainyake* (mother's son).
mwiitwa-mwendya	−	MZD	= daughter of *mwendya*.
ukulu	−	HB	leviratic heir of BW.

Note: −+ in column 2 refer to *kikio/kuthauka* respectively.

whom marriage was prohibited) with mother's sister [*mwendya*], and husband's elder sister with mother (and her husband with father). Generational skewing also merged grandfathers [*umau*] with three cross-cousins (FZS, MBS, FZD), in recognition that they were not *kikio* relations – none of these relatives was involved in institutions directly concerned with authority, inheritance or marriage. Spouse's siblings were differentiated according to whether they preceded or succeeded spouse in birth order – the former were marked by *kikio* and the latter by *kuthauka*.

Certain aspects of kinship terminology were explicable by reference to positive and negative marriage rules. As mentioned already, the ideal or preferred arrangement was for a man to marry where his father's father married – that is, to repeat marriage ties between descent-groups in alternate generations. A man should thus marry a second matrilateral cross-cousin, who came from *mbaa umau* – his father's mother's brother's clan – and was a classificatory *umau* in a relationship of *kuthauka*. As father's affines became matrilateral kin in the next generation, the son's marriage into a matrilateral clan made matrilateral ties into affinal ties again. Matrilateral kinship and affinity thus alternated across the generations. This made possible a network of firm ties between a minimum of four local descent-groups. It was not a four-section system, though, because Kamba had twenty-five exogamous clans and maximal lineages were also potentially exogamous, thus imposing no narrow restriction (other than practicalities of locality) on descent-group-directed marriage choice.

This interlocking system of ties within and across generations would have facilitated the creation of solidary local ties for migratory settlement groups under threat from a harsh physical and human environment. The pattern of marriages would theoretically have created a continuous flow of bridewealth payments to and fro between exogamous descent-groups, alternating in a non-hierarchial manner.[10] Relations of descent and affinity were thus both of major importance to the overall organization of the society, and the kinship rules and behavioural prescriptions associated with them shored up the system in operation.

How far this positive marriage rule was systematically followed in the past is difficult to know: in 1973 it was still set up as an example but did not appear to be systematically followed, although I had insufficient data to be sure of this. In contrast, there was a firmly upheld negative marriage rule that a man should not marry where his father married – that is to say, a girl who was a classificatory mother's brother's daughter [*mwendya*], a matrilateral cross-cousin, who could even be called 'mother' and was subject to extreme *kikio*.

The Village Economy

Kitui is generally a 'dry, marginal agricultural area', albeit with considerable variation of ecological zones.[11] It has an approximate average rainfall of 500–1,060 millimetres, but with wide variations between 183 and 1,900 millimetres falling in two rainy seasons (October to December and April to May). Its altitude ranges from 610 to 1,370 metres above sea level, except for higher mountainous areas rising to 1,830 metres. An economic survey of Kitui district published in the 1971–4 District Development Plan reported that crop failure was frequent and intensive agriculture was possible only in a few higher-altitude areas. In general, drier areas had a sparser population but with more livestock-breeding, while wetter, higher areas had a denser population with very little livestock-breeding. The district had many seasonal streams (such as the river Kyamukaa in Kamale – see Map 5) but only two permanent rivers – Tana and Athi – which formed the district's boundaries in the north, south and east. For most of the year, people obtained water with great difficulty from wells dug into dry river-beds or from earth dams dug in colonial days and by 1973 mostly in a poor state of repair.

Kamale was officially described as a 'high agricultural potential' area compared to much of Kitui. In Kamale, as in most of Kitui, slash-and-burn agriculture was practised, with maize as the main cereal crop. Maize had largely replaced the older, traditional staple crops of sorghum, bulrush millet and finger-millet (Plates 16 and 17). Pigeon-peas and cow-peas were

Plate 16   Pounding maize

Plate 17   Winnowing pounded maize

the main legumes. Important subsidiary crops were cassava, sweet potatoes, yams, sugar-cane (mainly used for brewing alcohol, as an alternative to honey, which was a prized resource, harvested from individually owned hives hung in baobab tres, and much used in ritual), bananas, pumpkin and squashes. Some modern farmers also grew onions and tomatoes, for which there was some local demand in markets and shops for cooking with vegetables or meat. Crops were inter-planted and rotated, and land was left fallow when crop yields started to diminish. Rainfall and soil were poor in most of the village, though there were important environmental differences within the village affecting the productivity of fields in different locations. Fresh gardens were dug from the bush fairly often, although the migration of domestic units and population expansion had led to the extension of cultivation on to what was previously pasture.[12]

Livestock were also an important form of wealth and economic activity. They were reckoned in monetary terms and might be sold at livestock markets to pay for a wide range of economic needs, such as court fines, school fees, or even food (during famine). Few people in Kamale had more than a few cows, though herds of goats and sheep were larger. Every household also kept chickens. Livestock products were an important part of the diet, as well as providing meat for social occasions. Livestock were also the medium of most important social transactions, such as marriage payments (bridewealth), bloodwealth payments, ritual payments, fines and gifts. Whereas the monetary market value of livestock perpetually changed, their 'social' value in monetary terms (in bridewealth payments, customary law fines, and so on) remained unaltered over years.

Production was based on the labour of the household domestic unit. Domestic labour was supplemented at times by workparties of varying size and composition. The main basic tools used in farming were the machete and the hoe, although some people still used a digging-stick for planting. Few had ploughing oxen (Plate 18) and tractors had not been used in the village.

Few people had any significant cash income from farming over and above their subsistence needs, even though everyone had certain cash requirements for basic and unavoidable expenses, both in pursuit of individual needs and also as a result of

Plate 18   Ploughing

national or community obligations, such as paying school fees and self-help dues. In addition, everyone looked for something better for themselves and their children, whether defined in terms of consumer items or more productive items.

Most farmers used traditional or semi-traditional techniques. In Kamale, only nineteen farmers could be categorized as 'progressive farmers' trained in modern farming methods. In addition, thirty-two youths and children (including several of the children of these progressive farmers) belonged to the 4K club for modern young farmers. About half the adult progressive farmers were moderately successful and had built modern rectangular houses, but their cash incomes were still very low. The poor soil quality, combined with erratic and insufficient rainfall, prevented them from attaining a reasonable cash income from modern farming techniques or crops. Cotton was grown by several progressive farmers and their children, but it yielded relatively little income. A few farmers also grew sugar-cane, tomatoes and onions, or cabbages for sale. Some others, both progressive and traditional farmers, sold bananas, mangoes or any other surplus crops, such as pigeon-peas or maize, in local markets or to local shops. However, produce of main crops was rarely sufficient to guarantee the family's food supply over the year and to provide a reserve in case of drought, which was common. Those who sold a new crop and then needed to buy food in time of drought usually had to pay two or three times as much for it.

About one-third of the men from the village were permanently away, spending most of their adult lives in towns outside Kitui and working regularly or intermittently in paid employment. Their occupations included: a primary school teacher, a postal clerk, two shop assistants, drivers, factory employees, railway workers, watchmen, domestic servants and petrol station attendants. Virtually all the men in the village had been outside to look for work, and many of the older men had worked in towns for several years or served in the army. Not all of those who were away from Kitui in 1973 had found regular employment, particularly those entering the labour market in recent years.

Virtually all younger men thought about or planned going outside to look for work, even the younger progressive farmers.

Incomes from manual jobs in a town might be higher than farm incomes, but high urban living costs were a major drawback. Several middle-aged Kamale men were established urban migrants, particularly in Mombasa (350 kilometres away), visiting the village only once or twice a year for a few days or a little longer. They sent remittances home to their wives and children, but with the cost of life in the town, and because they had to spend money on establishing themselves there or saving for larger items to bring back home eventually to the village, their rural-based families received little regular income from them, relying basically on their own farming for their livelihood. Some of these urban migrants had returned to Kamale with their retirement benefits, built modern houses and bought land. This was the aspiration of all the urban migrants.

Only five people in the village had regular local employment. Four were men: a schoolteacher in a nearby primary school, a shop assistant in the village, a clerk in Kitui town ginnery, and a self-employed mason. One Kamale woman worked in a bar at the coast – the only female urban migrant from the village. A few people regularly did casual labour [*kibarua*], which was often available for either men or women during the heavy agricultural season. A small number of people in Kamale had other non-farm incomes. For example, one man owned a sugar-grinder and charged for grinding sugar-cane; another had started a shop in the village; a few women sold home-brewed sugar-beer (illegally); a tailor made or repaired clothes on his home sewing-machine; some men who had built a kiln fired mud-bricks for sale. Two women were regular market traders, selling farm produce in the local market 'ring' (Plate 19) and using their income for children's school fees, buying land, and maintaining a slightly higher standard of living than their neighbours. Eleven other women were less frequent market traders. There were no traditional crafts which commanded any significant market, though one woman made clay cooking-pots which she sold in Kitui town market (Plate 20). One man occasionally made traditional stools similar to those collected by Lindblom in 1911 but no other traditional artistic skills were practised, by either traditional or modern practitioners. Ritual specialists, lineage 'moot' elders and the two village

Plate 19   Carrying bananas to market

Plate 20   Making pots

'local leaders' also had irregular incomes from the services they provided.

At least since the 1930s, money had been widely used in Kamale for new exchange functions and other new purposes – such as payment of poll tax, school fees, court fines, or bribes to officials. Modern markets had developed in Kitui in colonial times.[13] According to Stanner, there had been no traditional market places but internal trade was carried out from people's homes through a detailed system of barter [*ngwano*], which involved a degree of bargaining [*king'ang'a*]. Most goods were interchangeable, except for practical constraints on the exchange of large and valuable items for small or cheap items. There was no pre-colonial coinage or 'special purchase money', but there was a detailed system of value equivalences of goods, livestock and agricultural products, based on market principles. Food prices increased when there were shortages in time of famine but decreased in time of plenty. Trade in female cattle, which was called *kyuu* (the same term as for cattle-kraal), had a ritual attached to the sale. This consisted of a blessing ceremony [*kwathima*] in which beer was poured on the earth with prayers, thus creating a guarantee that if the cow did not produce calves, it had to be replaced from the original owner's kraal. Exchange of male cattle had no such ceremony and was merely called *kithuki* – 'a stump': there was no question of any further guarantee or 'insurance', and the material transaction was completed there and then without any supernatural sanction. These traditional means of exchange were still practised in 1973 in intra-village cattle sales in Kitui, although not in modern cattle-market sales.

In Nzambani in 1973 there was a weekly 'ring' of markets which had been established in colonial times. It had changed since then only in detail, as marketplaces developed or waned. Market traders travelled from one market to another each week within a radius of about twenty kilometres to sell the same goods. A small market on the outskirts of Kamale, at Nzewani (still known as Nzewani market – see Map 4), had become defunct as shops grew up around it, and shops had begun to sell some of the local produce previously only sold in the market. The same had happened at Chuluni 'market'

– Plate 21 – which in 1973 had become a small shopping centre without an actual market. Nzewani 'market' had three general shops selling basic items, a tea house, a butcher's shop, and a bar selling bottled beer, soft drinks and the traditional sugar-beer, *uki wa sukali*, which was mostly consumed by elders, who could often be seen weaving their drunken way home in the evening. Among elders alcoholism seemed to be quite prevalent, the only abstainers being Christians or former urban migrants who bought Kenya-produced bottled beer at 2.50 shs a bottle as opposed to 50 cents for a half-calabash of sugar-beer.

People occasionally went to the shops in Chuluni market, eight kilometres away by road, or even to shops or the big market in Kitui town, twice as far, if they needed modern items not sold elsewhere, such as tools or machine parts. They usually went on foot, or sometimes on a bus (which was very irregular) or a privately owned Land Rover service, costing 50 cents. A few basic items were available in the Kamale shop but everything was slightly cheaper in Kitui, as transport costs put up the price of goods outside town, larger measures were divided into relatively more expensive smaller units, and village traders sought more profit from smaller sales volumes.

A small minority of the urban migrants and 'progressive farmers' – the majority of them Christians with some primary education – had done well enough in recent years to erect rectangular brick houses (Plate 22), setting them apart from their neighbours with round mud-brick thatched or zinc-roofed houses. Many Kamale men and some of the women had had extensive contact with modern urban Kenya as a result of being labour migrants at the coast. Chains of migration had developed where fellow villagers (or, more particularly, fellow clansmen from the village) helped each other and often lived close together, in the search for employment, housing, friendship and partners, and other basic welfare needs. The village had an outside 'branch' or association in the coastal city of Mombasa, through which village social relationships were maintained.

This small 'village elite' was in several small but locally significant ways differentiated from the rest of the village in their home possessions, consumption profile, economic achievements, and ambitions for themselves and their children. Nevertheless,

Plate 21   Shops at Chuluni market

Plate 22   Progressive farmer with his wife, Kamale

few had cut themselves off socially from their neighbours or kin in any significant way.

Political Organization

Like the rest of Kitui, Kamale was involved in two different political systems: the modern, national political system, and traditional Kamba political institutions. In the former, people over eighteen could register as voters and vote for candidates for political office in the Kenya National Assembly, Kitui District Council and Kitui Area Council. They also elected two village 'local leaders' [*mutui*, plural *atui*], unpaid officials from the village whose function was to represent the villagers to the administration as well as represent the administration to the villagers and implement the subchief's instructions. People could join the Kenya African National Union (KANU), the only permitted political party, and stand for office in it. Apart from formal political activity of this kind, or informal political action in the same political areas, they might also involve themselves in a variety of local organizations, such as churches, traders' associations, administration-related development committees at district, division and location level, or self-help group committees.

In Kamale in 1973, no one was a member of any national or district-level political forum. There were a small number of Christians in the village who were active in local church affairs, but these activities did not in themselved confer political prestige outside their own churches. Some women belonged to *Maendeleo ya Wanawake*, the national women's organization, but their membership was not particularly active.

People's political activities were mainly concerned with their roles as voters at election time. National parliamentary elections were held in Kenya every five years, and the period of fieldwork was marked by pre-election 'fever' – elections could have been announced at any time up to late 1974. The election date in October 1974 was announced only the month before, just after I had left the country. Self-help and politics were closely intertwined at a certain level at all times: the connections between politics and the Harambee movement are discussed in Chapter 5.

At the same time, people were intensely involved in 'traditional' political activities and processes. These were less 'visible' than formal political activities and were principally related to informal status-definition processes in the village and the quest for local prestige and influence. Particularly important for the purposes of the examiniation of self-help activities was the structure of local leadership and decision-making as regards community action and objectives, as well as the processes of socialization into traditional and modern roles and values.

Kamba society was traditionally 'stateless' or 'acephalous', having no centralized political structures or statuses. Political organization was based on the patrilineal descent-group principle, which was cross-cut by forms of local organization deriving from co-residence – age-statuses in particular; and from socialization into Kamba beliefs and values – 'being a true Mukamba'. Much emphasis was placed on individual achievement in different institutional areas – economic, political, legal and ritual.

AGE-STATUS

Kamba society had a set of 'age-statuses' [*iika*] through which all Kamba passed in their life-cycle (see Table 7). These did not constitute corporate or named 'age-sets' or 'age-groups'. The transitions between these statuses were not themselves marked by dramatic group-based *rites de passage* – as, for example, among Kenyan pastoral societies such as the neighbouring Maasai.

There was traditionally some ornamental and symbolic differentiation between age-statuses in clothing, jewellery, hair-style and bodily decoration. Kamba youths and girls were noted for adopting rapidly changing fashions of hair and clothing design, scarification (such as having arrow designs etched on to their cheeks) and teeth-chipping (creating an inverted 'V' between the two front teeth), which came and went as quickly as dance fashions. There were important divisions of social functions between different statuses. For example, in pre-colonial and early colonial times, youths used to participate in hunting, raiding and trading enterprises, while elders stayed at home and had many tasks of jural and political management. Girls and boys danced and worked. Young men travelled and eventually married and started families. Male elders were the political and jural leaders of the society, performed elders' dances, did different jobs to those for younger men, and drank alcohol.

Table 7   *Kamba Age-Statuses*

Age	Male	Female	Initiation ritual
1–7	*kaana*	*kaana*	
8–11	*kavisi*	*kelitu*	*nzaiko nini/ikonde*
12+	*mwanake*	*mwiitu*	*nzaiko nene/mulili/mbusya*
25–35	*mwanake/nthele*	*kiveti*	*mbavani* (males only)
40+	*mutumia*	*kiveti*	
60+	*mutumia*	*kiveti/mutumia*	*mutumia wa ngulo* (males only)

Notes
kaana (with diminutive prefix *ka-*) = child
kelitu = small girl (with diminutive prefix)
nthele = 'finished', i.e. finished the dancing of *anake*
mutumia = male elder, but can refer also to older woman
kiveti = married woman/wife

The physical age for each life-cycle stage-change was not fixed. A girl was normally married shortly after puberty and became a 'wife' [*kiveti*] when the marriage seemed to have become established. Her name then changed from 'daughter of . . .', to 'wife of . . .'. A young man [*mwanake*] became *nthele* ('finished') when he married – usually in his twenties – had children, ceased to dance with younger bachelors and was allowed to drink beer with older men. The status of elder [*mutumia*] (Plate 23) was formalized at the age of about forty by a first payment of two goats and a later payment of a bull to the general community of elders. These payments were called *ngulo* – a term derived from the phrase *kukula mutwe* – 'eating a bull', part of a sacrificial *rite de passage*. Certain important social, jural and ritual tasks could be performed only by elders who had

Plate 23   Traditional elders in Kyuso

passed this stage – *atumia ma ngulo*. Women could also attain special status as 'elders', with corresponding gender-related prestige and tasks.

Among male elders there used to be a localized men's club, *kisuka*, which had consisted of ten ranks of elderhood, each marked by payment of livestock and subsequent entitlement to eat a certain part of the roasted meat of the goat or bull paid by others, ranging from the least privileged to the most privileged cut of the meat. However, this prestige ranking system had no significant political relevance: it represented hierarchical principles antithetical to the actual principles of political leadership, which were largely achievement-based. It thus constituted a fantasy of hierarchy – a principle which was absent from Kamba political institutions. The institution of the men's club no longer existed in Kamale in 1973, having died out two or three decades earlier.

TRADITIONAL LEADERSHIP AND CO-OPERATION

Traditional Kamba society was notably 'achievement-orienta-ted'.[14] Informal measures of influence clustered around achieved criteria of different kinds – jural, military, ritual or economic – where all positions were 'open' and none was hereditary. People were regarded as born equal, with differences in ability and achievement which were largely explained as supernaturally caused or contrived. On this belief, the means by which one man became rich and another poor might be use or purchase of magical medicines [*muthea*]. Relatively large wealth differentials were accepted as inevitable – for example, Lindblom mentions a man with fifty wives. But all Kamba were nevertheless bound together in a common value-system which limited individual influence and political power. There were important social sanctions against overstepping these bounds.

Moreover, leadership roles among the Kamba were function-ally specific, with no necessary or even common overlap between them. In jural areas, skilled litigators [*atumia ma nzama* or *asili*] were paid for their services by the contesting parties but had no more generalized office than this. Ritual specialists [*andu awe*] were paid for their services, each having one or more specialized skills and reputation in a particular field of ritual knowledge [*uwe*]. They were not, as such, regarded as expert in other social fields, and indeed in jural matters were excluded as being too dangerous (or possibly secretly partisan) because of the supernatural powers they were believed to possess. General social status was attained through success in any of these areas – economic wealth, jural skills, ritual expertise – but personal qualities and the ability to influence and persuade people were also highly regarded. Elders were particularly respected as having the most developed *ukuu* – knowledge of the society and traditional wisdom. This standing was reinforced by them through their command of obscure proverbs and semi-secret Kamba lore which they jealously guarded, rather than special rhetorical skills, which were not highly elaborated among the Kamba.

In pre-colonial times, for special enterprises, young men – irrespective of their different descent-groups – were traditionally organized by a skilled ritual leader or 'prophet' [*muthiani*] whose ability and experience were proven. He arranged the ritual details of the enterprise through divination and other means of ritual forecasting or decision-making, and deployment of ritual medicines and offerings. He held the group together through his possession and use of ritual medicines, and by these means directed the practical details of the project – for example travel, tactics or division of profits. Raiding was for cattle mainly, although women and children were captured too and brought home as domestic slaves. In the nineteenth century, hunting and trading were important Kamba occupations. Hunting parties killed elephant for ivory to trade for cloth and jewellery, each hunter keeping his own business separate but all trading in concert in the 'silent' trade with Swahilis and others at the coast.[15]

The submersion of individual self-interest for the purposes and duration of the enterprise was effected by an oath [*muma*] to stick together and not to flee or desert the others. Neither the oath nor the leader's prestige and medicines necessarily prevented conflict, but they allayed it and provided a basis for group co-operation. The institution of the loyalty oath was part of a system of belief and social organization relevant in other social contexts too. It was distinct from the oath of dispute-settlement [*kithitu*], which is described below. Loyalty oaths were used also for binding initiates to secrecy; incorporating an immigrant [*mbooswa*] into the neighbourhood; sealing an enterprise between two individuals – for example, involving secret use of the *kithitu* oath; secret sale of killing-sorcery [*uoi*]; or creating blood-brotherhood. The oath was sealed in a ritual which took the form of pricking the blood-filled intestine of a slaughtered goat with a thorn, saying the appropriate words of the oath, then joint eating of the meat. The oath also bound a person not to practise killing-sorcery against the oathed partner or group, on pain of a fatal affliction that was believed to fall automatically on a perjuror.

The role of *muthiani* as expedition leader was not institu-tionalized or established further than the particular enterprise, although some leaders were successful and wealthy enough to widen their areas of influence considerably. Such a person was Kivoi wa Mwendwa, a famous trader of Kitui in the mid-nineteenth century.[16] But this kind of authority never became hereditary or more generalized in a political sense. Kamba respected achievement and force of personality, but rejected being bound to general or permanent obedience to anyone possessing these virtues.

Co-operation was institutionally required in internal descent-group affairs relating to common property or genealogical ties – for instance, in organizing bridewealth payments, bloodwealth payments, descent-group rituals and inter- or intra-descent-group dispute-settlement.

Co-operation between members of different descent-groups was also necessary in certain economic, political or ritual tasks. Particularly important for the origins of modern community self-help development activities were traditional neighbourhood workparties. Rituals involving the whole community included sacrifices to avert threats to the basic concerns of life for the whole community when these were divined as mystically caused – such as drought and famine, epidemic or warfare – and where spirits affecting the whole community were believed to require placating. The community as a whole then sought ritual protection [*isyuka*] against the affliction.

The fundamental autonomy of the individual was thus modified in the direction of corporate action in certain spheres. New corporate bonds established by oaths created the basis for such co-operation where no other political basis for it existed. The autonomy of the individual was regarded as being subject to such restriction only where institutional or ritual restraints were imposed on it. This gave the obligation its prescriptive force and justified the individual commitment to a supra-individual corporate grouping, whether temporary or permanent. The benefits of the individual's merging with a group provided the reward for such restraints on individual freedom. The ways in which individuals acted within the group and for the objectives of the group were patterned along channels of corporate rights and duties, which were also perceived in terms of forms of reciprocal exchanges of different kinds between individuals.

MODERN LEADERSHIP AND COMMUNITY ACTION

In Kamale in 1973, leadership status was allocated, as in the traditional society, on the basis of a variety of measures of staus and prestige. This included traditional statuses relating to descent-group and kinship status; jural skills; traditional ritual skills or status in a religious sect; personal wealth originating from inherited or acquired land-holding and farming, or earned income in employment or other modern economic transactions; educational standing; and modern occupational or political status – for example as a government official, trader, and so on. None of these – with the exception of those which carried governmental authority – was automatically the basis of generalized community influence, but all could be.

The relative weight of these different status factors in respect of self-help group leadership is examined in Chapter 5, which also describes the relation between government officials and the village self-help group in Kamale. Decision-making in the self-help group closely resembled aspects of the traditional dispute-settlement process, which is described later in this chapter. Continuities appeared to be strong in the transfer of traditional statuses and values to the modern arena of community development, but they operated in specific ways which had evolved both as a result of an internal social dynamic and also in the course of the imposition of external factors such as the colonial administration, communal labour and the development of a new judicial system.

In Kamale, there was no automatic choice of the most 'modern' person as leader of the self-help group, nor did people hesitate to criticize government officials or party political officials when they felt the need to do so. For several months during fieldwork, there was a running dispute with the location chief.[17] Kamale people did not automatically do as government officials – even the most well-meaning and community-development-orientated – told them. At the same time, there was no automatic rejection of 'traditional' leaders for modern tasks. Choice of self-help group leaders fluctuated according to their success or otherwise, and several elected officials who were unable to mobilize support and action became the focus of major local conflict and criticism and, at least temporarily, suffered serious loss of prestige, as is described in Chapter 5.

Socialization

Socialization into Kitui Kamba society was an ongoing process throughout life. It was everyone's duty to make sure a young person was brought up in traditional ways and values, called *kithio* ('custom'), although the prime responsibility for inculcating these values lay with close relatives, both those in a relationship of authority or *kikio* (see above), such as father and mother, and those in the more relaxed kinship relationship of *kuthauka*, such as grandparents. The most knowledgeable members of the society were elder men and women, those possessing *ukuu*, traditional knowledge and wisdom.

INITIATION RITUALS

Particularly important to traditional socialization was the process whereby children and adults became 'true Kamba' through initiation rituals, *nzaiko* (see Table 7 above for a summary of age-statuses and associated initiation rituals). In Kitui, males used to pass through three 'initiation' rituals and females through two only. *Nzaiko* derived from the term for ritually prescribed sexual intercourse [vb. *kwaika*], which the initiate's ritual guardians [*aiki*] performed privately at their homes at night at the conclusion of certain phases of the ritual. Initiates were believed to be 'reborn' [vb. *kusyawa*] through this ritual. The Kamba of Machakos had only the first two of these *nzaiko* ceremonies, the third being peculiar to Kitui.[18]

The first *nzaiko*, separate for boys and girls, was called *nzaiko nini*, 'the small initiation', or *ikonde*, 'cutting'. It was conducted when some parents collected payments for the organizer, *mwaiki* – a particular kind of *mundu mue* (ritual specialist). It consisted of the circumcision of boys, cutting the foreskin of the penis all round – which distinguished Kamba circumcision from that of neighbouring societies such as the Kikuyu and Maasai – and the clitoridectomy of girls. Essential to the ritual was the prior sexual abstention of the initiate's parents, the ritual guardian, the ritual supervisor (who assisted the initiate through the operation) and the ritual operator, and their ritual intercourse with their spouses after it. There were also special initiation songs/dances, *mbovoi*, which were sung during and after the physical operation.

Traditionally all Kamba males and females had to undergo this operation of physical transformation to be regarded in later life as true Kamba. In Kamale in 1974, a girl aged ten was operated on in this way in a small ceremony attended only by immediate family and the ritual operator and ritual supervisor. No other ritual took place, not even the singing of ritual songs. The girl later said she had consented to the operation.

Most parents – whether as Christians who were forbidden by their church to observe this 'pagan' ceremony, or simply as parents who were committed to a modern education for their children – sent their male children to be circumcised at the local hospital, where the operation was conducted under a local anaesthetic and, of course, without ritual. The hospital did not perform clitoridectomy on girls for medical ethical reasons, and this practice had nearly died out under the pressure of religious prohibition and views about modern life, without ever having become an important political issue in Kitui. Whereas it was still regarded in 1974 as essential that Kamba males should be circumcised, the traditional view that Kamba women were incomplete if their clitoris was uncut had nearly disappeared. A *nzaiko* circumcision ceremony which I witnessed in Kyuso in northern Kitui in 1973 (Plates 24 and 25)[19] was much more elaborate and public than the one in Kamale in 1974 mentioned above, which was almost clandestine and was kept secret from the local administration, especially the chief, who disapproved of these 'pagan' practices and would probably have prohibited it.[20]

The second *nzaiko*, called *mulili* (an untranslatable term), *mbusya*, 'rhinoceros', or *nzaiko nene*, 'the big *nzaiko*', resembled an 'initiation school' in some respects. It was a bigger and more elaborate ceremony than the first *nzaiko*, and used to be held once a year in the dry season, with sometimes large numbers of boys and girls in the locality aged between twelve and twenty initiated together. Males were initiated before they could enter the age-status of *nthele*, and girls had to pass through it before they could be married, which was traditionally soon after puberty.

Preparations for the ceremony included the performance of the *kilumi* (spirit-possession) dance for several nights in order to placate troublesome spirits afflicting people, and of the *nzuma* dance by men who had passed through the third *nzaiko*. The initiates [*asingi*] were given two ritual guardians [*aiki*] to whom their parents made payments (2shs in later years, formerly a bottle of ghee), at whose homes they slept during the ceremony in specially built huts. They also had a ritual supervisor [*muvwikii*] who supervised their initiation rituals – perhaps one for ten or fifteen initiates. The ritual supervisors swore an oath [*muma*] not to divulge the details of the ritual.

On the first day of the ritual, the initiates were taken to the home of the first ritual guardian [*mwaiki*]; here they built a hut where they slept for the first stage. The hut had an entrance for them, with boys and girls sleeping separately, and a back entrance for the 'rhinoceros'. While they were there, their parents and the ritual guardian abstained from sex for the first night and on the second night had ritual intercourse [*kwaika*]. For those two days, the initiates, wearing only a headband and cloth, sang *nzaiko* songs – this was called *kutomba*, signifying the movement of the head from side to side and the arms up and

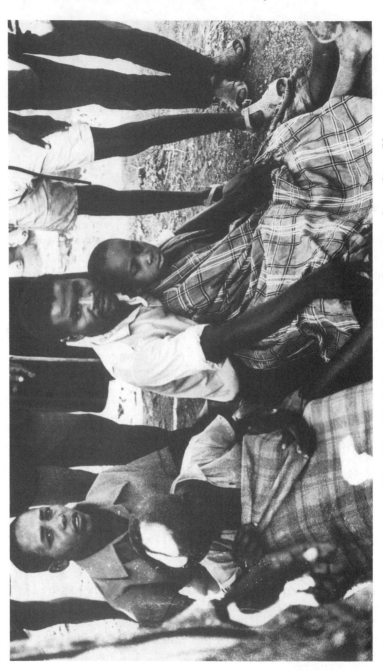

Plate 24   Newly circumcised boys with their ritual guardians, Kyuso

Plate 25   Men singing circumcision songs, Kyuso

down during the singing. Otherwise they did nothing, as they were in a state of ritual suspension [*mutindwa*]. They ate food cooked without salt, which was sent by their parents. On the third night, they performed the ritual of 'striking the rhinoceros' [*kwatha mbusya*]. A mock rhinoceros was constructed from leaves, branches and hides, with a man inside blowing through a reed into a clay pot hung from his neck to create a roaring sound. The rhinoceros, a creature of the wild, was traditionally not hunted or killed by Kamba (although they traded rhinoceros horns, which had reputed aphrodisiac and magical powers). The mock rhinoceros – only a small approximation of the animal, which was not paraded in public – was said 'to come from the river'. It entered the hut through the back entrance, while bystanders terrified the initiates with shouts that the rhinoceros was breaking free of the ropes by which it was tied, but they also called out to them not to be afraid of it.

The initiates entered the hut one at a time, with their ritual supervisors present to help them. Inside the hut there were two holes in the ground; the initiates had been told stories that their penis or clitoris would be cut off and put into one of these holes, and that boys must put their penis into the other hole and ejaculate into it, while girls would have a stick representing a penis put into their vagina. Informants told me that these stories referred to symbolic actions only, where a cutting movement by the ritual supervisor recalled the first *nzaiko* for boys and girls, and gestures hinted at the sexual act. Boys then had to strike the 'rhinoceros' with a stick and say the words: 'Don't break the arrow of the son ... who is the son of ... ' (thus identifying themselves). Girls had to strike with their fists a hide put in front of the 'rhinoceros'. That night parents, ritual guardians and ritual supervisors had ritual intercourse (each with their respective spouse) to make them 'reborn'.

On the fourth day the initiates moved to the house of a second ritual guardian and that day sang songs and did nothing else, though they were now allowed food cooked with salt as normal.

On the fifth day the ritual of 'eating the sap of the fig tree [*wumbu*]' took place. Fearsome stories were previously told to initiates that they had to climb the fig tree and jump down on to sharp sticks held by the ritual guardians, that the rhinoceros would eat them, but that they would then be reborn when the ritual guardians forced the rhinoceros to vomit them out. Good children would be reborn whole, while bad ones would be changed into things like caterpillars or headstraps.

For this ritual, the supervisors took offerings to a special sacred fig tree; the sap was smeared on the forehead and orifices of the initiates and they were made to taste it. They were then taken to the river and washed, and their headbands and cloths were abandoned there. Girls also left there a handful of soil which they had previously taken from their first ritual guardian's home, wrapped in cloth; this signified that they would not return there but would move on physically just as they were progressing in terms of social maturity. They were given special purificatory food (*kisuu*, honey mixed with blood from the ear of a sacrificed sheep). They sang more ritual songs and that night their guardians had ritual intercourse. The next day they went round the village collecting gifts of ornaments or jewellery to wear and singing songs, but otherwise doing nothing 'normal' as they were still in a state of ritual suspension.

On the eighth day they performed various actions symbolic of the real life to which they were gradually returning. Boys were given miniature bows and arrows to 'hunt' insects and frogs (said to symbolize their traditional enemies, the Maasai). They also pretended they were lost and then they happened to find livestock from their own family herds which they took home, carrying a calabash and strap, as if they had returned from a long journey to retrieve lost cattle. Girls pretended to steal sweet potatoes and sugar-cane. They were each given a knife and headstrap as if to collect firewood, but what they collected in fact was green twigs (that is, living branches, also miniature): on their return they were pelted by the boys with *ndongu* (yellow solanum berries, which featured in several rituals). Their parents and ritual guardians had ritual intercourse that night and on the ninth day the initiates returned home thus 'reborn'.

This second *nzaiko* ritual had been banned by the colonial authorities in Kitui in the late 1950s, although informants said that it had continued clandestinely for some years. In the end, missionaries reported to the district authorities that the ritual was continuing, some participants were caught and fined, and without major controversy or opposition the ritual died out. The younger generation in 1973 knew little about it and had no interest in reviving it, as it was not perceived as having any contemporary relevance. It had probably completely died out in Kitui by then.

The third *nzaiko*, called *mbavani* (rhinoceros), was performed only in Kitui and had never existed among the Kamba of Machakos – why this was so, nobody could say. Lasting six days and probably performed annually for varying numbers of initiates, it was much more 'secret' than the second *nzaiko*. It was for males only, aged between about twenty-five and fifty, and was a necessary *rite de passage* for full elderhood.

In this ritual, initiates had four ritual supervisors [*avwikii*], as with the other *nzaiko* rituals, and assistants called *ngala* ('fleas' or 'sparks'). Sexual abstention followed by ritual intercourse were as essential to the ritual as in the previous *nzaiko*. Initiates were taken to a bush enclosure cleared by four men who supervised and performed the ritual, *andu ma ndia* ('men of the pools'), who wore fibre bracelets on their arms, chests, and legs. During six days there, the initiates ate roasted meat from six bulls provided by their parents (one for each day). The ritual supervisors and their assistants carried sticks (four in each hand), kept other people away, and beat or reputedly even killed any non-initiates [*maengo*] who illegitimately witnessed the ritual. Oaths [*muma*] were sworn by ritual supervisors and initiates not to divulge details.

Initiates spent much time singing and listening to special initiation songs, *nzuma*. In one phase of the ceremony they lay face down on the ground, naked and smeared with ashes, in the presence of two mock rhinoceroses, called *mbavani*. These were constructed in the same way as the rhinoceroses in the second *nzaiko* – but they were more obviously *andu ma ndia* dressed up as 'rhinoceroses' and they were described to me as not particularly fearsome. Initiates got up when touched with sticks by ritual supervisors. There was no striking of the 'rhinoceros' as in the second *nzaiko*. The two 'rhinoceroses' moved around the circular enclosure and the circle of initiates in opposite directions, and this was described as *kwaika* (the same word as for ritual intercourse) or 'making them reborn'. The ritual guardians also lay down on top of the initiates to 'make them reborn'. Initiates were given special initiation sticks, *ukai*, to hold.[21] They were taught magic [*kyama*] to avert an enemy or sorcery, the knowledge of which later also identified them as initiates. They had to learn this magic before they would be given water to drink. I was told that these and other tests or ordeals were not so severe that some initiates might fail them.

After three days initiates washed off the ashes and were given their clothes back, and their mothers brought cooked salted food for them. They were then said to have 'become Kamba'. They visited their homes and on the fifth day herded their cattle. On the fifth night their parents and ritual guardians had ritual intercourse, and on the sixth day the initiates returned home. They were then regarded as complete Kamba and were also entitled to dance *nzuma* dances with the songs they had learnt during their initiation, and to participate in the initiation of others.

These three rituals were unified by the background of ritual sexual abstention and intercourse (as in other Kamba rituals) and by the structure of ritual guardionship. Classic initiatory symbols of rebirth appeared frequently in these rituals, based not only on sexual symbolism but also on the opposition between nature (represented by the mock rhinoceros) and culture (human society). The transformation of the initiate from the one to the other proceeded through distinct stages as well as gradually, and consisted of ritual instruction at certain points, psychological ordeals or tests at others. There was no actual social or practical instruction. Adjacent *nzaiko* rituals were linked – for example, the second ritual referred back to the physical operations of the first, and the third ritual featured the reappearance of the half-tamed, half-murderous rhinoceros of the second ritual, but shorn of terror.

The third *nzaiko* was formally banned by the colonial government in 1923, probably at the instigation of Christian missionaries. In central Kitui it probably never revived, but it may have continued for some years clandestinely in the remoter areas of the district. By 1974 there were few Kamba left alive who had passed through it and were also willing to break their oath and divulge information about it. Middle-aged and younger Kamba knew little about it. Political opponents of the colonial government claimed that the British had banned it so as to weaken the Kamba and prevent anti-colonial resistance,which may well have been a correct assessment. The ban no doubt contributed to the split between 'traditionalists' and 'modernizers' among the Kamba. The demise of the latter two initiation rituals did not destroy the sense of ethnic identity among Kamba *vis-à-vis* other ethnic groups in Kenya – this was maintained by all ethnic groups in Kenya through ethnic associations and their political activities, as well as cultural continuities in the rural areas especially.

MODERN SOCIALIZATION

Kamba society had changed drastically during the twentieth century, and modes of socialization had adapted too.[22] The major traditional social structural principles based on descent, age-status and gender were still fundamental in Kamale social organization and were inculcated as before, supplemented by people's increasing knowledge of the wider Kamba and Kenyan society. But social interaction with non-Kamba was a matter of everyday experience, and many people in Kamale had spent a long time outside the village as urban migrants or market traders, and thus spoke the Kenyan *lingua franca* and second language of Swahili, or had been to school. Only those who had been to secondary school spoke any English, as the English taught in primary schools was of a very poor standard.

Nevertheless, people recognized that new social values and skills were needed by the younger generation to enable them to cope with situations they would face in life. Kamba society, with a history of pre-colonial trading and travelling, had always been quite outward-looking, and so was not entrenched in the sense of seeking to preserve itself intact against external sociopolitical change. Kamba eventually welcomed modern education and sought to benefit from it. Since 1945 at least the acceptance of Western education had increased dramatically, and in 1973 every child in Kamale went to school (Plate 26). This was not seen as culturally disruptive but as a question of the right to education as a means of participating in the wider society and as

Plate 26   Nzambani schoolchildren

a key route to individual achievement and social mobility, both of these being a matter of family progress too.

The means of modern socialization were particularly the schools and other modern associational contacts (for example, the 4K young farmers' club for boys and girls – Plates 27 and 28), personal experience of the world outside, and vicarious experience gained from returning villagers, shopkeepers, townspeople, the radio (although only a few people in the village had a radio and there were only a few Kikamba programmes each week), and the fairly frequent contacts people had with government officials – the chief, subchiefs, and government officials from the agriculture, health, education and community development departments.

It was not the purpose of this research to study village-level social differentiation in depth, but it is worth noting that while even small socioeconomic differentials were important in indicating social prestige and elite–mass cleavages,[23] in 1974 these divisions had not yet become solidified and overriden countervailing egalitarian values and institutions. One important 'levelling mechanism' which partially prevented the Christian/-pagan, progressive farmer/traditional farmer, educated/illiterate contrasts[24] becoming all-important at village level was the self-help group, in which everyone participated and had a stake. Furthermore, these contrasts were not necessarily clear-cut; as indicated, there was still a substantial core of shared cultural experience and practice between both categories, reflecting commitment to change without totally abandoning the past.

Many traditional customs and values had been banned by the colonial administration (such as initiation rituals, some dances, community execution); others had been fiercely discouraged by churches and administrators (such as polygyny, alcohol and tobacco) or abandoned.

These official and unofficial bans on Kamba customs had been in some cases partially ignored, or the customs themselves might have been in a state of change or about to die out through people's own choice. The prohibition of rituals and dance was clearly intended to strike at the heart of Kamba religion. Songs and dances had been important in their educational role – relating to symbolic rather than secular instruction – and in the

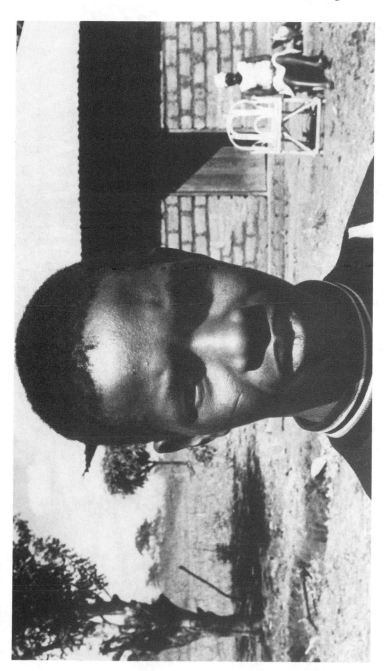

Plate 27 Modern young farmer, Kamale

Plate 28   Woman progressive farmer with youths and girls, Kamale

'transmission of sentiments' through their manifestation as ritual drama. The heightened languages of song and dance conveyed their messages through musical media rather than the language of normal discourse.[25] To replace these, churches promoted their own ritual songs (hymns and psalms) and modern African and Western popular music, heard on the radio and in bars, provided new secular musical entertainment – though whether or not it had the 'regenerative' social force that Kamba dances had provided in their social context could not be estimated. Self-help groups' songs performed new socially cohesive functions at village level, as analysed in Chapter 5.

In material terms, most of the artistic items depicted or photographed by Lindblom in 1911[26] were no longer made or used in Kamale, or even kept in people's possession: bead jewellery design and handicrafts had become obsolete except for those deliberately revived for a new market (such as the relaunching of designed calabashes for sale in Nairobi craft shops), and people had thrown away their old ornamental chains and beads in the 1950s, when much traditional dancing was banned and scarification and teeth-chipping were stopped too. In 1973, calabashes and stools were made for use but without traditional ornamentation; only traditional-design baobab and sisal baskets, made by women's groups encouraged by Community Development officials, had the national and international market to guarantee that these crafts would not become defunct.

Beliefs and Ritual

A full account of the traditional belief-system of the Kitui Kamba is not presented here. Some areas of traditional beliefs and rituals have already been described where these were important for understanding contemporary social processes – for example, initiation rituals as part of traditional socialization, and oaths as means of generating social co-operation. Certain other beliefs and rituals are described below, such as beliefs in spirits in connection with lineage structures, ritual means of settling disputes, and conflicts between traditional beliefs and the religion of social change – Christianity, of different denominations and sects.[27]

By 1973 there had been missionary activity in south and central Kitui for over eighty years. In Kamale, about 45 per cent of adults and young people claimed to be Christians rather than 'pagans' – the pejorative English term applied by Christians to those adhering to the traditional belief-system. Most of this 45 per cent were between fifteen and twenty-five and had been to school. Only about ninety of these were practising Christians and regular church-goers. The majority (thirty-seven) belonged to the Africa Inland Church (AIC), which was formed in 1943 out of the Africa Inland Mission (AIM), whose district headquarters were nearby at Mulango. The American-founded AIM remained as a missionary body separate from the new Kenyan AIC church. The AIC members in Kamale worshipped at a church they were building near Katothya AIC primary school. Twenty-four people belonged to the African Brotherhood Church (ABC), an independent Kamba church which had separated from the AIM in Machakos in the 1940s, and they were building their own church near the AIC church at Katothya and in evident competition with it. Thirteen belonged to the Roman Catholic Church, which was backed by a well-established mission station in Kitui town, and they had built a small church on the border of Kamale near Yanzuu rock; and fifteen were new members of the Anglican Church (also called the CMS – Church Missionary Society – but officially the Church of the Province of Kenya, the main Protestant Church in the country), a relative newcomer to Kitui, and had built a temporary mud-walled thatched building in Kamale to use as a church. The Christians were mainly from families of progressive farmers, or adults who had been to school or been successful urban migrants.

In certain respects Christianity was incompatible and in conflict and competition with traditional Kamba beliefs. Some Christians, such as the location chief, attempted to propagate a sharp dichotomy between modern ideas, beliefs, education and 'progress' on the one hand, and traditional beliefs and values on the other. The Anglican church in Kamale had deliberately been built on a traditional ancestral shrine [*ithembo*], in order to prove that their religion was more powerful and that traditional religious sanctions should not be feared. But acceptance of traditional beliefs in the power of ancestral or non-ancestral spirits to cause illnesses or other problems was situational rather than solid: even among non-Christians, shrines were neglected. Belief in the power of sorcery to cause harm was widespread among both Christians and pagans, and traditional ideas still retained their force in presenting an explanation of fortune or misfortune, suffering or prosperity, as an alternative or complement to modern systems of belief or medicine.

In the traditional Kamba belief-system, *Ngai* was the 'High God', believed to be the ultimate source of life and death, good and evil. *Ngai*, however, was invoked only in special sacrifices in connection with rainfall failure or general community afflictions. The more immediate spiritual agents relevant to the living and influencing everyday life were spirits [*aimu*] of different kinds. These were principally spirits of the dead which afflicted humans in different ways, rewarding or punishing them. To propitiate them, small offerings were made at meals, when drinking, on journeys, but special sacrifices (for example of a male goat, bull or ox) were made at special shrines, in caves (such as Kavia cave nearby, Plate 29[28], or in the undergrowth of certain trees). There were shrines of descent-group ancestors, approached by lineage heads, and shrines of spirits affecting non-descent-group kin, such as the spirit of a spirit-medium or prophet, or other spirits of human or non-human origin which might be divined as affecting the rainfall or fertility.

Spirits without shrines were also believed to range freely and affect people by possessing them.[29] Spirit-possession occurred mainly among women and some 'marginal' men – for example older men who had not married. It caused illness and other forms of affliction. After divination and identification of the spirit, the usual cure was to dance the spirit-dance [*kilumi*] and become possessed, in order to please the spirit, which would then stop troubling the patient. Other spirits required exorcism rituals. The dancers in the spirit-dance comprised both those who regularly danced and became possessed to please their spirit, and those who were in a conflictive relation with the spirit. The former danced and went into controlled trance, the latter

Plate 29   Cave paintings in traditional shrine, Kavia rock

went into uncontrolled trance. Some spirits demanded special gifts from their victims – some costly, some nominal.

Spirit-dances were organized by spirit-mediums or shamans, who beat the spirit-drum [*ngoma*], sang the spirit-songs which put patients in trance, and divined patients' spiritual affliction. Spirit-mediums had varying powers, including powers of prophecy both for individual questioners and in times of community crisis. The approach of an enemy, the aversion of disease, the timing of the rains, and other dramatic events affecting the whole community were the areas where prophecy [vb. *kwathana*, n. *muthiani*] sought to expand the boundaries of human knowledge and control over the external world. There were famous spirit-mediums and prophets in Kamba history which were said to have foreseen major social changes and also to have provided advice about avoiding or counteracting the dangers that would ensue.

Spirit-mediums were only one example of a wide range of ritual specialists in Kamba society. The ritual specialist was termed *mundu mue*, literally a person with *uwe* – ritual knowledge. This kind of knowledge differed from the social knowledge taught through forms of socialization and education which were called *ukuu*, meaning knowledge of *kithio* – 'custom' or 'culture'. Ritual specialists had a different form of knowledge, partly instinctual or spiritually acquired, partly taught by another ritual specialist. They used magical gestures [*kyama*] and magical medicines [*muthea*] to actualize and make known their ritual powers. Each had to establish and maintain a reputation for success in the chosen ritual field in order for people to utilize and pay for their services. People were believed to be born into the potential possession of the art by special indicators at their birth, but to actualize it only through apprenticeship or the onset of spiritual traumas and subsequent ritual supervision.

There were several kinds of ritual specialists, some nationally known – such as Kabwere, a sorcery cleanser at the coast – some locally well-known, such as Mutune, a shaman in Mbaa Liu village who performed *kilumi* dances in the Kamale area regularly during the dry season (see below); and others who had lesser skills or practised them rarely. The various kinds of ritual specialities, practised usually by one person each, were:

– spirit-mediumship, as described above;
– divination [*kwausya*] of different kinds, including interpretation of dreams or natural signs, divination in trance (usually with a special musical bow), and divination through oracles or ordeals (the 'bead-in-the-eye' and the 'heated knife', for example – see the next section on dispute-settlement);
– administering the loyalty oath of *muma* (see above) or the judicial oath of *kithitu* (see next section);
– preventing killing-sorcery [*uoi*] and remedying or warding off lesser forms of sorcery;
– protecting against enemies, rivals, farm pests or wild animals (Plates 30 and 31), or assisting in a person's ambitions – for example in business, politics, love, and so on – through making and selling magical charms or fetishes (*mbingu* if an ornament, *kithitu* if in the form of a horn, like that of the main oath-fetish of the same name);
– performing a cleansing ritual [*msebe*] to cleanse a person of sorcery or protect them from it, purifying someone of ritual pollution [*mwiio*];
– organizing initiation rituals [*nzaiko*];
– purifying a person, a home or a neighbourhood of some spiritually borne affliction, for example by smearing the victim with a purificatory substance [*ngondu*], the small intestine of a sacrificed goat mixed with magical medicines.

Lineage elders also had certain ritual functions and powers, but these were described as *ukuu*, traditional wisdom, rather than *uwe*, supernatural powers. These included the power to bless someone [*kwathima*] – spraying saliva over on the outstretched palms of the hands of the person being blessed, or pouring some drops of beer on the ground for the spirits, with ritual words. The use of magical medicines directed against someone was called *kuooa*, which Kamba translated into English as 'to bewitch', although in the generally accepted anthropological sense this was 'sorcery', not 'witchcraft'. The derivative verbal noun *uoi* was reserved for killing-sorcery. The ritual specialist for curing this might also be suspected of being able to use it. Suspicions, however, were usually not made public, except in special cases and after extensive divination.

Plate 30 Mundu mue (*ritual specialist*) *displaying magical medicine, near Kamale*

Plate 31   Mundu mue *supervising preparation of crop protection magic, Kamale*

If witchcraft is defined as an unconscious or innate power to harm by mystical means, without the use of materials, then the Kamba had no witchcraft, only sorcery.[30]

The use of such magical or ritual powers was distinct from the use of herbal medicines (*miti* – 'tree' or 'bush'). The practitioners of the former, however, were often also the practitioners of the latter, with demarcation lines between the two often blurred. The herbal doctor might have learnt particular pharmacological processes, but in diagnosing and treatment would also employ the skills of the ritual specialist, though to a lesser degree than where the affliction was being treated as if it were of spiritual or psychological aetiology.

Ritual specialists were of both sexes, but were often women or 'marginal' men.[31] The power to inflict *uoi* (killing-sorcery) was regarded as a female preserve, inherited in the gender-line but not active unless ritually transmitted from mother to daughter. It was believed to be performed through material means by the sorcerer, either for her own purposes or on behalf of a paying client. It was then used on the sorcerer's instructions against the enemy or rival by placing it in food, on footsteps, in the home, on the victim's exuviae, and so on. In Kamba belief, however, it had to be tested against the client's own child, which would then receive an 'antidote' and be cured. Purchase of *uoi* was secret, and the secrecy of the transaction was maintained by swearing a ritual oath [*muma*]. The effect of *uoi* and the agent of it could be revealed by divination. The direction of sorcery accusations – or, more accurately, suspicions of sorcery, because accusations were not publicly voiced – was socially patterned; it was believed that it was used, for example, by junior agnates against senior agnatic kin in property disputes, or by co-wives against one another. Verification of sorcery accusations was in theory materially possible only after death, through supposed physical post-mortem signs. This would not, however, affect the problem of knowing for sure whether or not a living person had or had not used these fatal powers.

An important traditional ritual of community purification involved a ritual specialist organizing the women of the polluted neighbourhood to demand compensation from the person responsible for the pollution. For example, a drought might have been divined as being caused by a man who had beaten his wife in the garden, or by the pollution of a shrine or the introduction of a ritually dangerous new cultural item (this was a Kamba reaction, for example, when the British flag was first raised in Kitui in 1897). The person causing the pollution would be asked for a goat, and if he refused the women would march naked to his home, waving branches to drive off spirits, singing sexually abusive songs to the beat of a special drum, assaulting any male they came across, and destroying the offender's home and harvest. If the goat was still refused, a fatal supernatural illness was believed to fall on the polluter. When the goat was paid, it was taken with other offerings to the shrine of the offended spirit, the women singing the same songs and waving branches, and a spirit-dance was performed at the shrine to please the angry spirit. There were no recent instances of this ritual, although it was cited by older Kamale women as still being available as a sanction against a particular abuse of a woman or women in general.

In the field of law, there was still regular recourse in the early 1970s to traditional methods of dispute-settlement involving oaths, divination and ordeals, which are described in the next section.

In Kamale in 1973, most of these beliefs and rituals were still active and all ritual specialists could be found in Kamale or a nearby village. There was still a general ideology that a person should be a 'true Mukamba' – even if he or she moved easily in the outside world of towns and salaried employment. The majority of the adult population were not practising Christians and rejected the discipline regarding beliefs and ritual practices that some churches sought to impose on their members – for example, by threatening to expel them from the church if they indulged in 'pagan' ritual practices, brewed or drank liquor, grew or smoked tobacco, or married more than one wife. Many of the 'Christian few' were not wholly committed to every aspect of the Christian belief-system, even though this was propagated as totally antithetical and superior to the traditional belief-system. In 1973, the spirit-possession dance, *kilumi*, was regularly held during the dry season at

Plate 32 Kilumi *shaman at Independence Day parade, Kitui town*

night, when the beat of the drum could be heard from afar. It was either performed at the home of a spirit-medium such as Mutune, who lived in the neighbouring village of Mbaa Liu, or organized by her at someone else's home. In 1974, for the first time, she also beat *kilumi* at a public meeting at the chief's camp in Nzambani (Plate 32). This represented partial public acceptance of a cultural tradition – which the chief and other Christians would have liked to ban – and a diminution of the significance of the dance as it became transformed into entertainment (without actual spirit-possession) rather than used for exorcism or control of spirits. The public performance mentioned above in Nzambani, however, was rather ambiguous, as some of the dancers (Plate 33) seemed to be in trance. In Machakos district, *kilumi* was already widely performed as a daytime entertainment at public and political rallies and Harambee Days (Plate 34), although at the same time it was also performed semi-clandestinely at people's homes at night for its original spirit-possession purposes.

Beliefs in sorcery were also still widespread in 1973, and ritual specialists were known and frequently consulted. One had a white flag as a marker at his home on the outskirts of Kamale. Divination by the 'bead-in-the-eye' oracle [*chuma*] was practised at a public session in 1974 (see next section). The owner of an important and much-feared *kithitu* oath-fetish, Sumbi wa Ndisya, lived in the neighbouring village of Ithimula and regularly administered the *kithitu* oath on the instructions of the Kitui magistrates' court in the presence of the subchief (see next section). This ritual specialist was also rumoured to provide a private and secret client service for the oath-ritual as well, which he denied. Other lesser ritual specialists were consulted and paid for their work in detecting sorcery, making charms, banishing crop pests, and curing milder forms of spirit-possession and other forms of spiritual affliction.

Traditional herbal medicines were also widely used, particularly for minor physiological or psychological complaints which were culturally regarded as being healed normally through these means rather than by modern medicines, and also for

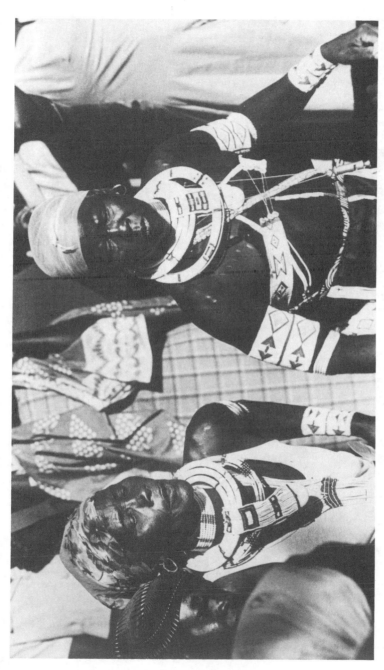

Plate 33   Kilumi dancers at chief's installation, Nzambani

Plate 34   Kilumi dancers at Harambee Day in Machakos district

major complaints where modern medical treatments – whether purchased in a shop or prescribed by a doctor or medical orderly at the town hospital or a health centre – were not found to be effective.[32] Belief in the efficacy of one belief-system as against another, or one ritual specialist against another, was very fluid and situational. This was probably a feature of the traditional belief-system itself: just as in the political arena Kamba had to establish and maintain their influence and prestige, so spirits had to demonstrate their power, and ritual specialists had to produce results, for people to respect or fear them. People were then willing or obliged to pay for the services they obtained.

Law and Dispute-Settlement

In Kamale, people were notionally involved in two different legal systems which overlapped at different points. There was the nationwide formal system of laws and courts, deriving from the Kenyan Constitution, Penal Code and Code of Criminal Procedure, ranging from the location chief's court up to the Kenya Court of Appeal. At the same time there was also a modified traditional Kamba customary legal system which operated at village level and according to traditional Kamba norms and values. Since colonial times these two systems had worked together, and colonial administrators had successively sought to marry them together in Kitui and adapt one to the other. This continued after Independence, with considerable recognition given by formal courts to customary law and legal procedures. This went further than strict application of the Kenya Penal Code and other written laws and statutes. In Kitui, it involved jural concepts deriving from wider social control mechanisms than the prohibition of crimes and torts.[33]

Traditional ritual socialization and secular training in the roles and values of Kamba society were far-reaching and supported by numerous institutional controls aimed at making individuals conform to the norms and values of the society. Nevertheless Kamba recognized that disputes occurred and needed to be resolved through established means. One of the most important functions of an elder [*mutumia*] was to assist in the management of the society, particularly through dispute-settlement institutions. Mechanisms existed for peacefully settling disputes both among Kamba and also between Kamba and members of other societies, although the latter disputes were more problematic because of the weaker sense of a common moral and cultural community.

In Kamale in 1973, the procedure for settling disputes outside the household (within which the jural authority of the homestead head was recognized) was that all elders of the descent-group were called to discuss the matter openly, with each disputing party presenting their case. The meeting was held at a clearing [*thome*] at the disputant's home. One elder was chosen as the '*thome* elder' of the day to organize the hearing. After sufficient discussion, each party chose two elders of their descent-group who were recognized as skilled in jural matters [*asili*] to be their representatives [*ngosi*]. The *thome* elder then nominated two other elders who were not interested parties in the case – that is to say, were members of different descent-groups to either disputant. The six chosen elders [*atumia ma nzama*] retired to a secret conclave [*nzama*] to finalize the settlement if the offence was explicitly or implicitly admitted. After making their decision, they had to receive their fees from both parties (nicknamed *usuu*, the word for maize-meal or millet porridge, although it was a cash payment, the rate being determined by the issue at stake and the status of the disputants) and then gave their judgement. This was binding on both parties and the conclave elders could order attachment of property, carried out by youths, if the fine was not paid within a reasonable time. These settlements were supervised by the subchief, who recorded the judgements and also received 'porridge' for his services.

Where there was no agreement between the disputants, traditional supernatural means could be used to arrive at the 'truth'. These were believed to have automatic validity and to be beyond human manipulation. The three main traditional means of arriving at the truth were:

Plate 35   Divination with the 'bead-in-the-eye' oracle, Kamale

(i) the 'bead-in-the-eye' oracle (*chuma* – meaning 'iron', i.e. an iron bead): a ritual specialist placed the magic bead on the lower eyelid of a neutral subject (Plate 35) and asked the bead a number of questions requiring a positive or negative answer. If the bead, smeared with white magical medicine, stuck to the eye, that signified 'yes' – for example the guilt of the person then being named as a theft suspect. If it slipped down, the person named was thus found innocent. This was administered in public in Kamale in 1974 under the supervision of a 'local leader' to test the truth of a statement made by a Kamale man denying theft of a beehive. The result was written down as evidence for the chief's court. The oracle was also consulted by several other people who paid a fee for asking about private matters.

(ii) the 'heated knife' ordeal, *kivyu* (knife): each suspect had to lick a heated knife, with the innocent party said to suffer no burn, while the guilty party was burned. This had been banned by the British authorities in 1910, although people said it could still be used if the appropriate ritual specialist could be found to operate it, which was probably impossible.

(iii) the *kithitu* oath: this was the most serious supernatural means of dispute-settlement, and was still used by court order or through private arrangement in serious disputes in 1973–4. In Kamale, for example, I witnessed an instance of this when Sumbi wa Ndisya (see above) brought his *kithitu* to settle a land dispute (Plate 36). The fetish, named Yolanzua, was placed on the ground (Plate 37) and each disputant had to swear an oath on it in the presence of the subchief and other witnesses (Plate 38). The oath was in the following form: 'Let me be eaten by this *kithitu* if I did so-and-so'. At the same time, each swearer struck the fetish with a small stick (Plate 39). The effect was believed to ensue within seven months and to cause the death of whoever swore falsely. The pollution created by the perjury was believed to be perpetuated through the perjuror's descent-group unless a purification ritual was carried out and compensation paid.

These supernatural methods of dispute-settlement took the conflict beyond the range of human decision-making, which was reckoned to be partial and liable to be affected by sorcery. It gave no person the ultimate power to judge or punish another. The ritual specialist himself had no jural influence or any special prestige apart from this expertise, as he might be suspected of bias or abuse of the powers of the fetish.[34]

Such was the respect and fear in which the *kithitu* oath was

Plate 36   Kithitu *ritual specialist with assistant carrying fetish bag*

Plate 37   Kithitu oath fetish

still held, by both 'traditional Kamba' and Christians alike, that the modern magistrates' court permitted disputing parties to have resort to it. The matter was then supervised by an administration official such as the subchief, who recorded the swearing of the oath and its consequences and reported them to the court.

In Kamba tradition, there were also situations where individuals were seriously at odds with the community – that is to say, had committed 'public delicts' requiring a public retaliatory response. These offences included persistent killing-sorcery, persistent theft, or general antisocial activity. They could traditionally be punished by public communal execution [*king'ole*], where a gathering of elders unanimously condemned the offender to death and forthwith ordered him or her to be stoned to death wherever he or she was found. The closest relative was said to have to cast the first stone. Such offences as these had gone beyond the possibilities of compensation or moral exhortation. However, since the early colonial period the state had asserted its exclusive right to apply the death penalty and *king'ole* had been banned. No cases of it were known in recent decades in Kitui.

Mystical sanctions lay behind other areas of social action where conflict tended to arise. These fitted into a wider set of beliefs and rituals concerned with the supernatural and explanation of basic social concerns. The main mystical sanctions – some of which were described in the section above, and all of which were potentially operational in 1973 – were:

– the power of a jural senior to curse a dependant or descendant;
– affliction by an ancestral spirit for neglect of social obligation;
– affliction by a 'peripheral' non-ancestral spirit;
– 'automatic' affliction for certain offences causing ritual pollution [*mwiio*] – for example incest, perverting inheritance procedures, and so forth;
– 'automatic' affliction causing the whole community to be ritually polluted – for example by affecting the rainfall, crops or childbirth in general;
– the risk of a slighted rival using sorcery, to the extent of purchasing killing-sorcery [*uoi*].

Plate 38   Subchief's meeting to prepare for the kithitu oath ritual, near Kamale

Plate 39   Swearing the kithitu *oath*

Certain offences against the Kenyan Penal Code, such as robbery or homicide, attracted penalties in both the modern and the traditional jural systems. Thus in the case of a murder the murderer could be tried, convicted and condemned to death, then executed or have the sentence commuted to life imprisonment if the President exercised his prerogative of clemency. In addition, the guilty person's descent-group could be obliged to pay bloodwealth in cattle to the victim's descent-group. A person falsely accused of a crime could resort to mystical means of clearing his or her name, discovering the criminal, or taking revenge on the malicious accuser by secretly using killing-sorcery.

4 Workparties

The ideology of Harambee stressed that the Harambee movement was based on African traditions of community co-operation and mutual aid. This referred specifically to the institutions of workparties which existed in many Kenyan societies, including the Kamba. Workparties are found in many pre-capitalist and peasant societies throughout the world.[1] The term 'workparty' embraces a variety of forms of co-operative labour-assistance. It is often the major institutional form through which heavy and onerous tasks or a series of such tasks are regularly carried out. Typically these include work at certain stages of the agricultural cycle, and building and construction tasks. Socioeconomic changes associated with the expansion of the market economy, wage-labour, labour-migration and urbanization have been linked with a steady decline in workparties, leading to their virtual demise in modern industrial societies.

In Kitui in 1973, workparties still played an important part in the rural economy. Their role in the agricultural economy and their significance in the allocation of labour resources were hardly recognized by economists or development planners. There are numerous brief references to workparties in the social anthropological literature, but 'detailed accounts of the mode of organization [of the workparty] and its relation to the general social system are most uncommon'.[2] There are few mentions of workparties in the ethnographic literature on the Kamba, even in the otherwise detailed descriptions by Lindblom and Stanner.[3]

This chapter describes the different tasks undertaken by workparties in Kamale, the different kinds of workparties there were, and the socioeconomic changes which had affected them.

Workparty Tasks

In Kamale in 1973, although the economy was predominantly household-based, there were specific tasks for which extra labour was regularly sought outside the household, with specific institutions for regulating the provision of supplementary labour to the household. Even though this comprised a small proportion of the total flow of labour, there was nothing random or casual about it. It was not simply a matter of 'everyone pitching in' but a system of various forms of labour-assistance through workparties.

Workparties took place during 1973–4 for the following tasks:

(i) Weeding the crops each rainy season, twice a year, using a hand-hoe [*iembe*]. This was the hardest regular work of the agricultural cycle, and it was the task for which most workparties were called (Plate 40).

(ii) Cutting a new garden from the bush. This was regarded as men's work and took place during the dry season. It consisted of cutting and burning trees and bushes, digging out their roots, moving rocks and stones, and clearing the land ready for digging over and planting. It was not a regular or frequent task, since most cultivation took place on existing gardens or cultivated land that had lain fallow for a season or two.

(iii) Harvesting a large crop. This was done mostly by women, boys and girls, but it was undertaken by a workparty, as distinct from household labour alone, only if the yield was unusually large.

(iv) Threshing millet or sorghum. Women threshed the harvested crop with long sticks on a dung-plastered threshing floor. Since, however, these crops were rarely grown any more, having been replaced mostly by maize, this workparty barely existed. There was occasionally a workparty for cobbing maize, if a large crop had been harvested.

(v) Collecting building materials. Women cut and carried thatching-grass, while men cut and carried wood for poles and roof-supports. These tasks involved lengthy journeys into the bush during the dry season, and the heavy job of carrying the materials back to the house site by means of a headstrap balancing the load on the back. These workparties were not very frequent.

(vi) Building a house, granary, kitchen or livestock hut. The typical house in Kamale consisted of a circular frame of woven branches, plastered with mud, on which a roof-frame was mounted, supported on a central pole and with about a dozen external struts, then thatched (see Plate 2). When the materials had been collected and prepared, the construction of the building could be completed

Plate 40   Women's weeding mwethya, *Kamale*

in a day by means of one workparty of men and another of women. The men wove the frames, the women fetched water for making mud; the men tramped the mud, plastered the wall-frame and set the roof on the wall-frame and struts, and the women thatched it. No other specialist skills were required. Such buildings could last about ten years, with minor repairs. Granaries on stilts, kitchens and livestock huts were built in a similar style, though on a smaller scale. By 1973, sun-dried mud-bricks, made from a simple brick mould, had often come to be used instead of the plastered wall-frame. Mud-bricks could be made either by a workparty or by hired labour.

(vii) Collecting tree branches for firewood, which was the only fire fuel used. This task was done by women and girls, usually in small numbers but occasionally with larger workparties going some distance into the bush. They carried the firewood on their backs, supported by headstraps.

Two other traditional workparty tasks, which were still practised occasionally in remoter parts of Kitui, were not in evidence in Kamale. These were the construction of a large basket for storing millet [*kiinga*] (Plate 41), which was set on a raised platform with a shelter built over it; and the grinding of a large quantity of sugar-cane in a manual grinding mill for brewing beer. In Kamale, noone grew sufficient millet to need such a large store, and sugar-cane was ground only in small quantities, with people individually paying the owner of the mill to grind the cane.

Even the larger tasks just described, however, were rarely done wholly by workparties. Rather, the workparty supplemented the household labour in the more labour-intensive or final stages of the task, or served to finish off quickly a task which had been mostly done by household labour. For example, weeding workparties started only after considerable early weeding had already been done by household labour, and the second main weeding of the season was usually light enough to be done by household labour alone. Building repairs, as distinct from new building, rarely required sufficient extra labour to warrant a workparty. In general, where the actual job was small enough it was done by household labour, not by a workparty, even for jobs mentioned above as usual workparty tasks.

The main three types of workparty observed in Kamale are now

Plate 41 Traditional millet granary and modern maize-grinder, Yatta

described. These were the neighbourhood workparty, *mwethya*; the small rotating work-team, *mwilaso*; and less formalized help from friends, which had no specific term in Kikamba. All three were *kithio*, customary institutions. Their main features, which are summarized in Table 8, were described by villagers as elicited through discussion with villagers, direct observation, and analysis of a survey of weeding workparties in Kamale in the first (long) rains of 1974.

Table 8   *Types of Workparty*

Type	Numbers range	av.	Immediate reward	Later return	Sanction
Mwethya (neighbourhood)	5–32	13	special meal	labour	fine-ostracism
Mwilaso rotating work-team	2–3	2	none	labour	end friendship
Friendship help	3–8		none	labour	end friendship
Utethyo (free help)	5–30	17	none	none	–
Friendship help	4–8	6	feast/cash	none	end friendship
Mwethya for feast/cash	6–30	20	feast/cash	none	–

Mwethya – the Neighbourhood Workparty

Mwethya [plural *myethya*] was the term used to refer specifically to the neighbourhood workparty. *Utethyo*, the verbal noun derived from the same verb [*kutethya*, to help] but belonging to a different noun-class, meant 'help' generally. *Mwethya* could refer to (a) an actual workparty, (b) the system of neighbourhood workparties, or (c) the collectivity of people in the neighbourhood in respect of their working together in neighbourhood workparties (for example 'the Utuneeni *mwethya*').

MWETHYA ORGANIZATION

A *mwethya* neighbourhood workparty consisted of the members of the neighbourhood working for an individual (called the 'owner' of that particular *mwethya* [*mwene mwethya*]) on his or her selected task. A *mwethya* was summoned not by the owner but by an intermediary who was termed the 'caller' [*mwaisya*].

A person who wanted to have a *mwethya* had to have someone to call it for him or her, and they met and decided together on the time and approximate numbers of people required. The caller then issued a general summons at the end of a previous workparty, or alternatively (and sometimes in addition too) went round people's homes to call or remind them. There was an ongoing series of *myethya*, one after another, during the height of the weeding season. Forward planning was necessary to ensure that people were available and not engaged in another person's workparty. The owner had to provide the *mwethya* with an immediate reward for its work – a meal and drinks (beer for the men and tea for women, girls or boys).

On the appointed day, the caller gave general directions on the work to be done but did not function as an overseer or manager and could not give orders. The work was done on a co-operative basis according to the usual work patterns. There was no division of labour according to levels of skill, since everyone could do the job. People said that in the past some elders used to watch and criticize any poor work, but that this responsibility was now left to fellow workers. Neither the owner or the caller could criticize the workers. Work usually lasted half a day, for a morning or an afternoon.

Work-songs were sung when women, girls or boys were working, particularly when the nature of the work was repetitive and rhythmic, as in a weeding party where the line of workers proceeded evenly across the field, swinging their hoes in rhythm (Plate 42). The songs were led by a songleader [*ngui*] and the others responded in chorus. There were traditional workparty songs for weeding and threshing into which the songleader might introduce new elements, but modern songs composed by self-help groups for self-help community work or political rallies (see Chapter 5) were also sung. Traditional or modern work-songs followed the rhythm of the work and were meant to encourage and entertain. Having a good songleader was important for the success of the *mwethya*.[4]

Plate 42   Women's mwethya finishing weeding, Kamale

After work, the workparty returned to the owner's home for the meal and drinks. It was the owner's responsibility to ensure that these were ready and that they were of the required quality and quantity. It was not necessary for the owner or members of the owner's household to participate in the workparty if they were busy with these preparations.

The workers could stay some time, particularly if beer was brewed, in which case the occasion turned into a beer party, with singing, general ribaldry and inebriation late into the night. In Kamale most workparties were for women or youths and girls, and they ended with just a meal and tea. Beer was brewed only for men's workparties comprising men who did not belong to any of the Christian sects which prohibited alcohol (such as the AIC).

While relaxing after work, people discussed any shortcomings on the part of either the workers or the owner and could consider imposing on them the available institutional sanction. For example, they could collectively impose a fine on someone for failing to attend without good reason, or on the owner if the food or drink was inadequate. The standard fine was three shillings, paid to the elders of the neighbourhood (who bought beer with it to drink together). In the event of persistent unjustified absenteeism on the part of a neighbourhood member, this penalty could be increased to a fine of ten shillings, or ultimately to exclusion (*kuvingwa*, being cut off) from the neighbourhood *mwethya* system. A person excluded in this way and therefore regarded as persistently uncooperative and unneighbourly would have to pay designated fines in order to return [*kusyokiana*] to the *mwethya* system. People said that in the past, someone so excluded was also subject to general community ostracism – people were ordered not to assist them in any way or so much as greet them, on pain of being fined themselves. In one neighbourhood (Kiliku) this sanction was regarded as still being available in 1973, but it was not seriously considered in the other neighbourhoods and there were no recent instances of this sanction being invoked.

Three progressive farmers in the village had opted out of the system, neither working in *myethya* nor having the right to have a *mwethya*. This was a different situation from absenteeism, as they were regarded as being in full-time employment or self-employment, and their families still worked in *myethya* and could have *myethya* for their own tasks.

SURVEY OF WEEDING *MYETHYA*

A survey of weeding *myethya* in Kamale during the long rains of 1974 showed a total of sixty-five *myethya* in the three central neighbourhoods over a period of seven weeks, during April and May.[5] Over half of these were crowded into the middle three weeks of this period, when many people worked twice a week in workparties. The weeding season began and ended with people weeding alone or in small household groups. The fields weeded were maize, cow-peas and pigeon-peas.

People worked in separate categories according to age-status[6] and gender, as follows:

– Men, including unmarried men [*anake*], younger married men [*nthele*, a category of *anake*], and younger elders [*atumia*];
– Women, i.e. *iveti*, married women;
– Boys [*anake*] and girls [*eitu*], aged between about ten and twenty (by which time all girls were married), working in single-sex or mixed-sex workparties.

Elderly people, aged about sixty or over, no longer worked in *myethya* and were regarded as retired, although they still performed the same tasks as other elders according to their ability. If they lived alone and unassisted they could receive 'free help' [*utethyo*], as described below.

Table 9 gives the frequency of these weeding *myethya*. Only eight were of men, compared to thirty-nine of women and eighteen of boys and/or girls, Numbers of participants ranged from five to thirty-two, averaging thirteen overall. The greater number of women's *myethya* was mainly due to the absence from the village of about one-third of the able-bodied males through labour-migration, and the partial absence of many boys and girls who were attending school.

No household had two *myethya* from the same neighbourhood, and the very few examples of any household having more than one *mwethya* were due to *myethya* coming from two different neighbourhoods. This maintained the ideology that the *mwethya* system should not be exploited or overused by any household. However, approximately 60 per cent of households (78 out of the 129 households in the three neighbourhoods surveyed) had no *mwethya* at all. Many of these were small households with only one member, or with one adult and small children, and others were very poor; neither category had planted a sufficient area to need so much extra labour. The explanation generally given by people as to why they had no *mwethya* was that 'there was no need'. Most such households had also been forced to buy grain before the new harvest was in, their previous harvest having been exhausted too early. Having no food from their own store to provide the *mwethya* meal deterred such families from having a *mwethya* unless they had some source of cash income to buy food without special difficulty, which most did not.

Table 9   *Weeding Myethya in Kamale*

Neighbourhood	Kamale	Kiliku	Utuneeni	Total	Numbers Range	Average
Men	2	2	4	8	6–20	11
Women	9	5	25	39	5–32	15
Boys/Girls	1	6	11	18	7–29	14
TOTAL	12	13	40	65	5–32	13

Table 10 shows the numbers of people potentially available for any one *mwethya* in comparison to the actual participants in the weeding *myethya* in the survey. This shows that on average fewer than half the available people worked in a *mwethya*, and that only occasionally was the actual number close to the potential total. Some *myethya* had only a quarter or less of the available participants. The explanation was not that people were failing to attend *myethya* when called – though there were some cases of this – but that the number of people needed and called for a *mwethya* was in most cases much less than the full neighbourhood total.

Table 10   *Mwethya Workparty Participants*

Neighbourhood	Kamale total	range	av.	Kiliku total	range	av.	Utuneeni total	range	av.	Average
Men	24	12	12	16	7	7	11	?	?	50%
Women	37	8–32	17	31	8–15	12	32	12–19	12	43%
Boys/Girls	31	6–29	13	25	18	18	49	8–19	11	40%

In theory, the neighbourhood *mwethya* was coterminous with the neighbourhood, with each *mwethya* supposedly comprising all neighbours of the appropriate age or sex category. In the past, when neighbourhoods were smaller, this was probably usually the case. With the increase of population and settlement density, there were by 1973 far more people in each neighbourhood than the amount of labour required in a single *mwethya*. Few wanted a *mwethya* of more than about twenty workers, which was greater than the number of potential workers of any category in each neighbourhood – between 25 and 37 boys/girls, 31 to 37 women and 22 to 36 men (figures from Table 4 above). In other words, the supply of neighbourhood labour had exceeded the demand for extra labour in any single workparty. The *mwethya* workparty had thus become a selection made by the caller from the total neighbourhood members. It was an 'action set'[7] rather than a 'team', since it had no existence except on the one occasion of the workparty, nor was it a defined grouping performing any other function.

Both in ideology and in practice, however, the obligation to work for a *mwethya*, when called, remained strong. Only those in full-time employment or self-employment (for example the three progressive farmers mentioned above) had left the *mwethya* system. In Kiliku neighbourhood – which was regarded as particularly 'solidary', perhaps because of its geographical isolation and the close proximity of its households – fines were imposed in 1973 on four people who had failed to attend a *mwethya*. In another neighbourhood there were a few instances reported during the survey of people failing to turn up and not being penalized, though it was suggested that they might have had a sufficient excuse for not attending.

A few *myethya* surveyed had one or two extra workers informally recruited at the last minute by the owner rather than the caller. Such people were called 'increasers' [*ekaisya*], as distinct from people 'called' [*eaisywa*]. This appeared to represent the intrusion of a different form of labour-assistance (namely that associated with friendship groupings, as described below) into the *mwethya* system.

The sanctions on non-attendance at a *mwethya* were still regarded as fully operative. Valid excuses were accepted – if someone was attending hospital or court, or engaged in some pressing business or social obligation. Of the four people fined in Kiliku neighbourhood in 1973, three paid the fine but the fourth, living on the borders of Kiliku and Utuneeni neighbourhoods, refused to pay and maintained that he had transferred his neighbourhood membership from Kiliku to Utuneeni. This dispute was unresolved at the end of fieldwork.

Instances were also mentioned – anecdotally but probably with a factual basis – of situations where sanctions had been applied in the past by workers against owners who had tried to exploit the *mwethya* system to their excessive advantage. In one case, the story was that the workers said that they would attend but insisted that food must be prepared beforehand; when the time came they failed to attend, thus causing the food to be wasted, and in this way punishing the owner for trying to have a *mwethya* without previously working for others. Another story related how some years earlier a wealthy man had a large *mwethya* called to repair the houses of each of his four wives; the workers agreed to do this but demanded that an ox should be slaughtered for them before they would start – this was acceded to and they then did the work, which was too heavy for the owner to have had completed in any other way.

THE OWNER AND THE CALLER

The differentiation of the roles of the owner [*mwene mwethya*] and caller [*mwaisya*], unusual in the sociological literature on workparties, was explained by a Kamale elder as follows:

'If you go to the people directly and ask them to work for you, they will ask for money. If you want a *mwethya*, you must invite someone and give him food and ask him to call people for you.'

The caller was told how many people were required, of which age or sex category, when they should work, and on what task. The caller received no payment or gift for this, other than probably the immediate reward of a meal that would have been prepared and served anyway at the owner's household. There was no instituted office of caller and no special prestige was required for it – anyone could do it, provided they were an active *mwethya* member with the right to call a *mwethya*. As far as could be ascertained, this had always been the way *myethya* had been organized in Kamale.

Kamba political values stressed the notion that no one could order anyone to do something for them without payment or return except under the obligations of close kinship or affinity. A service performed for someone else had to be agreed upon in advance, and payment or other reciprocation had to be made. Even before the introduction of money as a means of payment for work, there was an identical obligation on someone to 'pay' someone else for doing a specific job for them – for example with a goat or other non-monetary means of payment. The rate of payment was determined by the approximate standard of equivalence prevailing. The institution of the intermediary (the caller) recruiting people for a workparty was principally related to this avoidance of 'giving orders' when seeking to activate people's obligations to join in a workparty – in other words, it was consistent with the absence in Kamba society of instituted leadership statuses. The use of the intermediary also reduced the confrontational element that might otherwise have arisen from the direct imposition of the demand, whether resulting in acceptance or non-acceptance. The intermediary thus functioned as a 'broker', distanced to some degree from both the owner and the workparty participants, though linked to both.[8]

An examination of the relationship between the owner and the caller in forty *myethya* covered in the Kamale *mwethya* survey brought out two important aspects of the system and provided confirmation of informants' statements that many *myethya* worked outside their own neighbourhood and that many such *myethya* were '*myethya* of affinity' [*myethya ya uthoni*].[9]

The survey showed, first, that half of the *myethya* were from the same neighbourhood as the owner, being called by a member of that neighbourhood too. The workparty members thus worked on behalf of and for someone who usually worked with them. The other half of the *myethya* worked in a different neighbourhood and for someone who did not work for or with them. Of the latter, two-thirds were from other neighbourhoods in Kamale (mostly those adjacent to their own) but a third were from a different village altogether – including all the villages bordering on Kamale and one which was two hours' walking distance away on a steep bush path.

Secondly, the relationship between caller and owner was found to be one of close or fairly close kinship or affinity. For example, one man called a *mwethya* for his sister and a woman did the same for her brother; a wife called a *mwethya* for her husband; a son and a daughter for their mothers; a son and a daughter for their father's sisters; a granddaughter for her grandmother; and a husband for his wife's mother. Other cases included relationships based on a similar range of classificatory kinship ties. A common feature of all these relationships was the unequal relationship between the owner and the caller: the owner's request to the caller to call a *mwethya* could not be refused because of the strong respect/avoidance [*kikio*] characteristic of the relationship between them, whether based on descent [*mbai*] or affinity [*uthoni*].

Third, affinal relations between owners and callers were of special significance. The particular '*mwethya* of affinity' had a special place in Kamba social relationships – for example the *mwethya* called by a new husband for his wife's mother from his own neighbourhood. It was an obligatory marriage gift of a kind that is sometimes called 'bride service', although this term usually refers to a more formalized and prolonged pre-marital institution. It was recorded with other marriage payments (bridewealth) and written down in the 'bride-price book', as people called it in English – a notebook kept by both descent-groups containing a record of all marriage payments made and due. This special '*mwethya* of affinity' was valued in 1973 at 2 shs per worker. It was separate from the actual marriage payments and required no return from the wife's descent-group.

Many ordinary *myethya* in the past were said also to have followed the paths of affinity, outside the neighbourhood in particular, but without being counted as marriage payments. It was also quite usual for a *mwethya* to be called by a new wife for her husband from among the boys and girls she used to work with in her original (natal) neighbourhood. Workparties thus appeared to establish links in both directions between 'wife-receiving' and 'wife-giving' groups, which hinged on the intermediary caller. These links were consistent with the importance of affinity in Kamba society and with the interconnectedness through alternate generations of affinally linked descent-groups, which was established by the preferential marriage-rule described above.[10]

The key elements of *mwethya* organization were (a) the obligation on someone to call a *mwethya* when requested to do so by someone who had the right to ask for it; and (b) the obligation on a neighbourhood member to work when justifiably called.

The caller called people for the workparty from his or her own neighbourhood. That is, the caller had the right to call people from the *mwethya* where he or she usually worked to work for someone else, who might not be a member of the same neighbourhood or *mwethya*. Put another way, regular work in *mwethya* in one's neighbourhood entitled one to take that *mwethya* to work for someone to whom one was obligated through kinship or affinal links, but who was not from the same neighbourhood, as well as for someone from the same neighbourhood. As an extension of this principle, a wife who had left her natal neighbourhood upon marriage still had the right to call her natal neighbourhood *mwethya* to work for her new husband.

Where owner and caller were of the same neighbourhood, the help received by the owner was regarded as reciprocating help given to others at other times in the past. In contrast, where they were of different neighbourhoods – or, more precisely, where the *mwethya* came from outside – there was no inherent reciprocation, although circumstantially and over time the owner would probably participate in a *mwethya* travelling in the reverse direction. However, there was no direct reckoning up of exchanges of *myethya* across different neighbourhoods to ensure an equal exchange.

The social gains for *myethya* working outside their own neighbourhoods were that these developed and expanded the range of participants' social networks in the direction of more distant kin and affines, as well as potential marriage partners. Indeed, in the past there were probably far more *myethya* of boys and girls travelling to nearby villages, where the after-work entertainment included not only food and drink but all-night dances and sexual liaisons. These 'visiting *myethya*' functionally assisted in creating and strengthening ties between different neighbourhoods and villages, particularly those linked by affinal exchanges, which were made systematic in nature by the preferential marriage-rule.

FOOD AND DRINK

The food and drink given by the owner of the *mwethya* to the workers after their work was prepared by the owner's household, often assisted by friends. The meal for a *mwethya* of adults normally consisted of pounded maize-meal [*ngima*] with a relish of peas or greens (the leaf-tops of peas – *nyunyi*) or tamarind-flavoured curds [*iia*]. It was followed by tea with milk and sugar for women and children, or home-brewed sugar-beer [*uki*] for men. The meal was the same as the meal prepared by a family for itself on a special occasion, but beer would not otherwise be brewed except for a social occasion or ritual, or for sale.

The special meal, which had no particular name, was more than 'refreshments' but less than a 'feast'[11] – although there were no specific terms in Kikamba for either of these, or for the workparty meal itself. A *mwethya* of boys and girls usually received an ordinary meal of husked maize mixed with peas [*isyo*].

There was an important distinction between the meal provided for a *mwethya* of the same neighbourhood as the owner (who of course worked in the same *mwethya* on other occasions) and the meal provided when a *mwethya* visited from a different neighbourhood, where the *mwethya* owner did not work at all. The latter was expected to contain meat, usually a couple of chickens at least, and a relish of onions and tomatoes. Bread and scones, bought from a shop or the bakery in Kitui town, were also usually served with the tea afterwards. The enhanced status and quality of this meal were a symbolic recompense for the absence of any institutional return of labour. All these items were 'luxury' foods, purchased mainly from shops and rarely part of people's ordinary diet. Many in the village could not afford them even for special meals. It would therefore be justifiable to call this a 'feast'.

When asked why they worked for *myethya*, people in Kamale strongly denied that they did it just for the sake of the meal or drinks afterwards. People worked because they were called to work, and they assented to that because of the social relationship obliging them to do so. Even if they enjoyed the occasion and the food and drinks after it, particularly those unable to afford such 'luxuries' themselves, that was not why they worked. The ideology was firmly and constantly expressed that 'working for *mwethya* is working for each other'. The term 'immediate reward'[12] best describes the function of the normal workparty meal, and this distinguishes it too from any question of 'payment'.

The 'immediate reward' also included the social value of the occasion or gathering at the owner's home. In the past this included dancing, particularly for boys and girls, but these traditional dances had died out or been banned in Kamale several years earlier under pressure from the churches. However, young girls and boys (all Christians and attending school) had evolved a new dance which lacked the vigour and erotic character of some of the traditional dances. It was called *msomeno* ('saw') and consisted of rhythmic dancing round a table, each person slapping the table with one hand as they moved around it and sang after the songleader. The owner could not refuse their request for a table – a modern carpentry-made table which few poorer families possessed.

For men's workparties (except for Christians) elders would require beer after work, and the owner had to arrange this well in advance. Beer parties ended in real or affected drunkenness and elders' songs and dances.

The literature on workparties refers to 'festive' workparties. Workparties followed by a 'feast' or by dances could certainly be described as festive, but these constituted a small proportion of the *mwethya* workparties in Kamale which, although 'fun' (see Plate 44), could not really be described as 'festive' in the usual sense.

FREE HELP

A *mwethya* could also provide special assistance to someone who was particularly old, sick, poor or unable to help themselves or obtain other assistance. This was called simply *utethyo* – 'help'. As with an ordinary *mwethya*, it was organized for the owner by a caller, who might in this case have taken the initiative in planning it, but the owner did not need to provide a meal or any other kind of immediate reward for the workers afterwards.

Free or charitable help of this kind, usually from their own neighbourhood, was given to a person in recognition of their general fulfilment of neighbourhood obligations in past years or in better times. The occasion for it was the risk that the owner's crops would be spoiled by being overgrown with weeds as a result of their helplessness and inability to obtain labour in any other way – for example, by hiring casual labour. It was not a regular or frequent form of labour-assistance. A few instances of it were recorded in Kamale during 1973–4.

Mwilaso – the Rotating Work-Team

A contrasting type of workparty in Kamale was the rotating work-team called *mwilaso*, from the verb *kwilasana*, 'to alternate'. The same kind of workparty was called by other names in other parts of Kitui and in Machakos.[13] Seven examples of *mwilaso* were recorded in Kamale in 1974, consisting mostly of only two persons in each. *Mwilaso* was said to have been a more important institution in the past, occurring more frequently and with a few more participants.

The principle of *mwilaso* was that two or a few more people decided by mutual agreement to work on each other's tasks in turn, giving and receiving exactly the same labour on the same tasks, with the least possible delay in return. The rotation was strictly observed, often on successive working days. In effect, a temporary 'team' of equals was formed which alternated for as long as desired, though usually for only a few rotations. As distinct from the *mwethya*, there was no intermediary role of caller and no immediate reward of food after work.

Mwilaso was thus a contractual relationship of limited purpose and limited duration. It carried no sanction on non-reciprocation except for the break-up of the team and the friendship which inspired it. It was an arrangement made privately between friends among whom there was no obligation of co-operation or relationship of superordination and subordination. It was practised mainly by boys or girls, and occasionally too by younger married women. In line with its informal nature and lack of wider institutional recognition or sanctions, its importance in the social structure was peripheral. It was based simply on friendship [*nduu* – see below] and equality of status, as opposed to formal or prescriptive relationships of obligation. The form of reciprocation inherent in it was correspondingly one of equal and direct exchange without delay. A *mwilaso* team never became permanent, although it could be reactivated another season.

Friendship Help

A considerable amount of labour-assistance took place in Kamale through the occasional help of a few friends. This form of mutual aid had no special name, although when a group of friends were weeding they were called *aimi* ('weeders' – from *kuima*, to weed). It was organized by a person individually asking between two and seven friends for help for herself or himself with a specific task on a specific day. People said they would not work twice for the same person in this way unless they received similar help in return. Labour was given and received on the basis of equal and direct exchange. No immediate reward of food was given after work. No sanctions were attached to the exchange other than the break-up of the friendship on which it was based. The return was expected within a reasonable and limited period – for example within the same weeding season – but there was no requirement for immediate return, as in *mwilaso*.

Friends who worked together did not form a 'team'. This was an 'ego-focused'[14] and *ad hoc* gathering of individuals who might not work together again, as each participant's friendship network was different. The exchange of labour was between the person for whom the workparty was working, who worked with it, and each of the members of the workparty separately. The latter were not necessarily engaged in exchanges of labour on a similar basis with each other.

This common type of workparty was based on friendship [*nduu*], a chosen interpersonal relationship distinct from formal prescriptive relationships of kinship or affinity where respect/ avoidance [*kikio*] was involved. Friendship was an informal relationship of equality with a context of mutual help, support and affection. It could not withstand interpersonal conflict and was often defined in terms of 'absence of jealousy [*wathe*]'. Friends helped each other in weeding and other small tasks. The commitments of friendship were to a reasonably balanced exchange, with some tolerance of short delays in return. Friends were likely to be related by kinship or affinity, though not closely, and might use a relational term in salutation. But the norms and values of the role-relationship of friendship were distinct from kinship, and the kinship relationship had no overriding relevance.

Workparties and Social Change

Older people in Kamale in 1973 recalled that there were far more *myethya* a generation or two previously, with more participants, more singing and dancing after work, and with meat and beer provided more often. There were also stricter sanctions for failing to work. They said that workparties were gradually declining in Kamale. One elder wryly said, 'Soon there will be only women's *myethya* left.' He was referring principally to the effects of labour-migration and education, which had reduced the participation of men and school-age children in workparties. Some people said that there were fewer because not many people could afford the special food required. One said perceptively, 'Money is killing *myethya*', meaning that the trend was away from reciprocation of labour to payment for labour, mostly on a casual-labour basis. However, the slow growth of cash incomes in Kamale and the precariousness of living standards due to economic factors external to the village economy, including periodic drought and international inflation, seemed likely to prevent any rapid transformation of the workparty system.

At the same time, workparties in Kamale had adapted to new conditions. New forms and variations of labour-assistance had developed in response to demographic, technological and sociocultural changes. Workparties had even incorporated certain aspects of the market economy, in that they could work for money payment without losing their characteristic form.

The main changes affecting the tasks performed by workparties and leading to the use of other forms of labour-assistance, as well as changes in the perceived value of workparties, are now described.

POPULATION CHANGES

Over the course of the twentieth century the residential parts of Kamale had grown from one to five neighbourhoods, with corresponding increases in the cultivated surrounding areas. This was the result of increased migration into the area from the denser-populated parts of central Kitui, as well as accelerated population growth through increased life expectancy. In the previous two decades, one new neighbourhood (Kamale Number 6) had sprung up in a remote bush area to the east of the village on a hill slope by a seasonal river. Also, the central neighbourhood (Kamale) had divided in two, creating a new southern neighbourhood (Kamale Itheo – 'Lower Kamale'), which was still expanding on to vacant land. In 1974 Kamale Itheo had itself expanded so much that an elder from it said, 'Nobody could call a *mwethya* from all the people of Itheo because there would be too many people to feed and nobody would need

so many people to work'. Another elder explained that Itheo
had separated itself from Kamale neighbourhood 'because the
mwethya became too big'.

Thus each of the four central neighbourhoods was too large
in population for people to want a full *mwethya* from it.
Consequently, as explained above, *myethya* in 1974 contained
a proportion of the neighbourhood but not the whole neighbourhood, although the norms and values of neighbourhood
obligation were still strong.

WAGE-LABOUR AND EDUCATION

Despite the overall population increase during this century, the
rural labour-force in Kitui in general had diminished through
labour-migration. This accounted for the almost permanent
absence from Kamale in 1973 of about one-third of adult males
and the permanent or temporary absence of 7 per cent of adult
women. Kitui as a whole was poor in agricultural potential, and
most adult males sought wage-employment not only outside the
village but also outside the district. Labour-migration entailed
looking for jobs in Mombasa or other towns.

The dramatic post-Independence expansion of education had
also reduced the amount of labour available from children. Some
of the traditional tasks done by children and youths – such as
livestock-herding, scaring birds off the crops, and some of the
farm work – had been affected by children going to school. In
1974, when Kamale's own primary school had been open for
a year, nearly all boys and girls in Kamale of the relevant age
(seven to twelve) were attending primary school. Only one older
youth had attended secondary school. Schoolchildren still often
did farm work before and after school and during weekends and
holidays, but much of their work had devolved on to women
or simply been abandoned because people did not have enough
money to hire someone to do it (for example scaring birds off the
crops). Children's *myethya* were much fewer as a consequence.
In addition, many of their traditional dances had succumbed to
pressures from administration officials and the churches in the
1950s to end these and other customs, which were regarded as
detrimental to their education and morals.

AGRICULTURE

The gradual replacement since the 1930s of bulrush millet, sorghum and finger-millet by maize as the main cereal crop had eliminated two workparties associated with the former crops – threshing the harvest and building the large grain store [*kiinga*]. More significant to labour arrangements had been the teaching in recent years of new agricultural methods in government extension courses, as at the Better Living Institute (BLI) in Kitui town. These short courses – which had been attended by all the nineteen progressive farmers and many of the thirty-two young farmers' club members in Kamale – gave instruction on new agricultural and livestock management techniques, such as ploughing, anti-soil erosion methods, the cultivation of more drought-resistant varieties of maize ('Katumani 2') and the planting of cash-crops such as cotton and tomatoes. The instructors had instilled the notion that many traditional farming techniques, such as inter-cropping, were incorrect and inefficient, and should be abandoned in favour of modern techniques. This served to inhibit the diffusion of agricultural innovation beyond the group of progressive farmers and to enhance the socioeconomic differentiation between progressive and traditional farmers. Already in 1973, three of Kamale's progressive farmers had left the *mwethya* system and it was probable that this trend would continue. There was no attempt by agricultural instructors to experiment with utilizing community institutions such as the *mwethya* for the teaching and diffusion of new agricultural techniques. Those who attended the BLI courses left with the impression that the best way to farm was for the farmer and his or her family to work hard by themselves for their own profit and hire extra labour when they needed it.

BUILDING STYLES

Until the 1950s, nearly all houses in Kamale were of the traditional 'beehive' style [*kikuli* – see Plate 12 above]. The house had a conical frame of tree branches with a centre pole and was thatched from top to bottom in layers, with a small entrance. A new style, copied from more developed parts of Ukambani, was forcefully introduced in the 1950s by a new chief in Nzambani location, Gideon Mumo Nzuki, as part of the Community Development-organized *mwethya* programme described in Chapter 2. This house-type, which became the new standard architectural form throughout Kitui, consisted of a round wall-frame plastered with mud, on which a separate roof-frame was positioned on a central pole, supported by external struts, and thatched in layers (see, for example, Plate 2). Further building changes since then, diffused from more developed parts of Kitui, led to many houses having circular walls made of sun-baked mud (adobe) bricks. A considerable number of houses in 1973 also had iron-sheet [*mabati*] roofs instead of thatch. The most modern houses in Kamale, which were nicknamed in Swahili *nyumba ya kona* ('house of corners'), were rectangular with fired-brick walls and an iron-sheet roof nailed to roofing timbers. Only one in six households in Kamale had a house of this kind as the main house in the compound. Only one house in the village was further modernized with plastered and painted interior walls, glass windows, modern furniture and an outside rainwater tank (Plate 12).

There were also important changes in internal architectural layout. The traditional 'beehive' house had been divided into sleeping area, hearth and tethering area for small livestock, with other space allotted for storage of grain, utensils and other domestic possessions. Since the 1950s, the functions of some parts of this house type had been removed to different buildings. Many households in Kamale in 1973 had a separate kitchen, livestock hut and granary. Each of these was built in the same style as the main house, except that the granary was usually on stilts to protect it from insects – as in traditional granaries or temporary constructions in the fields where youths often slept – and the non-dwelling constructions were smaller and more roughly finished.

The labour requirements for these changes in building patterns created additional tasks for workparties – mixing mud, plastering, making mud-bricks, and constructing the frames for the walls and roof. At the same time, several stages of the building process were transferred from 'unskilled' workparties to hired skilled labour, for specialized tasks such as firing bricks, bricklaying and carpentry. Moreover, many of the materials for modern houses had to be purchased with cash – for example, roof timbers had to be bought to the correct specification rather than cut from the forest by a workparty and carried home.

WORKING FOR A FEAST

An occasional variation of the workparties of either the *mwethya* type or the friendship group existed in the form of a workparty where there was a 'feast' without any further reciprocation of labour. This arrangement was sometimes made by a person of high status who did not work in the neighbourhood *mwethya* but possessed the means to provide the 'luxury' food required, as well as having the good standing in the community to be able to persuade people to participate in the workparty. Workparties of this kind were followed by a feast including meat (chicken or a goat) as well as drinks such as tea, bottles of soft drinks (Kenya-manufactured Coca-Cola or Fanta, for example) or home-brewed sugar-beer if non-Christian men were working.

Three instances of this kind of workparty will illustrate its characteristics. In the first, the local Member of Parliament had a large workparty comprising six village self-help *mwethya* groups numbering a few hundred people from villages near his home on the outskirts of Kitui town. The purpose was dual: to obtain a large short-term supply of labour to plant cotton on his farm, and also to win political favour among the electorate in his constituency. His representatives who organized it promised that two bulls would be slaughtered and roasted for the workers. A large number of people attended, worked for two days and had their feast – they ate some cooked meat there and carried some raw meat home too, and were also given bread and soft drinks. It probably cost the MP more than the hired-labour equivalent. The event was apparently not repeated by that MP or any other politician, though it was said to have been enjoyed by the *myethya* participating.

In the second, which occurred during fieldwork, a Community Development Assistant from just outside Nzambani location had a *mwethya* of about thirty-five women to weed her fields, and had a goat slaughtered for them to eat. She explained, 'I gave them a goat because I felt happy with them'. She herself did not work with the *mwethya*, being in full-time employment, but she knew the neighbourhood women well through her professional work with the self-help groups there. Giving a feast for a workparty was a sociable way of getting her fields weeded. At other times she employed casual workers for some of the farm work or paid money for a women's *mwethya*.

In the third, a woman in Kamale who was away most of the time trading agricultural produce in markets in Kitui or Mombasa gave a 'feast' for two *myethya* from her own neighbourhood in early 1974 for them to finish her weeding. She occasionally worked with the *mwethya* when she was at home, and was a popular songleader herself. At other times she hired casual labour or paid cash to a *mwethya* to get her farm work done.

The 'feast' type of *mwethya* resembled the usual kind of *mwethya* where the workparty went outside the neighbourhood and received a special meal. In contrast, however, it was founded on a socioeconomic differentiation between owner and workparty, and was outside the system of reciprocity of labour. The infrequency of this type of workparty was probably related to the perception expressed by progressive farmers that it was easier and cheaper to hire casual labour, or even pay a workparty in cash, than to provide a workparty with the feast required. Quite clearly, the increased cost of the food and drinks compared to the usual *mwethya* meal indicated a substantial increase in the quality and cost of the immediate reward required in lieu of any future reciprocation of labour and in relation to the owner's greater financial means. The feast was the only reward and was a direct exchange for labour. The feast was akin to 'payment' in that it was qualitatively distinct from the special meal prepared for a *mwethya* where future reciprocation of labour was involved. Some instances were also noted in Kamale where small friendship groups working for someone of high status were given a meal including meat bought from a butchery, or a chicken, and on one occasion uncooked food to take home at a time when food was scarce and expensive, as a substitute for the non-return of labour.

The larger 'feast' workparty was exceptional, particularly because Kamba opinion was against anyone trying to avoid payment when making a profit. With the growing demand for payment in cash by workparties outside the *mwethya* reciprocation system, it seemed unlikely that people would agree to work simply for a feast, except in special circumstances (such as the instances mentioned above) where there was a social reason for doing so.

WORKING FOR MONEY

The difference between *mwethya* work and wage-labour was expressed by people in Kamale as follows: 'In *mwethya*, there is no "must"' – in other words, nobody gave orders in *myethya*, whereas in wage-labour the employer gave orders and paid cash in return: a totally different socioeconomic relationship.

The most common form of wage-labour in Kamale was unskilled casual labour (called *kibarua*, a Swahili term). About two-thirds of Kamale adults – all except those with some other source of cash income for sudden or regular cash needs – worked from time to time on a casual-labour basis for better-off members of the village, earning about five shillings a day. Casual labour in theory created a relationship of solely economic exchange between employer and employee, although in practice other strands of the social relationship between them – in so far as it was between fellow villagers who were also related by kinship or affinity – were always in the background. Thus casual labourers were often given food after work, in the same way as a visiting relative would be given food, but not as part of the work 'contract' and not in lieu of payment or as part-payment.

In wage-labour, the exchange was perceived as being completed with the payment of money, in contrast to the social exchange inherent in the *mwethya*, where the immediate reward (the meal) was not the end of the exchange, did not constitute payment, and did not exclude future reciprocation of labour. A *mwethya* took place within an ongoing cycle of *myethya* which was built on a system of reciprocity and return of labour over and above the immediate reward of the meal. Before the introduction of money into the society, the concept of payment for services, involving non-monetary items such as beer or livestock, was well established. Where services were then undertaken outside the obligations of kinship or affinity, payment was necessary, since nobody took orders unless paid to do so or under threat of social sanctions. For example, a person sent on an errand was paid according to a well-understood rate, proportional to the time and effort expended. After the introduction of money in the early 1900s, payment in cash, which was additionally a means of exchange for most goods and services, constituted an even greater contrast to the concept of reciprocity contained in the *mwethya* system.

A new variation of the traditional *mwethya* had become established in Kamale, as elsewhere in Kitui, whereby the neighbourhood workparty worked for cash. One instance of this has already been mentioned above (p.159). In another instance, food and drink were not provided after work but a sum of money, negotiated beforehand by the *mwethya* representatives, was paid to the workers and pooled for their common use. This kind of workparty could do customary workparty tasks, such as weeding or harvesting, or modern tasks, such as making bricks. The payment it earned, calculated by the task rather than by the time taken to do the job, was probably not much different from the payment made to a casual labourer doing the job over a longer period, but it might be the only labour available at peak labour periods for completing the job quickly.

An instance of this in Kamale occurred when a work-team was formed to work for cash. In 1973, at the suggestion of Ngwenze lineage elders, the married women of the lineage (called *iveti sya mbai*, 'wives of the lineage') formed a team to work on people's fields for cash, which they put into a common fund for any of the team's members to draw on in an emergency. The amount collected, however, totalled only about 200 shs by 1974, and evidently the team was not very active or well organized. Teams of boys and girls also occasionally worked for cash – weeding, making bricks or cutting house-poles – and used the proceeds to buy cloth and other materials for dancing traditional dances, as well as food for a feast at the dance. In the past, such dances [*wathi*] regularly took place after *myethya* or communal labour.

The arrangement where women's neighbourhood *myethya* teams worked regularly for cash by weeding the fields of employed people was common in Kitui's more developed areas. These groups formed teams which pooled their earnings for each member to use in turn for a specified modern domestic item, such as iron-sheets [*mabati*] to replace a thatched roof. The prerequisite of this institutional development of the *mwethya* was clearly the existence of enough people with money (mainly from wage-employment) who required the labour – for example, on farms large enough to produce crops for sale over and above domestic consumption needs – and could pay for it. In Kamale, only a handful of villagers had a regular employment income or farm income of as much as 200 shs a month, and very few urban migrants (most of whom had low-paid jobs) appeared to be sending remittances of cash to their families for more than their basic or emergency needs. For the majority, there was no economic necessity to hire labour for farm work and no financial resources for it. There were hardly any instances of such teamwork in Kamale or Nzambani as a whole. Perhaps a determined effort by the Community Development Department might have led to the creation of such groups, but by 1974 this system had not been started in Nzambani.

The institutional innovation whereby the *mwethya* worked for cash provided an interesting example of a mixture of a traditional institution and a modern economic form. This had a parallel in the use of the *mwethya* principle in self-help community development projects, which are described in the next chapter. As we have already noted, certain other traditional Kamba institutions – in law, for example – had also changed in this way, preserving their traditional character and form while incorporating key elements of new externally derived or imposed institutions.

The probable future of the *mwethya* workparty system was towards the development of women's neighbourhood teams which not only worked for their own members when required, on both traditional and modern tasks, but also worked for others for cash payment. The cash proceeds were pooled to form a central fund from which each member took money in turn to buy a set item, such as iron-sheets for roofing [*mabati*], or to fulfil an emergency need. The *mwethya* system would reasonably be expected to develop towards the model of women's self-help groups of this kind already well established in more developed parts of Kenya and known as '*mabati* groups'.[15]

5 The Self-Help Group

This chapter describes the modern village self-help group, which in Kitui was called *mwethya* – the same as the traditional neighbourhood *mwethya* workparty described in the last chapter. In the 1950s the term *mwethya* had also been applied to the modified village 'communal labour' groups, as described in Chapter 2. In Kamale, as in most of Kitui, the groups which had been created by the colonial administration in the late 1950s to take on several 'communal labour' tasks, as well as more popular tasks such as building schools, had ceased any activity in the year or two before Independence, owing to nationalist opposition. The rapid revival in new form of many of Kitui's village *mwethya* groups within a year of Independence (1963) reflected the enormous enthusiasm for nation-building and local self-help Harambee development activity throughout the new nation. This revival was achieved through a combination of popular enthusiasm, encouragement by politicians seeking or gaining election to central and local political institutions, and the efforts of the new Africanized district administration to regenerate local development activity. By 1973 there were 732 village *mwethya* groups officially registered by the Community Development Department in Kitui district. The whole district had a uniform system of community self-help organization. As set out in Table 11, there were twenty-seven self-help *mwethya* groups in Nzambani, which are marked on Map 6. As far as could be judged from discussions with Community Development officials working in all parts of Kitui, the Kamale *mwethya* was typical of others in organizational terms.

Kamale Self-Help Group

In Kamale, the *mwethya* group which had existed before Independence was reconstituted in 1964. Between 1964 and

Table 11   *Self-Help Mwethya Groups in Nzambani*

Mwethya	Sublocation	Primary school	Numbers men	women	total
1 Kilonzo	Kyanika	Kilonzo	30	263	293
2 Ngangi			(no details)		
3 Kavalula		Kavalula	50	190	240
4 Mathulini			60	91	151
5 Kyani			60	100	160
6 Syombuku		Yumbiisye	35	145	180
7 Katitika	Maluma	Katothya	71	252	323
8 Kavingo			35	135	170
9 Ithimula			(no details)		
10 Kamale		Kamale	93	213	306
11 Mutuyu		Ikuyuni	24	261	285
12 Kiseuni			48	65	113
13 Nzangathi	Kaluva	Nzangathi	34	60	94
14 Kaluva			40	74	114
15 Ngeleki			(no details)		
16 Kavumbuni			30	40	70
17 'Safari-Safari'		Kanzauwu	(no details)		
18 Mumbuni			30	40	70
19 Kanduti	Kanduti	Kanduti	(no details)		
20 Gatumba		Kitho	„		
21 Kitho			„		
22 Mbaa Ngulo			„		
23 Ngungu			„		
24 Mbaa Ngwenze	Ngungi	Inyuu	30	70	100
25 Mbaa Aombe			(no details)		
26 Mbaa Nzunzu			„		
27 Mᵤ a Mutei			„		

Notes
1. The information was compiled from location and *mwethya* records in 1973–4
2. The groups were named after the village (e.g. Kamale), a place or physical feature (Mumbuni – "at the fig tree"), or a nickname (no. 17 – meaning "Travel Fast").
3. 22 of the groups were composed of a single village, fairly large and with several neighbourhoods; 5 consisted of a grouping of 2 or 3 small villages.
4. The numbers – which were of "working members" only – were taken from official registers or were estimates by *mwethya* officials.

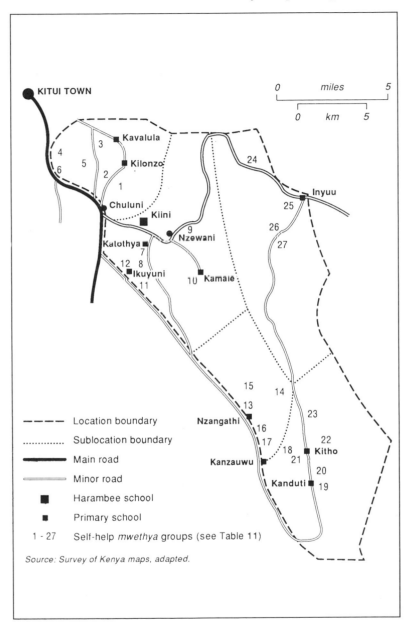

MAP 6 Nzambani Self-Help Groups

1974 it was engaged in the following projects, which are also set out in Table 12:

(i) Primary school building: it first worked on Katothya primary school, four kilometres north-west of the village, which was the project of three *myethya* from the nearby villages. The Kamale *mwethya* contributed labour and collected money for the building of classrooms, offices and teachers' houses, and cleared land for a playing-field and paths. In 1971, when the Kamale *mwethya* started to build its own village primary school, it gradually reduced its work for Katothya school. In 1973, Kamale primary school opened and the Kamale *mwethya* refused to work further on Katothya school, to which Kamale children had previously gone, and devoted its main efforts to working on Kamale school, which was to be the school for all Kamale children (Plate 43). A new classroom and teacher's house had to be built each year until the school reached its full complement of seven classes in 1977.

(ii) Building and repairing communal wells in the village: this was occasional work which was undertaken each year. Some progressive farmers preferred to dig their own wells as the water level in the village wells usually became very low in the dry season, when women sometimes had to wait for hours to get water. A new communal well was dug in 1972, but this did not fill the need adequately.

(iii) Clearing and extending village paths and the road from the village to the main Kitui–Zombe road at Nzewani: this was occasional work, usually necessary each year.

(iv) Building a nursery school for pre-school children in Kamale: a 'temporary' building with mud-brick walls and iron-sheet roof had been built in 1966. The nursery was temporarily rehoused in one of the two new Kamale primary school classrooms in 1973, and a new building in permanent materials (fired-brick walls, cemented floor, and better-quality roof) was finished in 1974.

(v) Repairing Syomukaa dam, a large water-catchment [*silanga*] at Nzewani, which created a permanent watering-lake from the seasonal river Kyemukaa. It had been built by communal labour in the 1950s and was used by Kamale and two other nearby villages as the only place for watering their livestock. The repair work was occasional, depending on the state of the dam, and was the responsibility of the *mwethya* groups from each of these three villages, co-ordinated by the subchief.

(vi) Joining with all other *myethya* in Nzambani location in an administration-organized project to collect money and contribute

Plate 43   Women of the self-help mwethya at Kamale primary school

labour for a Harambee secondary school for the location, to be sited at Kiini, five kilometres north-west of Kamale, using the buildings of the former Kiini intermediate school. This project was started in 1965, abandoned for several years, started again in 1973, and Nzambani Harambee School opened in 1974.

(vii) Building a cattle-dip near Kamale (Plate 44 – see also Plate 9 above) for all villages in Maluma sublocation: this project was co-ordinated by the subchief, begun in 1973, and nearly completed towards the end of 1974.

(viii) A 'cattle-crush' to facilitate the vaccination of cattle by the Veterinary Department was also built in 1973 at the department's request, by Kamale and two neighbouring *myethya*.

(ix) Collecting money in 1973 and 1974 for the proposed Ukamba Agricultural Institute (UKAI) to be sited on the Kitui/Machakos border at Yatta as a post-primary agricultural school intended mainly for students from Ukambani. This was co-ordinated by Machakos and Kitui district administration officials and planned by Kamba educationalists and politicians.

Table 12   *Kamale Self-Help Projects*

(A) Projects in the village

1964–74	Building and maintaining village wells
1964–74	Clearing and maintaining the village road
1966–74	Building and maintaining Kamale nursery
1971–4	Building Kamale primary school

(B) Projects outside the village

1964–72	Building and maintaining Katothya primary school
1965–6 and	Collecting money for Nzambani Harambee School
1971–4	School restarted 1973
1973–4	Building Maluma cattle-dip
1973	Repairing Syomukaa dam
1973	Constructing a cattle-crush
1973–4	Collecting money for the Ukamba Agricultural Institute

The main Kamale self-help projects in 1973–4 were building the village primary school and collecting money for the location Harambee school. Throughout Kenya, education was the

Plate 44   Myethya women carrying stones for Maluma cattle-dip

principal objective of the self-help movement. No one in Kamale was anything but keen to have their children go to school. As noted in Chapter 3 in the discussion of marriage institutions, everyone had – or potentially had – children who would need to go to school. Those who were initially childless in their first or later marriage would not be so for ever, as supplementary marriage institutions guaranteed the possibility of social paternity or maternity to everyone.[1]

All the self-help *mwethya* projects involved contributions either of unskilled labour and/or money. This was done on a *per capita* basis for villagers, with graduated amounts of money in lieu of labour collected from villagers in outside employment and other local people. Some projects involved only the village itself and were mostly initiated and carried out by the villagers themselves, albeit with some administrative supervision; others were initiated and organized by committees outside the village, requiring only the compliance of Kamale people through the *mwethya* structure. The latter projects were co-ordinated by administration officials – for example, the location chief for a location or district-level project, or the subchief for a sublocation projects.

Table 13 shows the money collected from people in Kamale in 1973–4. On average men paid 38 shs in 1973 and 50 shs in 1974; women paid 26 shs and 40 shs respectively. More payments were thus made for outside or supra-local projects than for village projects. Collections were made mainly in units of 5 shs. This could be earned by a day's casual labour or by selling a chicken (for 6 shs or 7 shs), thus not imposing a severe burden on people without any cash income, except when larger sums were demanded or when self-help payments for different projects had to be made at the same time. One progressive farmer expressed the widely held opinion that when people failed to pay their *mwethya* dues, this was 'not because of poverty but because of stubbornness'. Failure to pay up was penalized by sanctions which are explained below.

Kamale people in employment outside the village paid larger sums for both local and supra-local projects – approximately 155 shs each in 1973 and 195 shs in 1974. These payments were about four times what ordinary non-employed members of

Table 13   *Self-Help Project Payments in Kamale, 1973–4*

	Payment (in shs) m	f	
1973			
(A) Kamale projects:			
Kamale primary school	11	7	(in 2 instalments plus 1 sh for the opening day
Kamale nursery	5	3	
TOTAL	16	10	
(B) Outside projects:			
Katothya primary school	3	2	(refused to pay)
Syomukaa dam	2	2	
Nzambani Harambee School	15	10	
Ukamba Agricultural Institute	2	2	
TOTAL	22	17	
FULL TOTAL FOR 1973	38	26	
1974			
(A) Kamale projects:			
Kamale primary school	15	15	(in 3 instalments)
Kamale nursery	5	5	
TOTAL	20	20	
(B) Outside projects:			
Maluma cattle-dip	5	5	
Nzambani Harambee School	25	15	
TOTAL	30	20	
FULL TOTAL FOR 1974	50	40	

Notes
1. Non-working members (urban migrants) paid 10 shs in 1973 in lieu of working, raised to 50 shs in 1974. They also collected larger cash payments for projects, e.g. 25 shs each for Nzambani Harambee School in 1973 (1974 figures not known).
2. Data for 1974 covered only the first 9 months during fieldwork – there were other collections later in the year, of which I had no details.

the *mwethya* paid. Self-help contributions were thus 'graduated' according to income.

Self-Help Group Organization

The Kamale self-help *mwethya* group in 1973 had 306 regular members, comprising all active adult members of the village and 37 'outside' members who, while temporarily living elsewhere for employment purposes, had land rights and kinship ties in the village.

New members were placed on the *mwethya* register when they reached adulthood or were regarded as having formed an established marriage in the village – for example after one or two years of marriage and the birth of a child. People retired from the *mwethya* when they were too old or infirm to work in it.

Members were either working or non-working. The working members consisted of all resident villagers except those in full-time employment. Non-working members were those in full-time employment or self-employment, either living outside the village at their place of employment or living in the village but engaged in a full-time occupation other than farming. Thirty-five men and two women worked and lived more or less permanently outside the village, mostly in Mombasa, 350 kilometres away. Five were resident in the village, and the remainder – whose number varied as jobs were gained or lost – were away in Nairobi, other parts of Kitui, or elsewhere in Kenya, or occasionally in employment locally or away looking for work. They usually returned home only for short visits on annual leave or public holidays, or for family emergencies. Some had been away for several years without returning home, but none had severed ties with the village or with their kin in it. Most sent money remittances to their families from time to time and most had a wife (or wives) and children in Kamale.

Those who were in regular part-time employment with a skilled craft or trade, or engaged in commercial farming (the 'progressive farmers') or market trading, were given the option of either working with the *mwethya* when available or paying contributions in lieu of work. All such people in Kamale, who did not number more than a dozen, were reckoned as still belonging to the *mwethya* as working members and were excused their occasional absence from *mwethya* work. Although three no longer worked in neighbourhood *mwethya* workparties, none of these had yet decided to convert their status to being a permanent non-working member, because their income was not sufficiently stable from their non-farm or commercial farm ventures.

In 1973 there were 306 working members, with 93 men (30 per cent of the total) and 213 women (70 per cent – a male/female ratio of 1:2.3 (Table 14). There were in addition 37 non-working members (about 10 per cent of the total).

Table 14 *Kamale Mwethya Members*

Neighbourhood	Members
Kamale	60
Kiliku	48
Utuneeni	42
Itheo	135
No. 6	23
TOTAL	306 (93 men and 213 women)

Note: in addition there were 37 absent members (urban migrants).

Working members performed unskilled manual jobs on *mwethya* projects, on which they might work up to once or twice a week (usually Tuesday and Saturday mornings) for about seven months of the year, excepting only the heavy agricultural periods during the two rainy seasons, approximately during April and May and between October and December. In practice, however, the Kamale *mwethya* did not keep to such a regular and extensive schedule of work, and in 1973–4 it probably worked less than a quarter of this. This substantial divergence in *mwethya* performance between ideal and reality is discussed below.

Work involved such tasks as clearing land, carrying building materials, fetching firewood or water for brick-making, and tramping mud for bricks. People also contributed money at a fixed *per capita* rate decided by the *mwethya* committee to purchase materials or to employ skilled labour for specific jobs. The work and money payments were written down and recorded by the *mwethya* committee secretary. Non-working members paid a fixed yearly sum of money instead of working. This was called a 'goat' [*mbui*] – a customary unit of payment in the ongoing traditional jural institutions. At the beginning of 1973 this sum was 10 shs – the monetary value of a goat about ten years previously, which had not been revalued to match inflation or market changes. In late 1973 the *mwethya* committee decided to increase this to 50 shs, which was still below the market value of a goat – between 60 and 100 shs according to size and quality. Non-working members also contributed additional sums of money for purchasing materials or hiring skilled labour. Their regular and supplementary payments were about four times higher than working members' contributions, reflecting the higher cash incomes of labour migrants.

Kamale labour migrants in Mombasa, where Kamale people most often sought work, had formed an outside branch of the Kamale *mwethya* there some years previously. This was principally a mutual welfare association of urban migrants. It met every Saturday and enabled Kamale villagers to assist each other in coping with the problems of urban life – finding employment and accommodation, meeting emergency situations, repatriating the body of someone from the village who died there, and other similar purposes. In addition, it regularly collected money from its members for the self-help *mwethya* in Kamale. The regular payment was 10 shs a month. In 1973 the Mombasa branch had thirty-five members, many working in the same factory (Kenya Casements Ltd), but including some who were not permanently employed. Virtually all were employed in skilled or unskilled manual jobs, earning between 250 and 800 shs a month, mostly at the lower end of this range.

Kamale labour migrants in places other than Mombasa did not belong to any such association, because their numbers in any one place were insufficient and there was no such single workplace connection as in Mombasa. A larger urban mutual welfare association in Mombasa for all people in the adjoining

Mulango and Nzambani locations, called 'Munza', had existed earlier, but was defunct in 1973. Most Kamale urban migrants in Mombasa and Nairobi also belonged to the New Akamba Union (NAU), an ethnic association for all Kamba, which performed important political and welfare functions and also made substantial contributions to self-help projects in Machakos and Kitui districts. The NAU chairman attended the Harambee Day for Nzambani Harambee School in 1974.[2]

Elected officials from the Mombasa branch of the Kamale *mwethya* visited Kamale from time to time to present their contributions in the form of cash or building materials purchased in Mombasa, where these were cheaper. One such presentation was made in December 1973, when the *mwethya* assembled for a short semi-formal occasion described as 'our children from Mombasa bringing something'. Short speeches were made and the five Mombasa workers, wearing suits, created a favourable impression of urban employment success, when they presented the village *mwethya* committee with 386.45 shs and five bags of cement for the primary school.

Myethya also gained further financial contributions in three ways:

(i) '*Harambee Days*': these were public fund-raising events organized through the local government administration. They might take place every few years, or on a particular occasion such as the opening of a school or a new building. Before the Harambee Day, in addition to ordinary *mwethya* contributions, collections were taken from all local associations, businesses, politicians and individuals having any connection with the village. Prominent local people, politicians and administrative officials were invited to the Harambee Day and were expected to make contributions during the fund-raising, which was led by a senior administration official or politician. The occasion was festive, including songs and dances by *mwethya* song-groups, church choirs or traditional dance-groups, and guests were given food and drinks – for example chicken and rice with bottled soft drinks such as Coca-Cola, like a 'feast' after a workparty.

In 1973 and 1974 there were dozens of primary school 'Harambee Days' in Kitui, each of which often raised several thousand shillings. Kamale villagers were very annoyed that the public opening of their primary school in January 1973 by the

Kitui District Commissioner took place without any fund-raising of this kind.[3]

(ii) *Gifts from politicians*: politicians seeking votes sometimes visited *myethya* for unlicensed and illegal meetings. The Kitui County Council elections in mid-1974 and the Kenya parliamentary elections of late 1974 provided a dramatic impetus to politicians' interest in self-help projects. The official 'Harambee Day' provided an overt and legal arena for such contributions, even though directly political speeches were banned at such events. In the run-up to the 1974 parliamentary elections, political candidates occasionally visited *myethya* illicitly without the knowledge of the local administration to seek their votes and make contributions (see 'Politics and Self-Help' below). In early 1974 Kamale *mwethya* gained about 250 shs for its funds in this way.

(iii) *Cash earned by the mwethya*: self-help *myethya* occasionally worked for cash which was paid into the *mwethya* funds. The usual task involved was making bricks. Some *myethya* in Nzambani location had imposed informal local regulations that all brick-making should be done by *myethya* rather than by individual casual wage-labourers, in order to reserve this source of payment for the community self-help groups' funds. The chief estimated that *myethya* in Nzambani had earned between 300 and 1,000 shs in this way in 1973. In Kamale, though, there was not much work of this kind because there was little demand for fired bricks, and the *mwethya* failed to obtain any such paid work.

Decision-making

The organization of *mwethya* work and contributions depended on decisions taken by three bodies: the *mwethya* committee; the *mwethya* assembly; and the project management committee. Where the self-help project was planned on a wider or supra-local scale, administration officials were also involved.

THE COMMITTEE

The Kamale *mwethya* committee (called *komiti*, from the English term) was elected by the whole *mwethya* and consisted of a chairman, a treasurer and a secretary, deputies for each of these posts, and six or seven ordinary members (Plate 45). Relevant administration officials – the location chief, subchief,

Plate 45   Kamale mwethya committee at the primary school

Community Development Assistant and the two 'local leaders' [*atui*] – were *ex-officio* members. In addition, two people were appointed as *askaris* ('police' or 'soldiers' in Swahili) whose duties were to call meetings, preserve order, and enforce decisions and sanctions.

Committee meetings were private and were called *nzama*, the term for the private 'conclave' meeting of the traditional jural system, as distinct from the full gathering of those concerned in any particular dispute.[4] The committee was regarded as a conclave of the full *mwethya* assembly.

Committee meetings aimed at unanimity and consensus in their decisions and there was not usually any actual voting, except in elections for committee members. The main task at ordinary committee meetings was to examine proposals of the project management committee – for example the school management committee – and prepare decisions to be presented to the full *mwethya* assembly for discussion and approval. The treasurer was responsible for the accounts and funds of the *mwethya* and keeping the money safe until it could be deposited in the nearest bank, which was in Kitui town. The secretary kept a record of meetings and maintained the register of members and their work and money contributions.

The Kamale *mwethya* committee changed six times between 1964 and 1974. This was unusual among Nzambani *myethya*, most of which had a fairly stable and frequently re-elected leadership – even, in some cases, retaining some of the same leaders as before Independence. The frequent changes of leadership in Kamale, which are discussed further below, reflected disputes over leadership as well as problems over the *mwethya* projects. *Mwethya* leadership positions were among a small number of modern village-level leadership statuses, which included the administrative positions of *atui* ('local leaders') and political positions, such as KANU Party officers and elected councillors (of which there were none in Kamale).

The characteristics of the *mwethya* committee officials in Kamale in the ten years since Independence were as follows:

Chairmen: all were men in their fifties with long experience of wage-employment, literate in Kikamba and Swahili but without any formal education. None of them was a Christian, although one was a nominal or non-practising Christian. All were respected traditional elders and held the traditional jural staus of 'conclave elder'. All had either two or three wives, which indicated their high social status in the traditional value-system, though not all were economically better off than the average.

Singi Ndisya (chairman 1964–9 and 1973–4) was a former court police officer and a 'conclave elder' of Ngwenze lineage. Kaluma Kanyasya (chairman 1969–71 and also chairman of the Itheo section of the *mwethya* when it divided into two sections in 1971–2) was a self-employed carpenter and mason who had worked in Mombasa and Kamale, and a 'conclave elder'. Mutinda Ndinga (chairman during 1973 and chairman of the central section of the *mwethya* in 1971–2) was a self-employed tailor formerly working in Mombasa, a progressive farmer, and a 'conclave elder' of Ngwenze lineage. Nguthu Kisungu, who was elected chairman in 1974, was a retired police officer.

Treasurers: all four treasurers between 1964 and 1974 (some of whom had been re-elected more than once) were men in their thirties, all with a few years of primary education and basic literacy and numeracy skills. All were active or nominal Christians and were employed or self-employed locally in a modern occupation.

The treasurers during this period were: Mwalili Kilei, a clerk at Kitui cotton ginnery; Muthami Kyeli, a self-employed carpenter, mason and progressive farmer, and an elder and lay preacher of the African Brotherhood Church; Kilonzo Kathyaka, a progressive farmer; and Silo Kiliku, who brewed sugar-beer in the village for sale – an occupation which involved socializing skills as well as entrepreneurial talent.

Secretaries: three of the four *mwethya* secretaries in the previous ten years were of similar education, employment and standing as the treasurers, and included two who were at other times elected treasurers – Mwalili Kilei and Muthami Kyeli. The other two secretaries were King'oku Kung'ala, a retired welder and former secretary of the Mombasa branch of the *mwethya*, and Nzengula Maitha, who was literate in Kikamba but had never worked outside Kamale.

A survey of *mwethya* officials in other *myethya* in Nzambani locations[5] showed that the Kamale *mwethya* leadership had similar characteristics to others in that respect. Chairmen were mainly male elders with prestige and influence derived from both modern and traditional value-systems, which thus enabled them to integrate into the group's activities both those with least involvement in the modern value-system (who were the majority of *mwethya* members) and those with most involvement in it through education or employment (the small minority). Treasurers and secretaries, on the other hand, whose positions required certain modern clerical and administrative skills rather than traditional leadership qualities, were selected from among people possessing such skills (usually not at an advanced level) who had not found urban employment. Half of the treasurers in Nzambani location (though none in Kamale) were women. Women had a traditional role in safekeeping household valuables and were generally believed to be more trustworthy than men in that respect. The women treasurers all had basic literacy and numeracy skills acquired in market trading. Probably, as in Kamale, each *mwethya* committee also contained a balance of different neighbourhoods and different descent-groups in the village or villages from which it drew its members.

In addition to the holders of these three elected posts and their deputies, committees also had a varying number of ordinary members, usually between five and ten, who included several women and particularly the songleaders [*ngui* – see below] of the song/dance group, and two or three *mwethya* 'soldiers' [*askaris*].

None of the Kamale *mwethya* committee had any training for their self-help roles (for example, from the Community Development Department). Assistance and advice from Community Development officials was virtually non-existent, though there was some assistance and intervention from local administrative officials such as the 'local leaders' [*atui*], the subchief and the chief.

THE ASSEMBLY

This was the public meeting of all *mwethya* members,[6] which was called when it was needed. It met when summoned by the chief on a chief's tour of *myethya*, during which the chief made public announcements about a range of issues, including contributions to outside Harambee projects; or for a meeting called by the *mwethya* committee after a day's *mwethya* work to discuss problems, announce self-help contributions due, or discuss other *mwethya* business.

The assembly was called *baraza* (or *valasa*), from the Swahili term for meeting or assembly, which referred particularly to obligatory meetings called by government officials such as the chief or subchief. Attendance at *mwethya* assemblies was obligatory, subject in theory to a fine of 2 shs for non-attendance – although, like the official penalty of 75 shs for failing to attend a chief's *baraza*, this was not usually enforced. In practice, attendance at Kamale *mwethya* assemblies was low, averaging little more than a third of the members during 1973–4. *Mwethya* officials complained loudly about this and threatened penalties for non-attenders but these were not enforced, mainly because such threats alone usually increased attendance the next time to a sufficient number. The *mwethya* assembly met in the central village meeting-place – the primary school playground. Chairs were set out for the committee and other notables and the other members sat on the ground facing them, men separate from women.

The assembly meeting followed conventional proceedings common to chiefs' assemblies, with the chairman playing a strong directional role. Consensus was sought through acclamation and the absence of dissenting opinion, not usually by formal voting. Where important divisions of opinion existed, debates petered out without any decision being reached.

Speakers at assembly meetings were committee members reporting committee decisions; ordinary members speaking as 'opinion leaders' and representing a canvassed view; and individuals voicing their own views. Speeches were fairly direct without extended rhetoric, which in any case was not customary among the Kamba. Opinions were expressed in an orderly way, and fairly freely.

The *mwethya* assembly was an important arena of public expression in Kamale, alongside others – descent-group meet ings, which were usually jural moots dealing with disputes; government assemblies, which were more formal and directed by government officials, often flanked by an administrative police officer; and political rallies, which were supposed to be held only with a government licence and with government officials present. Although debate in the *mwethya* assembly was confined to *mwethya* business, it was the only community-wide forum for political display and mobilization. Women and younger men participated little in the debates, although non-verbal expressions and exclamations from the women were evidently of considerable importance. Their views were usually represented by a male spokesman.

One such *mwethya* assembly took place in Kamale on 16 October 1973. It consisted of about eighty people who gathered after a morning's rather desultory work carrying bricks and fetching water for about half an hour each. Only about half the *mwethya* members turned up for the work and the assembly. No record was kept of the workers. The rains were imminent and people were busy planting. The assembly started mid-afternoon after long delays and lasted about three hours. It was run by the chairman and committee, with no outside people present except for myself, who did not participate.

The two main topics were:

(a) a proposal to stop contributing to Katothya primary school on the grounds that Kamale now had its own school to build. This was opposed by other *myethya* working for Katothya school. An anonymous letter had circulated in Kamale calling on Kamale people to opt out of this work. The meeting unanimously approved the proposal and this resolution was subsequently conveyed to the chief, who eventually accepted it after initial opposition.
(b) a proposal to apply the sanction of *kithendu* ('attachment' – see below) to people who had failed to pay their contributions for the village school and nursery.

Money was urgently needed to complete the nursery roof before the rains started. The 'local leader' [*mutui*] proposed an immediate summons to the meeting of everyone who had not paid their nursery dues. This was rejected and instead the secretary read out a long list, comprising almost half the *mwethya* members, of those who had not paid the total of 11 shs for the nursery and primary school that year. The chairman announced without further debate and without opposition that *kithendu* would take place the following night. The *kithendu* 'soldiers' were selected, and the meeting ended. The next day, however, many people paid up and a total of 260 shs was collected, so *kithendu* was postponed. A further 70 shs was paid up during the week, so *kithendu* was again postponed, though some payments were still outstanding. The amount collected was sufficient to pay for the most urgent work to the nursery roof.

The *mwethya* leadership changes referred to above occurred after periods of tension and disputes which led in each case to the resignation of the committee and election of a new one. One such crisis led to a *mwethya* assembly on 19 February 1974 attended by the subchief and chaired by the village 'local leader'. Several items were discussed, but the most important was the election of a new committee, attended by fifty-two people. The meeting started when the subchief arrived, three and a half hours after the time set. The previous committee had resigned owing to the chairman's sudden departure to Mombasa to look for work, which may or may not have been linked to the *mwethya's* problems and its inactivity over the previous three months – it had failed to resume work after the December rains. There were also accusations of embezzlement against a committee member, which he denied.

These issues and what lay behind them were not openly discussed, though the subchief set a date for public examination of the treasurer's accounts, in accordance with the latter's offer to open his books to public scrutiny. Nominations for new officials were made and voting took place immediately, each person raising a hand to vote, with eyes covered during the counting of the votes. A former chairman was re-elected, with a younger man as deputy; the former secretary of the Mombasa branch of the *mwethya* was elected secretary; and the person who made the embezzlement accusation was elected treasurer, with a woman deputy. Five women and two men (including the former treasurer) were elected to the committee as ordinary members, and three *askaris* were elected.

The embezzlement accusation came to nothing. No one turned up to say anything on the day set by the subchief, and nothing more was heard publicly on the subject. The new elected committee lasted only seven months before being forced to resign because of its inability to get people to work or pay money. Accusations of embezzlement were made against one of its members, too, again without any result. Another committee elected in its place in late 1974 had a former police officer as chairman – 'to make it tougher', as someone said.

Accusations of embezzlement, phrased as 'eating the *mwethya*'s money', had appeared frequently in the history of the Kamale *mwethya* committee. Embezzlement, mismanagement of funds and poor accounting were chronic problems in the self-help movement. Some larger projects in Kitui had lost substantial amounts of money through embezzlement. Such accusations were usually difficult to substantiate and procedures for auditing self-help accounts were virtually non-existent, with hardly any assistance from official quarters. The administration, Community Development Department and police were notably unwilling to initiate investigations, and court actions were very rare. If a case was regarded as 'proven', there was a preference to seek to recover the funds rather than go to the trouble and expense of taking the offender to court. Thus two members of one Nzambani *mwethya* were each ordered to repay 60 shs which they were judged by the chief, in an informal hearing, to have illegitimately taken as 'expenses'. I could not determine the truth of the allegations of embezzlement in Kamale in early 1974, nor did I try to investigate far. The allegations were made by someone of a different descent-group, neighbourhood and Christian sect who replaced him on the committee until he too was voted out after facing similar allegations himself. It appeared probable that the allegations were politically motivated and without any real basis, as there was no serious attempt to substantiate them.

Although no one expected that elected *mwethya* officials should be paid for their services – apart from being refunded necessary expenses incurred (such as transport expenses) – there was often suspicion of embezzlement of funds or clandestine receipt of money in exchange for a service or favour. In traditional jural moots, jural elders were paid 'porridge' [*usuu*] for their services, in the form of cash payments by the litigants. Administration officials were often subject to accusations of embezzlement or receiving bribes, which might have been well-based in some cases, but in other cases appeared to be no more than political attempts to remove them from office in favour of someone else.

Twice before in the history of the *mwethya*, embezzlement accusations had been made against officials leading to their resignation and replacement. In 1971 the village *mwethya* divided into two, Itheo neighbourhood forming its own *mwethya* and the rest of the village working separately. Each formed its own separate committee. They worked in competition, which benefited the school project through the resultant speeding up of work and collection of money. The division was precipitated by accusations that the previous all-village committee had 'eaten the *mwethya*'s money'. Whether this was the case or not was impossible to discover. The split lasted only about a year, after which the two divisions came back together again into a single group with a single committee, in time for the school's opening in 1973. Where a committee was unable to mobilize the *mwethya*, the allegations of embezzlement appeared to function as means to sharpen and then resolve the leadership problem in political terms.

There may be a parallel here with the accusations of witchcraft or sorcery which have been described among the Kamba and several other societies in east and central Africa and had the function of facilitating the ecologically and politically necessary segmentation of a descent-group and the migration to new land of a new section of an expanding lineage.[7] The accusations, which were objectively not provable or disprovable, represented an oblique demand for new leadership, each side being righteously indignant about the alleged offence or libel. In Kamale, sorcery accusations were made obliquely and privately (but not publicly) in some serious interpersonal disputes in Kamale. Sometimes they were tested by various traditional ritual means, including divination and oath-taking, but these did not figure in the *mwethya* disputes described above. Although embezzlement did occur, the use of public accusations of embezzlement also appeared to be a weapon chosen by contenders for political leadership in community affairs.

THE PROJECT MANAGEMENT COMMITTEE

Each self-help project had its own management committee elected to manage the project when it was completed. The Kamale school management committee was established in accordance with national education regulations and included the school headmaster, who chaired the committee, the *mwethya* chairman, two or three villagers who had been to school and some parents whose children attended the school. Its function was to discuss the school's needs and problems with the headmaster and liaise with the *mwethya* committee on what was needed from it. Its decisions and proposals were submitted to the *mwethya* committee by its chairman – for example, requesting the *mwethya* to buy school equipment or proceed faster with the building work.

The Kamale school management committee met every two or three months or as needed. It had some of the formality of administration committee meetings, with written minutes, and some of the informality of the *mwethya* committee meetings.

LIAISON WITH DEVELOPMENT COMMITTEES

Each *mwethya* in Nzambani was in theory represented in the location development committee, a consultative body chaired by the location chief and intended to plan and monitor location development projects. This committee, meeting every few months, was part of a nationwide structure of development committees which had an input into district development planning (discussed below). In practice, only the district development committee, whose members included administrative department heads in the district and Members of Parliament, had any influence on the district development plans drafted by the regional planning team to form part of the five-yearly national development plan. The committees were intended to be more participative than their colonial antecedents had been, but in practice they were very administration-dominated and virtually all discussion in the location development committee's meeting was led by the location chief and decisions were virtually made by him.

Each *mwethya* committee planned and organized its own projects with relatively little input from location administration officials such as the chief, subchief, Community Development Assistant or location development committee. 'Supra-local' projects, like the Nzambani Harambee School, involved the location development committee to a greater extent and were also supposed to be approved in the planning stage by the district development committee.

In 1973 the location development committee, which the chief regarded as having insufficient experience or understanding of local development planning, was taken by him to visit all *myethya* in the location.

Sanctions

Mwethya contributions were not 'free gifts' made when and how individuals chose. They were obligatory and sanctioned, with penalties imposed on those who failed to pay the set amount of money or work the required amount. The *mwethya* committee set these contributions and the secretary recorded payments, gave written receipts and listed defaulters. The Mombasa branch of the *mwethya* operated in a similar way.

The sanction employed in Kamale (and also in most of Kitui district) was called *kithendu*. This term derived from the verb *kuthendua*, 'to strip something off' – for example to strip bark off a tree. The term had no other specific application. Its meaning in this context was immediately understandable, even to Kamba not familiar with the sanction itself. As a sanction it meant 'attachment of property', similar to the judicial penalty for non-payment of a fine as ordered by a court or a local lineage 'moot'.

As described earlier, when there were a large number of payment defaulters and the money was urgently needed, the *mwethya* committee imposed *kithendu* and appointed *kithendu askaris* to go round the homes of defaulters at night to collect outstanding payments. They first asked politely for the payment and, if this was paid to them, collected in addition a payment of one shilling for their services. If it was not paid, they seized some item of the defaulter's property and took it away. One *kithendu* haul in Kamale in 1973 included three kerosene lamps, two hens, one hoe, one hoe-handle, two dresses, one bedsheet, two winnowing baskets and a pair of trousers. Most of these items were later reclaimed by their owners and the dues paid, plus the *askaris'* 'expenses', but some were sold in the village later as the owners refused to pay up. They were sold for the amount of the debt, irrespective of the value of the item, and the proceeds were paid into the *mwethya* fund. People said that even a goat valued at 60 shs could be sold for 10 shs if that was the amount owed, though most items seized were not worth much more than the debt.

If anyone physically resisted the *kithendu askari* group, they would be arrested, probably beaten up, taken to the subchief, and possibly prosecuted for assault. The local administration supported this practice. One Kamale elder had offered physical resistance to *kithendu* some years previously and was beaten up, charged with assault, convicted in the chief's court and fined 600 shs with the alternative of a prison sentence in the event of non-payment. He sold a cow to pay the fine.

It was said that the committee of the Mombasa branch of the *mwethya* could also instruct the Kamale *mwethya* committee to execute *kithendu* at the defaulter's home for non-payment of a *mwethya* due. The *mwethya* committee, however, was reluctant to penalize the defaulter's family for a debt that was not theirs, and preferred other sanctions. For example, one former *mwethya* chairman had his bicycle seized while he was on a home visit in early 1973 for non-payment of 40 shs to the *mwethya* – the bicycle was returned to him when he paid up.

An alternative sanction was also available. One Kamale man working as a post office clerk in Northeast Province accumulated unpaid dues of 160 shs but had not returned home for several years. The *mwethya* committee decided that when his child reached school age they would charge a special 'admission fee' of the amount owed before admitting the child to the school. This sanction had no legality as far as the education authorities were concerned, but it was widely used in other parts of Kitui where there were many urban migrants who did not return home frequently.

Asked about the significance of *kithendu*, people in Kamale generally said, 'Without *kithendu*, nobody will pay'. In 1973–4 *kithendu* was threatened numerous times but applied only twice. Some instances of threats and application of *kithendu* have been mentioned above. On another occasion a *mwethya* assembly on 5 March 1974 decided to impose *kithendu* for money required for Nzambani Harambee School. There had been a *mwethya* assembly two weeks previously when demands were made for payment of 5 shs for the first Kamale school payment for 1974, and also for the 15 shs payment required at the same time for the Harambee school. A former *mwethya* leader said at the meeting, 'Some people have money but don't want to pay, they're just waiting for *kithendu*.' There was widespread support for collecting the 5 shs village payment first, but instead the 'local leader' ordered *kithendu* for the Harambee school money first, as this had been requested months previously and there was now a final demand from the chief as the Harambee Day was approaching. *Kithendu askaris* were chosen. People then started paying up, and with 478 shs collected by 9 p.m. *kithendu* was postponed until the following night. As many others paid the next day, *kithendu* was again postponed and never in fact took place.

On another occasion, on 16 July 1974, a *mwethya* assembly was called after the treasurer informed the committee that there was no money left for the Kamale school building work. At the meeting the chairman criticized people for not working and not paying their dues – although 115 shs had been paid in the previous few days after the meeting was announced. Others criticized the committee for allowing this to happen. The rains had finished a month before and the *mwethya* should have begun a period of intense activity during the dry season. The treasurer said they had been wrong to expect a lot of money from politicians – very little had been given by them, contrary to expectations. The pressure for *kithendu* was obvious. The chairman announced that work would start twice a week and the money for the school had to be paid by the next working day.

The consequence was that 130 shs was paid after the assembly and 395 shs the following week, leaving only twenty payments outstanding. *Kithendu* for the remaining payments was ordered for 23 July. The *kithendu askaris*, however, failed to turn up at the required time that night, so it was again postponed but finally took place on 28 July, taking all night until halfway through the following morning. Most defaulters paid up when the *askaris* arrived at their homes, without offering resistance, but a few items of property were seized – they were returned later when the dues were finally paid. There seemed to be no particular pattern in the defaulting, and in the end no one escaped paying.

The sanction of attachment of property had been a traditional Kamba penalty which could be imposed by a descent-group jural conclave [*nzama*] for non-payment of a fine.[8] The conclave instructed a group of youths [*anake*] to seize a goat from the offender – beating him if he resisted. They slaughtered the goat and roasted the meat for the descent-group elders to eat at a formal gathering. Those applying the sanction were rewarded with some of the meat. This penalty, however, was not traditionally termed *kithendu*, and indeed had no special name. It was still available in 1973, but not used.

Attachment of property was also an official judicial penalty, both in the colonial period and after Independence, applied by the courts for non-payment of a fine. A fine of or seizure of a goat had also been a penalty imposed by chiefs or subchiefs for those failing to attend 'communal labour' in colonial times. Some chiefs had reputedly acquired considerable livestock as a result of keeping confiscated livestock for themselves, which was illegal.

There was thus a correspondence of form between the traditional and modern form of this penalty, but with different social and political meanings. The traditional penalty involved a goat which was eaten by the elders. The modern judicial penalty was the confiscation and sale of the goat, with the proceeds put into a government fund (or perhaps sometimes a government official's 'pocket') – in either case it removed the community orientation signified by the consumption of the attached livestock by the elders.

Kithendu as a *mwethya* sanction entailed the attached item being sold for the *mwethya* funds rather than appropriated by an individual or consumed by the community or its leaders. The sanction was associated with the whole community and its objectives. It expressed community disapproval and established reparation beneficial to the community. It was widely recognized that unless there was some sanction to ensure that everyone paid, no one would pay. It was evident that large numbers of people commonly delayed paying until *kithendu* was applied, when they could be sure that everyone else would pay too. *Kithendu* was clearly an institution of last resort, applied after numerous threats when all other means of collecting the money had failed, and the money was urgently needed.

The existence of a sanction to uphold a social institution need cause no surprise, nor does this in itself indicate a lack of social cohesion or solidarity in respect of the self-help group. As explained above, the group contained people related by kinship, descent and affinity, but its basis was shared residence, and decision-making was effected by an elected leadership who needed means of enforcing decisions. Kamale *mwethya* had not worked very actively or vigorously during the period of research, and this was probably owing not just to a predictable gap between the rhetoric and the reality of Harambee self-help, but also to political factors which appeared not to affect most of the other *myethya* in Nzambani so much. These political factors were the disputes over the *mwethya* leadership, as well as the dispute in 1973 between the *mwethya* and the local chief and subchief. The *mwethya* had worked much more enthusiastically when starting its primary school in 1970–71, but by 1973 the work had become more routine and less dramatic. Combined with a lack of stimulation from the committee and the local administrative officials, these circumstances had resulted in a slow pace of work, although in the end the *kithendu* sanction ensured that the work and collection of money were carried out.

Songs and Dances

A further integral part of the Kamale *mwethya* – and all other *myethya* in Kitui – was the *mwethya* song-group. Each of these had a songleader [*ngui*] (Plate 46) and a chorus group [*aseli*], all women, who sang and danced without instrumental accompaniment or band. Most songleaders, though not all, were women. The songs and dances went together and were both called by the same term, *mbathi* [plural *wathi*], just as the word 'to sing', *kwina*, also meant 'to dance'. Songs were composed by songleaders, taught by them to the song-group, and practised for public performance. They were also sung during self-help work and at other times too – for example at a customary workparty or the meal afterwards. They belonged to a continuing and continually changing tradition of secular songs for entertainment. Neither musically nor textually did they have any connection with ritual songs, such as the initiation [*nzaiko*] songs or spirit-possession [*kilumi*] songs mentioned above, or with ordinary workparty songs, which were of a more rhythmically and textually simple form. Nor did they have any resemblance to traditional Kamba entertainment songs and dances of the 'acrobatic' kind (Plates 47–50),[9] which were sometimes part of the Harambee Day celebrations. These were performed by youths and girls, were physically very strenuous, and were still to be found in only a few remote areas such as Kyuso, where they featured at a Harambee Day in 1973 (Plate 50).

The *mwethya* songs contained great variety and originality in both musical and textual terms. Their form was remarkably similar in many parts of Kitui, as were the dances accompanying them. This was probably because they were based on the same traditional unaccompanied song forms, *kiole* and *nzai*,[10] and because they received the same encouragement from government officials and politicians. They also performed the same functions in connection with *mwethya* and self-help activities.

Mwethya dances (Plate 51) were performed on public occasions, such as the Nzambani chief's installation, an administration official's visit or the Independence Day parade in Kitui town. However, the main occasion for the performance of *mwethya* songs was the Harambee Day (Plate 52), where each *mwethya* was represented by its song-group, which had its own dancing uniform, consisting typically of white blouse, plaid skirt,

Plate 46   Inyuu mwethya song-leader

Plate 47   Kamba "acrobatic" dance group, Kyuso

headscarf, soft shoes, and beaded jewellery worn as necklaces, headbands, waistbands, anklets or armlets. Dancers often wore strings of dried seeds or flattened bottle-tops around the waist to create a percussive and jangling sound which was accompanied and punctuated by the dancers' metal whistles (Plates 53 and 54). The songleader, facing the chorus group, usually waved a beaded ornamental fly-whisk, such as politicians often carried, and blew a whistle. Women's song-groups often had a male elder accompanying them, carrying a flag enblazoned with the name and origin of the *mwethya*. The position of songleader was an important one, requiring musical talent and carrying special prestige and social or political influence.

A performance piece[11] could start with a solo recitative by the songleader (termed *mwali*), followed by a half-sung, half-spoken dialogue between songleader and chorus in the form of questions and answers (termed *kisyio*). It then proceeded to the main part of the performance – the song, which was perhaps accompanied by some dancing, ending with the last phase. The last section was the high point of the performance, called *kutilangila* ('cutting into pieces'), and it consisted of a series of practised set-piece periods of singing with dancing or dancing alone, each called *kisomo* ('teaching'), accompanied by the blowing of whistles. The songleader sang the song and the chorus repeated it in unison or sang a separate chorus part, or just danced.

The songs were listened to carefully by the audience. They consisted of narrative stories, praise of individuals – particularly government leaders, chiefs and politicians – and a wide range of social comment on such subjects as jealousy, sorcery, love and marriage, national events (colonialism and Independence), Harambee and political matters (especially during election time).

Many of the songs were called *siasa* ('politics'), the term being used in its widest sense, but sometimes referring to specific politicians, usually with the purpose of soliciting money from them for the song-group or its *mwethya* projects. The more directly political songs were sung at illegal political meetings not attended by government officials – virtually all political meetings were prohibited except for those officially licensed and

Plate 48   Traditional dancers, Kyuso

Plate 49   Traditional dance group, Kyuso

held under strict conditions and in the presence of government officials. The traditional custom of 'calling' [*kwitita*] individuals in the songs, particularly prominent people who would respond to the praise by giving the songleader a gift of money, fitted neatly into the newly institutionalized relationship between politicians and self-help groups described later.

The following are some examples of *mwethya* songs recorded in Kamale and other villages in Nzambani, mostly at Harambee Days:

SONGLEADER
Where are you coming from?
CHORUS
We're coming from Kamale
And River Kyemukaa where we take our clothes off.
SONGLEADER
What are you doing?
CHORUS
We're taking our clothes off.
SONGLEADER
Listen, *atui*, people are talking about you,
Mutisya, watch your step.
People are talking about you, important people.
Mutisya, step higher.
Kenyatta's government helps those who help themselves.
Anyone who doesn't want help, let him go away.
Musyoka has been installed,
The light of Nzambani.
Hurry, watch Musyoka step higher.
I told you, Musyoka,
Take a whip and beat some people I see.

This song was sung by Kamale *mwethya* (Plate 43 above), and it referred to a local river (Kyemukaa), where people often bathed, the subchief (Mutisya) and the location chief (Musyoka – Plate 1 above). The first part evoked laughter, and the second was fairly light-hearted too.

The following song was specially composed for the Kamale school opening day in 1973. Such events usually included

Plate 50   'Acrobatic' dancers at a Harambee Day, Kyuso

Plate 51   Mwethya dancers, Nzambani

fund-raising from official guests, though on that occasion there was no fund-raising, which caused major disappointment in the village. The songleader addressed the Kamale *mwethya* chairman (Kaluma wa Kanyasya) and 'called' Chief Musyoka, Subchief Mutisya and Councillor Mutua to make donations to the school funds. They would have had their contributions prepared and would have expected to be 'called' in the songs, as a mark of their prestige.

Yes, recording from Kamale,
Mr DC is coming to open our school here in Kamale.
This is a happy day.
We want blessings on Kamale.
Let Mutisya the subchief, Matali's father, come early.
Don't be late, Mutisya,
Write a letter, Mutisya,
And send it to Chuluni to Musyoka, the chief of Nzambani,
Telling him not to be late.
I'm calling Kaluma wa Kanyasya,
Set the chairs out.
Friends, come here,
Wipe the dust off before sitting down.
It's open, yes, Kamale is open.
Mutua, take your wallet out
And open your coat,
Give us what you can
To build our school at Kamale.
It's open, Musyoka,
Take your wallet out
And open your coat,
Give us what you can
To build our school at Kamale.

Kanzauwu *mwethya* sang the following song, referring to their subchief (Wilson Mundewa) and the same location chief (Musyoka Matuku):

I raise the flag for Kanzauwu.
Everyone knows I'm singing for the chief –

Plate 52   Mwethya dancers at a primary school Harambee Day, Matinyani

Plate 53   Mwethya *dancer*

I'm calling Musyoka,
And I'm happy to call Wilson.
I've been shown how much Nzambani has advanced.
It has got wise people
And darkness has gone.
Yes, our subchief is Mundewa's son.
Give him a 'crown'.
Musyoka, son of Matuku, these people are yours.
Tell them to send their children to school,
Only this will help our people.

These songs and many others like them were composed for official occasions such as Harambee Days and government assemblies, where *mwethya* song-groups provided the main entertainment. They expressed support for the government and the local administrative officials, such as chiefs and subchiefs.

The following song from Inyuu *mwethya* had a nation-level political focus. It also mentioned the song-group's visit to the Gatundu home of President Kenyatta in Kiambu District near Nairobi. They had been chosen for this privilege at the request of a local KANU Party representative in Inyuu. The song mentioned their main problems – pasture was needed for cattle, dams were wanted to provide water for people and cattle, and they complained of the cost of goods in the shops, which, they said, only seemed to make the shopkeepers rich:

Yes, Kenya's problems are many.
Kenya's problems are many.
How many are they?
Pasture for cattle,
Dams,
And rich men's shops.
Who was calling?
It was Mr Kenyatta.
We even went there to visit him,
To greet Chief Mr Kenyatta.

The Inyuu songleader in the following song speaks like a politician – 'I'm the Member for Kamuli' – to the politicians

Plate 54 Mwethya *dancer*

present. The subject was the lack of medicines in the local health
centre, which was headed by a medical orderly, 'Doctor' Ngovi:

I'm the Member for Kamuli.
Go and lead me, Mother.
I'm worried, very worried,
I'm speaking Kikamba.
Our hospital can't be *kithendu*-ed.
It has no medicine.
Medicine isn't like school that you can miss for a week.
Officer Ngama, ask our Doctor Ngovi –
It has no medicine.
Medicine isn't like school that you can miss for a week.
I'm speaking out and telling the important people the problem.
See the troubles that have come on us.
Chiefs, do you know, they've forgotten us.
I hear rumours that the chair is ours
And I must tell this to Kenyatta.

Inyuu *mwethya* had a talented songleader (Plate 46 above) and
an important political backer (the KANU representative). The
following song complained about the health centre as well as the
depredation of monkeys. It was both lighthearted and serious –
saying that their local problems were a national political issue.
Although it focused on the *kithendu* attachment sanction, Inyuu
mwethya reputedly had to use *kithendu* very little – much less than
Kamale, for example.

Whoever can't pay, you want his clothes snatched instead.
Chief Musyoka, Chief Musyoka wa Matuku,
Number One, switch on the tape-recorder,
Listen to our troubles.
We want you to take them to Kenyatta.
Another thing I tell you, Chiefs,
I want you to help us with our hospital.
Let us all work to bring progress here.
Whoever can't pay, his clothes will be snatched instead.
Use your power, Chief Musyoka.
Whoever can't pay, his clothes will be snatched instead.

I'm calling you, Chiefs of Kenyatta,
I'm calling you, Mutua,
And Musyoka, my brother.
I ask our chief Musyoka,
And I'm really asking nicely,
Has Mr Monkey paid his tax,
His poll tax, which hasn't yet been abolished?
I'm tired out and for nothing.
I planted millet and took the first maize to plant.
But this isn't Harambee.
Oh, so much trouble –
Mr Monkey threw me out.
I want to be sent to Gatundu
To ask Kenyatta what I should do.
Mr Monkey finished off my field first thing in the morning.
And if these monkeys are yours, Kenyatta,
Send them to find their own fields
And stop troubling me.
Mr Monkey finished off my field first thing in the morning.
Now I want to greet our chiefs:
I greet Kivui, number one, Chiefs, and Nyeki, Kaloko's father,
I praise his mother just to please him.
I go home and greet Kivili and his lorry called 'I don't care'.
I greet Itiku,
Our chiefs of Kenya.
There's a school,
A hospital,
And all the monkeys.
I want to be sent to Gatundu
To ask Kenyatta what I should do.
Mr Monkey finished off my field first thing in the morning.

Some of these songs were performed on the chief's tour of the location, on which I accompanied him. They were recorded by him (as well as by myself) on a cassette tape-recorder, so that he could later listen to the complaints, which were one form of *siasa* – 'politics'. The expression of complaints in the Inyuu songs represented an appeal to him by the community, reinforced by direct verbal explanation of local problems made to him privately afterwards in a meeting with Inyuu *mwethya* officials. Chiefs' *barazas* rarely allowed much direct open exchange of complaints – audiences were expected to be conformist and officials might take complaints as unwarranted criticism of them personally or of the government. *Mwethya* songs, which were basically not antagonistic to the government, enjoyed a greater freedom of expression of opinion than was possible in direct speech, due to the distancing element involved in the use of a musical medium to carry the message, and to the community form of the expression.

Mwethya songs, in an important sense, represented the community and were a dynamic expression of its relationship with the government, politicians and the wider society. The singers, who wore attractive dance uniforms and sang for cassette recorders or even radio sound recordists, were the official representatives of the self-help group, conveying to the audience and the group itself the ideology and purpose of the Harambee movement, both locally and nationally. Through song they sought to maintain or revive commitment to the group and its projects. The singing was 'political' in these aims. In addition, the songs represented the community to the local authorities and politicians, not only in soliciting contributions from them in songs which 'called' politicians and prominent people to give money to self-help projects and thus gain prestige, but also in making appeals for development assistance and even expressing complaints.

The songs and dances, at the same time, had a special entertainment value both in motivating work, as workparty work-songs did, and in celebrating it publicly. Their creative use of traditional song and dance forms in a modern arena was also a strong symbolic expression of how traditional co-operative institutions lay at the heart of this modern community movement.

Government Involvement

Local administration officials, particularly location chiefs and sublocation subchiefs, kept regular watch over *mwethya* activities.

They became most involved when the projects were supra-local – that is, involved a wider catchment area than the *mwethya* itself – or when problems arose. The officials were designated *ex-officio* members of *mwethya* committees.

For supra-local projects, *myethya* collected money on a *per capita* basis for projects outside the village and worked from time to time on such projects which were located nearby. They also attended Harambee Days for nearby projects. There were often complaints in Kamale that outside projects conflicted with their own in terms of the payments due for them, and there was scepticism about whether some such projects would really benefit them in the same way as their own village projects. The administration was aware of the dangers of too much coercion or external imposition in self-help activities. Officials were usually careful to restrict their interventions to providing advice on adherence to bureaucratic norms – for example in electing the committee, controlling the access to *myethya* sought by politicians, and trying to resolve their problems.

In October 1973 the Nzambani chief toured all *myethya* in the location in a borrowed government vehicle with the members of the Location Development Committee (LDC) (Plate 55). He was in chief's uniform with a uniformed administrative policeman. The purposes were to see how *myethya* were functioning, to encourage them, advise on use of *kithendu* for collecting unpaid self-help dues, answer queries and settle disputes. He was also registering his presence in all parts of the location, some of which were remote and rarely visited by him or the LDC members. He also conveyed advice from government departments or proposals, such as a proposal that *myethya* in each sublocation should build an office for the subchief (a proposal which was universally ignored), advice on planting cotton, countering soil erosion, digging wells, and other development activities. In this way he familiarized the LDC with the problems of the location as a whole. During the tour he had private meetings [*nzama*] with local leaders to discuss problems, on one occasion adjudicating on an accusation that two *mwethya* officials had wrongly claimed expenses.

Some *myethya* he visited during their regular work and had a more formal meeting with them later, but others were

Plate 55   Nzambani chief visiting Inyuu mwethya

instructed to assemble at particular times on his itinerary. As his schedule ran very late, an average of only about a third of each *mwethya* actually met him. These meetings were similar to formal government assemblies [*barazas*], with little opportunity for discussion. Some local problems were presented in the songs of the song-group (see above), to which the chief gave close attention, recording them on his cassette recorder.

One project initiated by the chief in 1973 caused major problems in Kamale. His plan was that each *mwethya* in Nzambani should contribute 200 shs a month to a rotating fund for the ten primary schools in the location, from which each school would receive in turn the whole 'pool' of 2,000 shs. The money would then be publicly presented to that school on a Harambee Day, when more funds would be obtained through donations from guests. This project started at Kanduti school, where an additional 400 shs was raised on the Harambee Day, which was attended by the chief. The plan, however, collapsed after that, with Kamale *mwethya* saying that their school had only one *mwethya* building it, so their members would be paying proportionally more than others where several *myethya* worked for the one school. The chief made an alternative proposal for each schoolchild to bring 2 shs from its parents to the fund, but this was not accepted either, as parents of school-age children would have had to pay more than those who did not happen to have a child in school at the time. In addition, this was criticized as representing school 'fees', which had recently been nationally abolished by the President of Kenya.

There was also a lack of confidence generated by rumours (almost certainly false) that some of the money collected for Kanduti school had 'disappeared'. There were fears that the money would not come round to all the schools in turn without some of it 'disappearing'. The chief responded to this opposition by dismissing the Kamale school committee, which was the forum of opposition rather than the *mwethya*, although in fact only the District Education Officer had the power to do this. The chief also refused to visit Kamale for several months while this dispute persisted. The following exchange took place in a *mwethya* assembly in Kamale in June 1974 when this conflict was discussed in the presence of the subchief:

SUBCHIEF: I dismissed the committee because of politics – people asking questions and objecting instead of doing as they were told. The committee's job is only to decide how much money to collect. The *mwethya* will lead you. You are killing the power of the government. You should not compete with the government. I have power to lead you in any way, and if you refuse I can make a charge against you. Government uses the 'crown' [the symbol of authority] and wants obedience.

ELDER: I don't attend secret meetings [i.e. for political purposes to oppose the government] but I want to know, is this a plan for all locations [in Kitui]?

SUBCHIEF: No, each location does its own planning.

ANOTHER ELDER: Is the money to be all mixed together or kept separate for each school?

ANOTHER ELDER: We would know more if we were told. We have no representative who can tell us anything more.

SUBCHIEF: So you support what your committee decided [i.e. to reject the chief's plan]?

ELDER: Yes, its not right to dismiss a committe like that. Why should you tell parents to pay without calling it 'fees'? There are no fees now.

SUBSHIEF: I can do anything I like at any time.

The meeting closed soon after this exchange, without any more discussion on this point. Criticism was not particularly heated and the subchief took no further steps to press the matter. The *mwethya* continued to stay out of the plan – which the chief still said was voluntary – and Kamale *mwethya* continued to work on its own school by itself. The dispute was still unresolved at the end of fieldwork in September 1974.

Another instance of resistance to official pressure in self-help work occurred when the subchief tried to get people to do repair work on Syomukaa dam the previous year. Many people turned up late or not at all, and much time was spent arguing with the subchief about whether the work was worth doing. After some weeks of inactivity the rains started and it was too late to fill in the deep gullies that had appeared in the dam basin and seemed likely to prevent the dam holding water. In the event, sufficient water stayed in the dam, but the problem remained for another year. Nevertheless the arguments for and against doing further work on the dam – which are referred to in Chapter 7 – were not easily resolved.

One writer has commented on the question of these dams:

> From a detailed technical dam construction point of view we should note that the Kelly revolution [i.e. District Commissioner Kelly's plan to build 50 dams a year in the 1950s] was a failure. Dams were marked by any officer. Sites and techniques were poor and most of the dams have been washed away. When they washed away, they accelerated soil erosion. Yet it contributed new techniques for harnessing water, i.e. rock catchment dams, earth dams and sand river dams.[12]

Politics and Self-Help

Self-help was an important arena of political activity. This is illustrated by the two songs below from Kamale which were overtly political and related to the 1974 local council elections. Overt politics of this kind was not permitted by the government on official or other occasions or on Harambee Days. However, during the 1974 election campaign, candidates sometimes visited self-help projects, either meeting *mwethya* leaders privately at night or illegally meeting with the *mwethya* assembly, visiting it at work. Politicians on such occasions could not avoid making or at least promising a financial contribution or contribution of materials to the self-help project. One council candidate visiting Kamale gave 100 shs to the *mwethya* songleader, 20 shs for the elders to drink beer, and 10 shs for the women to buy tea and scones. The *mwethya* chairman later tried to make the songleader give the money to the *mwethya* funds, but instead she used it to buy uniforms for the song-group. Other candidates donated a total of about 250 shs to the *mwethya* during that period – much less than everyone hoped. In this third set of elections since Independence, people did not seem to take too seriously the promises of self-help contributions in return for their votes. Conversely, politicians knew they could not rely too much on people's promises of their votes in return for self-help contributions. Those involved in self-help projects tried to use the campaigning period to obtain as much money as possible for their projects from the election candidates. *Mwethya* songs, which 'called' politicians and directly or indirectly solicited gifts, were an important part of this 'extractive' process and placed *mwethya* songleaders in potentially important local political roles.

The first song below was sung by the Kamale *mwethya* song-group and called Kamale people to meet a local political candidate (Munyalo) whose election symbol was '*panga*' (machete). It was in fact composed so that it could be adapted (with appropriate name changes) for any of several politicians likely to visit the village – Kyanza, Munyalo or Muthungu. The demand was that each or any of them should give money for the school – a classroom might cost 5,000 shs. However, the actual amounts received were very small and a great disappointment to the hopeful voters.

I'm blowing my whistle to call everybody to Kamale and wait.
The *mwethya* leader has come, Singi wa Ndisya.
I'm blowing my whistle to call you all to come and gather.
Parents, let's talk together before '*panga*' comes.
Yes, we want a classroom for our children.
Let him build a classroom –
He'll be given our votes
And a golden seat to sit on.
I'm calling our 'member', Matali's father.
I'm looking for work.
Open up, I said,
We're all Kenyatta's children.
Kyanza, you want our vote –
Build us a classroom for our children.
I'm selling my vote,
I'm taking it out of my pocket,
I'm giving it to you.
Munyalo, you want our vote –
Build us a school for our children.
I'm selling my vote,
I'm taking it out of my pocket,
I'm giving it to you.

Muthungu, I'll gladly give you my vote –
Come and meet me in the morning.
I'll wait up all night for you.
I told our teacher, Ndunda's son,
Don't be afraid of anything.
The line's getting bad.
Teacher, Ndunda's son, show us the way.
I told Makenzi to take you there for me.
I praise Munyalo and sing,
I know his '*panga*' will 'cut' Nzambani.

It is worth remarking that some people criticized Kamale *mwethya* for trying to get money from politicians rather than working for it. There may well have been some truth in this, as donations from politicians turned out to be disappointingly small.

By the time of the 1974 local and national elections – the latter being held after fieldwork ended – the relationships of reciprocity and exchange inherent in the self-help concept had spread far and wide in social terms. Those involved in self-help projects sought contributions from all people involved in social relationships with the community. Politicians, who often involved themselves centrally in Harambee projects in their own constituencies, were just one of several categories of people in relationship with the 'self-help community'. Their particular resources of and access to power, influence and wealth made them prime targets for Harambee fund-raisers. Election time was when the self-help groups could exercise most influence on them and make their greatest demands.[13]

6 The Harambee Schools Movement

The most visible and dramatic realization of the Harambee movement in the first years of Independence was the building of Harambee schools at secondary school level. Soon after Independence, local communities started to build secondary schools by self-help, using organizational methods similar to those in primary school development, but on a larger scale.[1] In Kenya there was deliberate government encouragement of Harambee schools and a corresponding restriction on the growth of government and mission secondary schools. Private profit-making schools were limited to the urban areas so that they did not compete with self-help non-profit-making schools. The pressure to build Harambee schools arose in large part from the massive expansion of primary education in the last few years before Independence, as seen in Tables 2 and 3 above. Primary education statistics for Kitui and Nzambani in 1974 are set out in Table 15. The growth of 'unaided' schools (mostly Harambee schools) between 1963 and 1973 may be seen in Tables 16 and 17.

The traditional link in Kenya between education and Christianity was preserved in the role assigned to and welcomed by the churches – to manage Harambee schools. Politicians also joined in the Harambee movement, and an important claim to political support was active involvement in and financial donation to Harambee school building. The speed with which the Harambee schools movement took off exceeded expectations and led to hasty imposition of regulations to prevent the movement getting totally out of hand and leading to the low standards which characterized much primary school development through self-help action.

The Ministry of Education quickly established regulations for the registration of Harambee schools as follows:

(i) There had to be sufficient 'feeder' primary schools in the catchment area to justify building a secondary school for local primary school leavers;

(ii) 40,000 shs had to be raised in advance and buildings had to be provided for a two-form intake, to a defined building standard;

(iii) the school had to be managed by a recognized church or lay

Table 15 *Primary Education in Kitui, 1974*

Enrolment 1968–74		Enrolment per class 1974	
1968	31,811	Standard 1	30,042
1969	35,418	2	12,982
1970	42,615	3	9,997
1971	41,443[1]	4	8,177
1972	45,982	5	6,929
1973	52,889[2]	6	5,907
1974	79,601[3]	7	5,567[4]

Primary Schools in Kitui, 1974

Number of schools: 275 (about 75% were full 7-class schools)
Number of classes: 1,624 (average size 33 pupils)
Number of new schools opening 1974: 10
Number of new classes starting 1974: 371

Source: Ministry of Education reports and District Education figures

Notes

1. The fall in enrolment was due to severe drought and parental difficulties in paying school fees.
2. The sudden increase exceeded official projections by over 3,000.
3. 1974 marked the beginning of free primary education for the first four years, with the expectation that those entering Standard 1 in 1974 would have free education through to Standard 7. The increase in enrolment benefited girls particularly, resulting in a 2:3 male:female sex ratio.
4. Standard 7 pupils sat the Certificate of Primary Education (CPE) exam, from which 14% would proceed to government secondary schools, while others would end their education or might go to Harambee, mission or private secondary schools. About one-third of the total repeated the exam the next year, to get better grades for further educational purposes. The total of 5,567 pupils finishing primary school meant that there was 17.5% 'wastage' of the cohort which had started primary school seven years earlier.

organization, which would be responsible for it in liaison with the Harambee committee (which organized the fund-raising and started the school) and the headmaster;
(iv) there had to be an adequate water supply, access to roads, proximity to medical facilities, and sufficient land for relevant facilities and future expansion (30 acres).

Table 16   *Kenya Secondary School Pupils, 1963–73*

schools

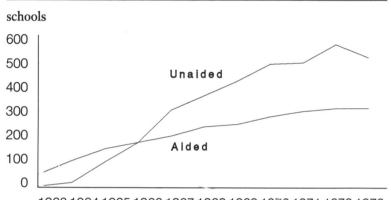

1963 1964 1965 1966 1967 1968 1969 1970 1971 1972 1973

Source: Ministry of Education Annual Reports, 1963–73

Notes
1. The 'aided' schools consisted of government-built schools, government-aided former mission schools, and Harambee schools which had become government-aided.
2. The 'unaided' schools were Harambee schools (which comprised the majority), mission schools and private schools.

These regulations were not strictly enforced, despite the legal necessity for schools to comply with them to secure official registration and to be legally open. Registration was supposed to be provisional for two years, during which time education officials would monitor the school's progress. But no new education officers were appointed to supervise the Harambee schools and the task of monitoring an annually increasing number of Harambee schools was added to the already overwhelming duties of provincial and district education officers. Many problems arose from the failure of the education authorities to hold schools to these regulations. At the same time, there was an often overriding aim 'not to spoil the spirit of Harambee' and not to discourage or be unnecessarily negative about this most crucial movement of the early post-Independence years.

Table 17 *Kenya Secondary Students, 1963–73*

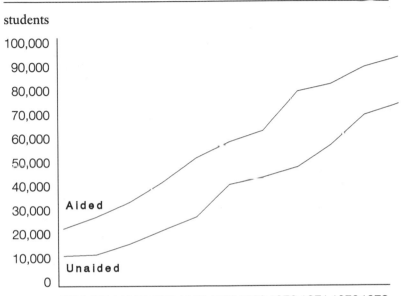

Source: Ministry of Education Annual Reports, 1963–73

Note: For meaning of 'aided' and 'unaided', see Table 16.

The pressure created by the popular expansion of education in the Harambee schools movement was keenly felt by the government, and within two years of Independence the Ministry of Education was forced by public and political pressure to begin a programme of government assistance to Harambee schools.[2] Various measures were undertaken, such as providing qualified teachers to a few successful Harambee schools; proposing to set up a Harambee schools advisory service (which never materialized); allowing the best Harambee school pupils to transfer to government schools by means of a halfway examination after Form 2 – the Kenya Junior Secondary Examination. The only measure which satisfied the demands was the take-over by the Ministry of Education of over thirty Harambee schools throughout the country each year – approximately one per district, with a corresponding cutback in the Ministry's own secondary school building programme.

These measures were inadequate either to restrict the number of the Harambee schools that were springing up at a very rapid rate, or to impose reasonable educational standards. In late 1974, when fieldwork was concluded, new proposals were still being discussed in educational and planning circles to limit severely the growth of the Harambee schools as a result of increasing anxiety and scepticism about their benefits. However, government aid continued, together with the trend of allocating government funds for improving or taking over selected Harambee schools.

By 1973 about 650 Harambee schools had been built in Kenya, with probably a further fifty or more opening in 1974. Of these, about 470 were still Harambee schools in 1973, 500 or more in 1974, since by then some 180 had been taken over into the government system.[3] The facilities and educational standards in the Harambee schools were poorer than in the government-built schools. Harambee schools outnumbered government schools, but they had fewer pupil places and less than half of them proceeded beyond the first two years of the four-year secondary school course. (Table 18 summarizes Kenya's educational structure.)

Harambee schools were, in most cases, inferior to government schools in the quality of their buildings, the educational level of their pupil intake, their facilities of all kinds, and the qualifications of their teachers. Their student fees were sometimes almost double the highly subsidized government school fees. The Harambee schools were modelled on the government schools, sticking to the basic formal academic curriculum. This was the simplest curriculum model to follow. They were not 'alternative' schools; they were a 'second-chance' institution for those who failed to get a government secondary school

Table 18 *Kenya's Educational Structure*

Primary							Secondary						Tertiary		
1	2	3	4	5	6	7	1	2	3	4	5	6	1	2	3
Exams:						CPE		KJSE		EACE		EAACE			BA etc.
Alternatives:							Village Polytechnic						University		
								Teacher Training							
											Teacher Training				
													Other higher education		

Notes

CPE = Certificate of Primary Education
KJSE = Kenya Junior Secondary Examination
EACE = East African Certificate of Education
EAACE = East African Advanced Certificate of Education
BA = Bachelor of Arts

(This system is called the '7–6–3' system, denoting the number of years/grades of primary, secondary and tertiary education respectively.)

place. With few exceptions, Harambee school leavers also had worse chances than government school leavers in continuing with their education or finding employment in a worsening job market. Nevertheless, local communities persisted in building these schools and sending their children to them. Some Harambee schools, particularly those closely controlled by missions, were well organized and efficient and were as good as or sometimes better than some government schools. A minority were extremely badly organized and of little or no educational value.

The Growth of Harambee Schools in Kitui

The first four Harambee schools in Kitui all opened in 1966, having started collecting funds in 1965 or earlier. Two years later, each administrative division in Kitui district had its own Harambee school (mostly for boys only) and the more developed locations were already starting their second Harambee school (mostly a girls' school). Table 19 lists details of all the secondary schools in Kitui,[4] which are located on Map 7. By 1974, nineteen Harambee schools had been opened in Kitui, of which six had become government-aided schools, and one other had become a mission school. There were twelve Harambee schools in the district at the time, including Nzambani Harambee School, which was the subject of particular study (see p.242 below). Two more Harambee schools were scheduled to open in 1975, having failed to open in 1974. Thirty-five more were proposed for 1974–8 in the draft Kitui District Development Plan for that period, which would have resulted in the doubling of the number of Harambee schools in the district.[5]

The year-by-year growth of Harambee schools in Kitui may be seen in Table 20. Their distribution throughout the district (see Map 7) correlated approximately with areas of greater population density, more provision of primary schools, better rainfall and agricultural potential, and improved level of infrastructure. People in those areas which scored highest on these closely related variables had more interest in education and more Harambee schools. This process operated at both local

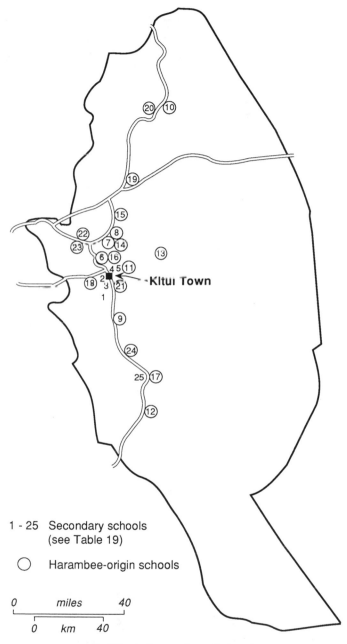

1 - 25   Secondary schools
         (see Table 19)

◯   Harambee-origin schools

0   miles   40

0   km   40

MAP 7 Kitui Secondary Schools

Table 19 *Kitui Secondary Schools, 1974*

School	Founded	Type[1]	Church[2]	Intake[3] fms	Intake[3] sex	Intake[3] d/b	Division	Location
1 Mulango[4]	1903	Govt (Miss)	AIM	4–3	f	B/d	Central	Mulango
2 Kitui[4]	1909	Govt	–	6–3	m	B/d	Central	Changwithya
3 St Angela's[4]	1946	Govt (Miss)	RCM	4–3	f	B/d	Central	Changwithya
4 St Joseph's	1961	Govt (Miss)	RCM	4–2	m	B/d	Mwingi	Mwingi
5 St Charles Lwanga	1964	Govt (Miss)	RCM	4–2	m	B/d	Central	Changwithya
6 Matinyani	1966	Govt (Har)	RCM	4–1	m	D/b	Central	Matinyani
7 Mutonguni	1966	Govt (Har)	AIC	4–1	m	D	Mwingi	Mutonguni
8 Kyome	1966	Miss (Har)	AIC	4–1	m	B/d	Mwingi	Mutonguni
9 Kisasi	1966	Govt (Har)	AIC	2–1	m	D/b	Central	Kisasi
10 Kyuso	1967	Govt (Har)	AIC	4–1	m	D/b	Kyuso	Mivukoni
11 Kalawa	1968	Har	RCM	4–1	m	D	Central	Changwithya
12 Ikutha	1968	Govt (Har)	RCM	4–1	m	D/b	Southern	Ikutha
13 Mutito	1968	Govt (Har)	RCM	4–1	m	D/b	Eastern	Mutito
14 Muthale	1970	Har	RCM	4–1	f	B/d	Mwingi	Mutonguni
15 Migwani	1970	Har	RCM	4–1	m	D/b	Mwingi	Migwani
16 Kauma	1970	Har	RCM	2–1	m	D	Central	Matinyani
17 Mutomo	1970	Har	RCM	4–1	f	B/d	Southern	Mutomo

18	Tiva	1970	Har	AIC	1–1	mf	D	Central	Changwithya
19	Mwingi	1971	Har	RCM	2–1	m	D	Mwingi	Mwingi
20	Kimangao	1973	Har	RCM	2–1	f	B/d	Kyuso	Mivukoni
21	Nzambani	1974	Har	RCM	1–1	mf	D	Central	Nzambani
22	Katheka	1974	Har	RCM	1–1	mf	D	Mwingi	Mutonguni
23	Kakeani	1974	Har	AIC	1–1	mf	D	Mwingi	Mutonguni
24	Ikanga	1974	Har	RCM	1–1	mf	D	Southern	Ikanga
25	Mutomo High	1974	Priv	–	2–1	m/f	D/b	Southern	Mutomo

(Two more schools were being planned in 1974: Zombe AIC Harambee school for girls in Eastern division, Zombe location; and Tseikuru AIC Harambee school for boys and girls in Kyuso division, Tseikuru location.)

Notes

1. Govt = government school; Har = Harambee school; Miss = missionary school; Priv = private school; Bracket ( ) indicates previous status.
2. AIM = Africa Inland Mission; AIC = Africa Inland Church; RCM = Roman Catholic Mission.
3. fms = number of forms (grades); 4–2 = four grades of two streams (classes) each; m/f = male/female; b/d = boarding/day school (whichever is the greater in the school is capitalized, e.g. B/d).
4. Started as a primary school, developed further later.

and national level, increasing development differentials between wealthier and poorer areas. More developed areas had better organizational resources, more money, improved infrastructure support and greater development orientation. This process, however, was modified by the government and Community Development policy of giving special encouragement to self-help activities in less developed areas through more extensive administrative involvement. Central development planning through district development committees sought to ensure that all areas had Harambee schools; that where a boys' school was started first in a particular area, the second Harambee school there was for girls; and that government aid to Harambee schools was given in a planned way.

Table 20   *Growth and Distribution of Harambee Schools in Kitui*

Division	1966*	1967	1968	1969*	1970	1971	1972	1973	1974*	Total
Eastern		1								1
Kyuso	1						1			2
Southern		1		1				1		3
Mwingi	2			2	1			2		7
Central	2	1		2				1		6

* general election year

Harambee schools were initiated as a result of lengthy discussion through local and district-level administrative and political channels. Who exactly started any particular school in Kitui was virtually impossible to pin down, as so many people were involved at different stages, even before the official fund-raising started. Many such claims by individual politicians or administrators were probably exaggerated or spurious. Parliamentary election campaigning in 1966, 1969 and 1974 (see Table 20) generated considerable extra support and funds for Harambee schools, and spurred on their growth.

    The relatively large-scale mobilization of resources for Harambee schools took place through the only possible social unit available − the relevant unit of local administration, which in most cases meant the division or the location. There was thus automatically considerable involvement by local administrative officials, whose responsibilities included the encouragement of self-help development. Chiefs' involvement was mainly in an executive capacity, organizing the Harambee committee and the Harambee school fund-raising. Each school had its Harambee committee and, after opening, its management committee. Much effort was made to explain the project to people through the chief's regular assemblies [*barazas*] throughout the location. In half of the nineteen Harambee schools in Kitui, chiefs were closely involved in initiating the school project, and in several cases their pressure and enthusiasm were crucial.

In half the cases, there was also extensive involvement by the local Member of Parliament. In Nzambani, for example, the MP made the first donation of money for a Harambee school in 1965 and raised a further large sum of money in 1974, although he had no day-to-day involvement with the school. MPs were not allowed by the government to be members of Harambee committees and were actively prevented as much as possible by the administration from being closely identified with particular schools. Harambee committees were obvious targets for political manipulation, but in general they attempted to distance themselves from political conflicts. They drew their members from local notables in the church, business and other fields, including elected councillors, and sought to draw everyone into the project, leaving out no social or political category in their efforts to raise as much money as possible.

Schools were started with the intention of imitating government schools, which were the only role-models available. Harambee committees would aim to build a four-year full secondary school of an academic type, although all started as a two-year school in the first instance. They then hoped to add boarding accommodation to attract sufficient pupils, and the facilities required to offer the secondary school certificate in the fourth year – a science laboratory, better-qualified teachers, sufficient books and other equipment, and improved basic pupil facilities. Form 1 and 2 equipment was moderately easy to provide but substantially greater funds were needed for Forms 3 and 4, involving a further major fund-raising effort. Schools often halted for some years at Form 2, which was previously a junior secondary school dividing point. To proceed further, which all wanted to do, they needed official permission based on their ability to provide the requisite facilities. Form 2 leavers had few job prospects and most tried to move to other Harambee schools to complete the four-year secondary course.

With the decision made to start a school and a Harambee committee elected, the school site had to be selected. The first preference was usually to take over an existing school, such as a former 'intermediate' school in the area. (Intermediate schools were 'upper primary' schools, containing classes of standards 5 to 8, and were usually built by the district council and of a higher building standard than community-built 'lower primary' schools of standards 1 to 4.) The former intermediate classes were transferred to new buildings which were usually not so well built and were sometimes very poorly constructed with temporary materials. This policy had the advantage of ensuring that the new Harambee school was centrally located and started with reasonably good buildings and sufficient land, thus eliminating the initial need to buy land, which was extremely expensive in more developed locations. In 1974 the District Education Board tried to stop the practice of Harambee schools taking over the best primary school buildings in the area, but without much effect. If they had done so earlier, it would have been a major barrier on Harambee school development, as the extra money required to buy land would have taken up a large part of the money raised to erect buildings.

The other long-term intention of Harambee committees was usually to try to get their school aided by the government as soon as possible. This was easier in 1966 than in 1974. Government policy was to aid or take over one or two Harambee schools each year from each district, often the longest established and most successful. In Kitui, this was the case in half the instances but other factors sometimes intervened – for example where a school in a less developed and remoter area was aided ahead of one built before it, or where a school required rescue in order to prevent a major Harambee failure.

The aiding policy with regard to individual schools is shown in Table 21. Of the seven Kitui Harambee schools aided between

1967 and 1974, political influence appeared not to have been an overriding factor, even in a campaign for government aid involving a Kitui MP who was Assistant Minister of Education. However, in people's perceptions political influence was usually regarded as important, if not crucial, in any local development, and many people thought it was the only influence that counted. All schools thus lobbied any possible political figure to support their case. By 1974 there was enormous competition for government aid within the district.

Church Management

The most far-reaching decision made by each Harambee committee was about the management of the school. The historical role of the churches in Kenya in school management and development formed a logical basis for Harambee school involvement,[6] although government regulations did not restrict management to churches. Where churches were managers, as they were in virtually all cases, government regulations still specified that Harambee schools should be secular schools, with their religious nature much more limited than that of private mission schools. In Kitui, the four longest-established schools, all originally mission schools, had become government-aided some years before.

The only possible managers in Kitui were the two major churches, the Protestant Africa Inland Church (AIC) and the Roman Catholic Mission (RCM). Local communities, traders' associations or urban migrants' associations were not equipped in any respect to take on such projects. In Kenya in general, there were hardly any Harambee schools which were not church-managed. Private sponsorship of Harambee schools for profit-making purposes was banned.

Both the AIC and Catholics in 1965 had a network of churches, Bible schools, religious training centres, clergy, sponsored primary schools and mission centres in Kitui. The AIC was the longer established, having developed out of the Africa Inland Mission (AIM), which entered Kitui in 1915 (see Chapter 2). Virtually all Christian worship and all

Table 21 *Government Aid to Kitui Harambee Schools*

(a) Aided School	Date aided	Years open	Top class	Explanation of provision of aid
1 Matinyani	1968	2	2	(i) First Harambee school in Kitui (ii) Influence of senior local education official
2 Kyuso	1969	2	2	(i) Remote area, only school in division (ii) Rescue of troubled school
3 Ikutha	1969	1	1	(i) First school in division to be aided (ii) Influence of MP/Assistant Minister of Education
4 Mutonguni	1970	4	2	(i) Oldest Harambee school not yet aided (ii) Political influence
5 Mutito	1971	3	2	(i) Remote area, only school in division
6 Kisasi	1973	6	2	(i) Rescue of troubled school (ii) Oldest Harambee school not yet aided
7 Mutomo	1974	4	4	(i) Remote area, girls' school (ii) Influence of MP (as in 3 above)

(b) *Explanation for other long-established schools not being aided (by 1974)*

1	Kyome	–	8	4	(i) There was another aided school in the location already*
2	Kalawa	–	6	6	(i) There were other aided schools in the location already (ii) Political opposition to local MP (iii) Successful school, no need to aid
3	Muthale	–	4	4	(i) One aided school in the location already
4	Migwani	–	4	4	(i) There were other aided schools in the division already

* Kyome, a Harambee school in Migwani location, was allowed to become a Mission (AIM) school in 1974, as a way out of its difficulties; government aid was refused in 1972 as there was another aided Harambee school in the location already.

education in Kitui up to the end of the Second World War was monopolized by the AIM. The Catholics were allowed to enter Kitui in 1946 after about fifteen years of applications to the Kitui district administration by the Machakos-based Holy Ghost Fathers. The AIM had up to then been successful in preventing their entry into the district, although colonial officials were not entirely sympathetic to the AIM, viewing it as of little help to the development of the district.

Nearly three decades later, by 1973, the Roman Catholic Mission had made a major impact in Kitui for its sponsorship and funding of development projects, but much less so in terms of Catholic Church membership. The majority of Christians in Kitui (estimated to be about one-quarter of the total adult population) were members of the AIC. Only a small minority of Christians belonged to the Catholic Church, probably just ahead in membership numbers of some small congregations of 'independent' churches such as the African Brotherhood Church, some Pentecostal churches, and affiliates of other small missionary or indigenous sects centred in other parts of the country.

One of the problems about AIC management of Harambee schools was that the church grew out of a missionary society (the AIM) which had no parent denomination abroad, no extensive funds, and few clergy or lay staff. The AIC educational effort could not draw on expatriate church teachers or foreign resources, although in Kitui there was an AIC district education secretary who supervised the AIC-sponsored primary schools and AIC-managed Harambee schools in the district.

The Roman Catholic Mission, on the other hand, represented a powerful international Christian denomination rather than a relatively small and poorly resourced sect. It had access to extensive foreign-collected funds for religious and developmental work. Several Catholic missionary societies were represented in Kenya. The main missionary society in Kitui was St Patrick's Society from Ireland, which staffed the mission centre in Kitui town and four other mission out-stations in the district. There were also several Irish nuns belonging to different Orders of Sisters (such as the Consolata Mission) at mission stations in Mwingi and Kimangao. The RCM had a bishop and a cathedral in Kitui town, and two hospitals and a leprosarium in other parts of the district. In 1973 there were thirty-five Catholic priests (Fathers) in Kitui district, of whom fourteen were working full-time as teachers, mostly as headmasters of RCM-managed Harambee schools. There was probably an equal number of Catholic nuns (Sisters) in the district, many of whom taught in girls' Harambee schools at mission centres. The presence of St Patrick's Society in Kitui was somewhat fortuitous. After the society had been expelled from Nigeria after the Biafran War because of its activities in Biafra (eastern Nigeria), it found a new working base in eastern Kenya. To co-ordinate RCM educational activities in Kitui the RCM had a district education officer. There was also an RCM development co-ordination officer responsible for Catholic-aided projects, such as a water scheme and a livestock ranch scheme, for which the Mission could draw on financial support from international Catholic charities such as Caritas and Misereor, which had regional offices in Nairobi backed by the Kenya Catholic Secretariat.

RCM involvement in development and education in Kitui was, as with AIM, both a historical connection (although as they came to Kitui a generation after the AIM, their influence was less) and also a reflection of a theological attitude to development which was more explicit in Catholic than in AIM thinking. It centred on the theme of 'liberation' – liberation from material deprivation and oppression, such as poverty, disease and lack of education and literacy, as well as liberation from spiritual confines. Involvement in development work was 'the continuation of creation'. In contrast the Mission's religious profile was kept fairly low – also, no doubt, because of government political criticism of 'religious divisiveness'.

Some Catholic priests, expressing dissatisfaction with this, said that their involvement in development had been 'used rather than utilized', and there was indeed, evidence of this. At one District Development Committee meeting which I attended in 1974, the District Commissioner jokingly said, 'We would accept aid from the Devil himself!' The RCM was aware that it had very low returns from its development work in terms of Catholic Church membership, and that even in Catholic-managed Harambee schools few pupils changed church affiliation from AIC to the Catholic Church. In most of the Catholic-managed schools, only about one-third of pupils were Catholics and no school had more than a handful of pupils who went through a Catholic baptism course.

Table 22   *Church Management of Kitui Harambee Schools*

	Africa Inland Church	Roman Catholic Mission
1966	3	1
1967	1	0
1968	0	3
1969	0	0
1970	1	4
1971	0	1
1972	0	0
1973	0	1
1974	1	3
TOTAL	6	13

In Kitui between 1965 and 1974, six Harambee schools were managed by the AIC and thirteen by the RCM (see Table 22). The first Harambee schools in the district were all AIC-managed, in accordance with the majority religious affiliation. After that, very few schools chose AIC management, as the committees quickly perceived the material advantages of RCM management in a Harambee school in terms of access to financial and staff resources. Some AIC schools ran into serious problems as a result of financial deficits and poor management. The AIC district education secretary had no resources to assist the AIC Harambee schools. Three failing AIC schools became government-aided schools in 'rescue' take-overs (see Table 21 above).

After 1966, virtually every Harambee committee, of whatever religious orientation, sought RCM management because of the resources it could call on and its commitment to Harambee education. It was sometimes even said that 'Catholic Harambee schools were not Harambee schools at all', as they received so much RCM asistance. They were usually allocated a priest as headmaster (paid by the Harambee committee at the local salary rate) and proportional assistance for several items of school capital expenditure – for example, where they gave a second teacher's house when the local community had built the first one; half the cost of a science laboratory for Form 4; loans or grants in a financial crisis; and access to funds for major expansion – for example, water facilities – which might fit in with other local development objectives.

There were several cases of RCM management being requested simply on the basis that it had more to offer. In Nzambani, as described in the case study below, RCM management was requested by the chief, an AIC member, and supported by the Harambee committee chairman, an ABC member. There was very little RCM membership in the location. In three other instances, RCM management was requested in areas without any significant RCM foothold. For example, at Ikutha Harambee School in the south, sited near the first Protestant mission in Kitui (1891), the division development committee voted 16:13 in 1968 on the chief's proposal to request RCM rather than AIC management, although he was an active AIC figure. This gave the RCM a chance to break into an established Protestant area.

In Kyuso in the north, an AIC-managed school committee appointed a Catholic Father as headmaster after the previous AIC-appointed head had been dismissed. AIC pressure, however, reversed this, but the Catholic headmaster stayed on for some time. Kisasi Harambee School, an AIC-managed school first sited at the AIM headquarters in Mulango, had moved to Kisasi because of shortage of land for the school's expansion. The move was badly planned, there was a bitter wrangle, the committee accused the AIC and AIM of 'never helping the school in any way', and the committee took a decision to request RCM management. The RCM quickly agreed, and an RCM headmaster was put in without any delay. However, he had to leave three weeks later after vigorous AIC complaints. The school was finally saved from its problems by being given government aid. In Kyome, the AIC Harambee school had endless problems of funding and was nearly closed several times. Finally in 1974 the AIM offered to take it over as a mission school, to which the government District Education Officer reluctantly agreed. Kyome thus became a private mission school without local fund-raising. It was financially viable only because the American missionaries working there taught unpaid.

The RCM did not, however, automatically agree to manage any AIC school that was in difficulties or any new school being proposed. They had no interest in helping Tiva AIC-managed Harambee School in central Kitui, which was badly sited and poorly managed and on several occasions was closed by the district education authorities. A girls' Harambee school had been planned by people and politicians in Zombe in the east but had never managed to open, because of political disputes and financial problems. The RCM had refused to manage it, as they did not want to commit the Mission to opening a mission station there to house resident Sisters to teach in the school. Their alternative offer to manage a technical school in Zombe, which they would help establish, was rejected by the school committee. The two proposed Harambee schools in Zombe and Tseikuru had no alternative to AIC management as a result of the RCM refusal to manage them.

Church management was thus decided 'instrumentally'. The church role in management was never allowed to become dominant or to lead to the school, its pupils or its curriculum taking on a religious character. Of fifteen Harambee chairmen interviewed in Kitui, ten were AIC members chairing committees of RCM-managed schools. Pupils were selected without regard to religious affiliation – though all were Christians – and school management rules (identical throughout all government and non-government schools in the country) prevented the church manager from increasing the small religious elements in the school. To people in Kitui, education thus meant modernization rather than proselytization. Education was seen as a process related to economic modernization and individual social mobility rather than religion.

In 1974 it was rumoured that government take-overs of Harambee schools would soon be ended. This would have meant that in the future there would be total and indefinite reliance on church management as well as community efforts to run Harambee schools. The role of church management and its access to outside funds would thus have become even more crucial. The RCM in Kitui would have been well placed to provide and benefit from such services. However, these rumours of the end of government aid to Harambee schools proved incorrect – such a move, even if recommended by planners, would have proved politically impossible.

Harambee Fund-raising

Fund-raising was organized by the Harambee committee, not the school manager. It rested not on voluntary donations but on assessed contributions required from all people living and working in the school's catchment area. It was regarded as an obligation on them all, from which they would all derive benefit, either indirectly or because their child would have access to secondary education. In both cases there were various sanctions against non-contribution.

Harambee school contributions derived from the following three areas of social involvement, exempting no one and drawing on existing sociopolitical and economic networks:

(I) PER CAPITA ASSESSMENT

People in the area were assessed for their contribution according to different criteria – for example non-employed men, non-employed women, the self-employed, the employed (according to their level of employment and wages), urban migrants, primary and secondary pupils, chiefs and subchiefs, etcetera. These were collected by village self-help *mwethya* committees over a period of several months, with receipts given, and were presented by each *mwethya* or sublocation on the 'Harambee Day'. Between 2 and 15 shs was often the basic men's rate, women paying only half, with the employed paying about twice as much.

(II) HARAMBEE DAYS

'Harambee Days' were government-licensed fund-raising rallies at which the fund-raising collections were presented in the presence of guests and local notables, with additional contributions by guests. Ministers, MPs and politicians regularly attended such functions. Entertainment was provided by *myethya* song groups, who sang the same songs as at their village Harambee Days, and by church and school choirs, and sometimes by traditional dance-groups. Prominent guests made speeches. The highlights were the presentation of locally collected funds and the competitive fund-raising where all guests contributed, including administrative officials. Guests made their contributions publicly by presenting them to the master of ceremonies, or chairman of fund-raising, who was usually the chief guest, and they often made a short speech at the microphone. The most prominent guest – for example, a government Minister – was expected to out-give the others – this could be done only by bringing 'contributions from friends' (see below). 'Modern' fund-raising methods were also sometimes used to enhance guests' contributions – for example auctioning donated goods. Guests were usually given food and drinks afterwards.

(III) EXTERNAL SOURCES OF FUNDS

Harambee committees also solicited aid from external agencies, such as district development committees (whose funds were very limited), different government departments (for example requesting assistance with water supplies from the Water Department), commercial firms, the Kenya Charity Sweepstake, overseas agencies (for example Oxfam, Misereor, Caritas, Christian Aid – some of which might be linked to the school manager) or even foreign government aid agencies. Some such funds were widely believed to be allocated through political influence.

The basic fund-raising by *per capita* assessment was made through the district administration and supervised by administration officials down to village level. The same sanction which was employed by *myethya* – *kithendu*[7] – was used for these collections and, as with *myethya*, people could not delay paying for ever. *Myethya* were often faced with potential conflicts between Harambee school fund-raising and fund-raising for their own projects. Occasionally people from nearby *myethya* could be called to do some manual work on the school grounds in addition to their cash payments, but most of the building work, which had to be of a higher standard than for a village primary school, was done by a hired local building contractor.

Funds raised in this way could be increased substantially – often doubled or more – on Harambee Days. The ideology of Harambee contributions was expressed as follows: 'No matter how much or how little you give, it is welcomed, whether it is 5 cents or 5 shillings' . . . 'Harambee is not a matter of competition or trying to give more than someone else for some reasons.' At the same time, the political reality was that Harambee Days were the major platform for bidding for or confirming prestige and influence, including political status. Although overt political campaigning and vote-seeking were prohibited by the administration, these took place indirectly – or sometimes directly, when the administrative officer was absent. The amounts of money given or promised – by 1974 people were becoming distrustful of cheques, as so many had 'bounced' in the past – were expected to relate to the giver's means and the reputation they desired. The amounts given were carefully calculated by donors *vis-à-vis* what others gave and within limits regarded as locally appropriate. There were strong social pressures on local notables to give more than their regular 'assessed' contribution, and they probably did, if they valued their reputations and wanted to use the project facility.

Harambee Days were also a major opportunity for national politicians to make contact with local people. President Kenyatta and his Ministers often organized their tours of the districts around Harambee Days. Important national political statements were sometimes made on such occasions, as well as development propaganda.

Harambee Days were organized for the first collection of funds for the school preceding the school's opening the following year, and also for subsequent major fund-raising – for example for opening a new classroom. Amounts raised in Kitui for Harambee schools in the early 1970s ranged from 70,000 shs raised for

Kimangao Harambee School for girls in 1971 by the then Vice-President (President since 1978) Daniel arap Moi, to the 33,000 shs raised for Nzambani Harambee School in 1974. Harambee Days were frequently reported in the national news media, the amount raised usually including local *per capita* contributions as well as the most important guests' contributions and any other financial or material assistance – for example from church managers. Guests' contributions often included money described as 'raised from their friends'. Politicians obtained such funds by pressing their supporters and contacts for contributions, as they did during political campaigning. Thus a Minister's Harambee contribution might normally include, as well as his own money, cheques sent from companies which had business dealings with the Minister.[8]

Harambee Students

The educational side of Harambee schools differed little from that of government schools.[9] Major restraints were the lack of central administration and supervision, and the reduced and often very unstable financial state of Harambee schools. Continually in financial difficulties, these schools could not afford the qualified staff, textbooks, equipment and extra items to which they aspired. They were modelled on government schools, followed the same syllabus and curriculum, reflected the same kind of school organization and intra-school role structure, and took the same examinations. There was nothing especially different about the running of the Harambee school. There were usually no special ideas or activities associated with the Harambee ideology and no special interest in Harambee from the students, whose concern was to pass examinations and gain qualifications which would make the financial investment in their education worthwhile. Internal school processes did not reveal anything distinctive about Harambee schools as against secondary schools in general. The Harambee element in the school had no effect on its operation.

Harambee students differed from government school students in that their primary school leaving achievement was lower.

Success at gaining entry to secondary schools was rather arbitrary because in Kenya each year almost half of primary school certificate failures re-sat the Primary School Leaving Examination the following year. Harambee schools, as well as private schools – which were strongly discouraged outside the main towns – offered the chance of secondary education to primary school leavers who failed to obtain entry into government secondary schools and could raise the school fees, which were between 750 shs and 1000 shs per year, higher than the government school fees of 500 shs per year.

My survey of Harambee schools and students in Kitui, comparing them to their counterparts in government schools in the district, showed that there was little difference in occupational status between students' fathers at either kind of school. Fees were paid by students' fathers in three-quarters of all cases, with brothers paying them in one-sixth of cases and a variety of other relatives for the remainder. Slightly more Harambee students had fathers who were farmers, but the number in paid employment was close. In about two-thirds of all cases their fathers had no education, though fathers of government school students who had some education tended to have slightly more education than fathers of Harambee students. In both cases 90 per cent of mothers of secondary students had no education, but of those who had been to school at all, those with government school children had more education. Regarding other close relatives, government and Harambee students tended to differ only slightly in social and educational background. This was probably to be expected in a district where educational levels for the previous generation were low, as a result of poor provision.

Harambee students' views of their school were generally positive. They listed their main demands for their school as having trained teachers, boarding accommodation and science facilities. Extra 'needs' mentioned included a school bus and television. Government students also tended to be fairly positive about Harambee schools, saying that Harambee students worked harder, mainly because most of them sat an examination in their second year, the Kenya Junior Secondary Examination, by means of which they had the opportunity to transfer to a government school; if their school was only a two-year school, they had to seek entry to a four-year Harambee school which proceeded to the secondary school certificate in the fourth year.

Both government and Harambee students recognized that going to school required different habits and behaviour patterns from home. All favoured boarding school as the place to acquire these. Day students had practical problems of travelling to school each day or finding local accommodation, setting aside the time away from other normal rural tasks to study at home, and having proper light to study by after night-fall (about 6.30 p.m. for most of the year). Students also understood that schools were instruments of resocialization, particularly for those from homes where their generation was the first to receive modern education. However, the main end-product was perceived as improved access to employment opportunities. Although for Harambee students the opportunities for social mobility and the likely economic rewards of their education were less than for government students, these were undoubtedly greater than the opportunities available to those with only primary education.[10]

Nzambani Harambee School: a Case Study

The Harambee school observed most closely during fieldwork was Nzambani Harambee School, which opened in 1974.[11] A Harambee school in Nzambani location was first proposed in 1965, when several other locations were planning their own Harambee schools in the first phase of the growth of these schools in Kitui. The local MP gave 1,000 shs and a bank account for the proposed Nzambani Harambee Secondary School was opened. However, there was no further progress until 1971, when the Roman Catholic Mission in Kitui was persuaded by the Nzambani chief to undertake the school's management. The Mission was expanding its educational activities and had appointed an education officer (a missionary) to supervise its educational work in the district. Apart from an application for formal registration of the school, there were no further moves with regard to the proposed school in Nzambani until the following year, when the location chief had been dismissed and a new chief appointed.

Plate 56   Kiini Intermediate School – later Nzambani Harambee School

The new chief of Nzambani location in 1972, Charles Musyoka Matuku (Plate 1 above), revived the Harambee school plan as his major project for developing the location and making his mark on it. At the same time, he also proposed that the location's Community Hall at his headquarters – or 'chief's camp', as it was called – should be converted to a village polytechnic – a secondary-level technical training institution. He was soliciting Anglican Church aid for this through the Protestant National Council of Churches in Kenya (NCCK), which was sponsoring several such village polytechnics in the country. He hoped to have either a Harambee school or a village polytechnic to promote the educational development of the location, which had ten primary schools but very few primary school-leavers gaining entrance to government secondary schools. He envisaged that the possibility of access to a local Harambee school would stimulate educational progress in the location and have a long-term and generally positive effect on development in his location.

The plan was to use the buildings of Kiini intermediate school (Plate 56 above) for the Harambee school and transfer its three classes to new classrooms to be built at the nearby Katothya lower primary school by local *myethya*. The chief selected a committee for the Harambee school consisting of local clergymen of different denominations, politicians, traders and officials. It was chaired by the pastor of the ABC church – an independent church with which the chief's own church, the AIC, had had poor relations ever since the ABC had seceded from the AIC during the 1940s. (The ABC had deliberately built its first church in Kitui close to the AIM mission station in Mulango, and was building another close to the AIC church at Katothya.)

Very relevant to the time schedule for starting the school in 1974 was the fact that elections were due in 1973 or 1974; thus a great deal of money was expected from the politicians' campaigns. The chief's declared aim was to oblige all politicians to compete in supporting it and giving it funds as a means of impressing the voters. The sitting local MP (who was also a government minister) had a major initial advantage. Having given 1,000 shs to start the school in 1965, he promised to raise a huge amount of funds for it to 'build it himself', as people put it. He said he would bring 15,000 shs for the school and that if he didn't honour this promise 'they shouldn't vote for him'. This naturally attracted the hostility of the other candidates, whom the chief at the same time wanted to attract to give money to the school in competition with the MP, even if they could not command the same resources as he could. The MP had farms in central Kitui and a business in Kitui town.

Harambee committees invariably pressed their MPs to make big Harambee contributions for the sake of their political reputations, and MPs had no choice but to comply, particularly at election time. If in the Nzambani case the MP had not taken the initiative to commit funds for the school, the Harambee committee would have campaigned him to do it. This would have been the same whoever happened to be the MP at the time. Nzambani was a poor area and would have been unlikely to raise sufficient funds for the school from its own resources without this substantial extra injection of funds. No other comparable source of additional funds was available. In the context of the established link between Harambee and politics in Kenya (see 'The Political Phenomenon', Chapter 7), this was not seen by people in Kitui as at all reprehensible or different from what all other Harambee committees sought.

The committee started the collection of money in the location in early 1973. It was organized through the administration – that is, by the chief and subchiefs. The amount to be paid by each category of person or organization (such as *myethya*) was fixed by the committee and collection was made through administration officials. Men in the location were to pay 15 shs, women 10 shs, and the employed 25 shs. A Harambee Day was planned for August 1973. Little support for the school was forthcoming from traders, possibly because an important political opponent of the MP was a prominent trader. By August 1973, 17,000 shs had been collected by *myethya* in the location and banked, and work had started on the building of a teacher's house. The Harambee Day, however, was postponed, both at the MP's request and because insufficient money had been collected in the location. The Catholic Mission had undertaken to put in a Father as headmaster if the school was ready by November that year, but as it was not, the Father designated was appointed to another Harambee school in Kitui.

By January 1974, thirty students (mostly boys) had been selected for entry to the as yet unopened school from primary school-leaver applicants who had failed to get places in government schools. Only two or three of the selected students were up to the standard of government school entrants, and some had very poor results in the primary school-leaving examination and thus no chance of government school admission. Most students were from Nzambani location, as there was no boarding accommodation to attract pupils from further than walking distance (about five miles) from the school. A local sixth-form leaver, who had no teaching experience or qualifications, was appointed temporary headmaster.

The school did not open in January 1974, as the building work had not been completed and the upper section of the primary school was still occupying the Kiini site – their new classrooms at Katothya had not been completed either. The Catholic Mission blamed the committee for inactivity, the committee blamed the Mission for not doing more, the chief was away for an extended period on a chief's course, and there were political disputes looming in the background. Location collection proceeded, however, and *kithendu* was beginning to be used by *myethya* to increase the rate of payment, resulting in 26,000 shs being collected and put in the bank by the end of that month.

In February 1974, the chief returned from his course and started planning for a Harambee Day the following month with the MP as chief guest. He also invited the chairman of the New Akamba Union and the District Commissioner to attend. The local traders were continuing to be uncooperative, even though the chief, as owner of a small shop at Chuluni, knew them well. The District Education Officer opposed the opening of the school until the buildings were completed. In late February the Harambee chairman added more pressure to collect money, telling people, 'If we miss opening the school this year [i.e. election year], it will take years to get it'. In late February the school committee lent 5,000 shs to Katothya primary school to complete the new classrooms so that the Kiini classrooms could be vacated for the Harambee school. The Catholic Mission lent money to buy desks and books, so as not to deplete the total of the banked funds, which remained intact for the purpose of trying to reach the 40,000 shs target. This amount had to be collected for official permission to open but more money would be needed, even in its first year, to ensure the school was financially viable.

Nzambani Harambee school opened unofficially in late February 1974, without quite meeting the official requirements regarding money in the bank. As the school year had begun in early January, the committee felt it was vital for pupils to start as soon as possible, to avoid a year's delay in opening the school. Adding the MP's promised 15,000 shs to what had been collected in the location, the committee regarded the 40,000 shs target as achieved, and likely to be surpassed when the long-delayed Harambee Day took place. The school opened with only six paid-up students. Other selected students who came without their fees were sent home to fetch the money required. The fees were set at 750 shs for the year, on which basis a class of forty would be sufficient to keep the school running. The school opened with three teachers: the previously appointed sixth-form leaver, who was awaiting university entrance, and two other voluntary temporary part-time teachers (unpaid) – the Catholic Mission's District Education Secretary and myself. A woman domestic science teacher was appointed later in the term.

In mid-March, the Provincial Education Officer gave formal permission for the school to be open in advance of its official registration. The *fait accompli* of the school being open a month before official registration was apparently accepted in line with the policy of not wishing to disturb the spirit of Harambee. By late March the school had thirty paid-up students, as word got round that things were improving. Plans for the Harambee Day had to be postponed twice more, as the MP did not give a firm date when he could attend.

The Harambee Day finally took place on 31 March 1974. The chief guest was the MP. Other guests included the District Officer, the District Community Development Officer, a District Information Assistant, and district administration officials from the cotton, co-operatives and crop development

Plate 57   Mwethya song-groups arriving at start of Harambee Day

departments. 33,000 shs was presented or raised on the day, including 16,000 shs from the MP, more than he had promised. The MP brought contributions from business companies in Nairobi and 500 shs from Vice-President Moi. The MP said that his 'personal' contribution within this figure was 5,000 shs, excluding the cement he had previously given for a primary school classroom at Katothya School to house one of the displaced Kiini School classes. These business companies contributed because, as I was told, it was usual for MPs to write to them asking if they might wish to contribute to particular Harambee projects. The MP promised to return to Nzambani for the formal opening of the school later on, and said that he would give more on that occasion (which did not take place during my fieldwork). He also promised to donate glass for the school windows.

A local KANU official donated a cow to be a prize for a giving competition between the MP and the location – the former won, as his contribution outstripped what the location collected. One of the MP's political opponents gave a cup for the sublocation which collected the most (won by Maluma), but in the end he did not appear on the day and gave nothing himself.

The New Akamba Union (NAU) chairman arrived late in the evening after the MP had left. His contribution (from NAU funds collected from NAU members in the towns) was 1,000 shs. He also brought a further 300 shs from another Kitui MP, and gave 100 shs each to three *mwethya* dance groups – the chief tried to appropriate this money for the school but without success, as the *myethya* regarded it as gifts to themselves.

The Harambee Day started in the afternoon, with *mwethya* song-groups arriving on foot or by lorry, dancing and singing (Plate 57). The official ceremonies were led by a choir from the ABC church, the committee chairman's church (Plate 58). There were also songs and dancing from most of the *mwethya* song-groups in Nzambani, including Kamale's (Plate 59). The traditional spirit-possession dance [*kilumi*] was due to be performed too, but the song-leader/shaman (Mutune) pleaded illness. As at other Harambee Days, there were speeches and presentations of donations but there was no overt political campaigning.

The Harambee Day was a festive and informal occasion. It was not reported by the official radio or press. Possibly this was

Plate 58   African Brotherhood Church choir at Nzambani Harambee Day

Plate 59 Mwethya dancers at Nzambani Harambee Day

because the DC didn't attend, but also there was rumoured to be a strong campaign against the MP. Although seven candidates eventually stood in the October 1974 election, the MP had only one serious opponent, who stayed away from this Harambee Day but gave money for other Harambee projects in the constituency, as all candidates did according to their means.

The Harambee Day confirmed the school's ability to complete its initial building programme and other work, and it more than met the basic requirement of having 40,000 shs banked. It was successful enough for the Catholic Mission to confirm its support for the school and to promise a pump if the school dug a well, and a second teacher's house to match the one built by the school. Further money would still be needed for future expansion, and the chief promised he would collect it – 'like GPT', he said, referring to the General Poll Tax, which had just been abolished. He implied by this that there would be similar strong administrative efforts to collect it and that collection would continue year by year.

In May 1974 a new headmaster was appointed – an American national who had come to stay in the location the previous year. He had a US college degree and took on the job (at the local salary rate) because of educational interest and also so that he could get a work permit to allow him to stay in Kenya. He was strongly pressured by the chief to accept the post and thus offer his skills (which included practical knowledge of carpentry, farming and motorcycles) to the community. As the Catholic District Education Secretary and I were unable to continue teaching for long, two other teachers were temporarily employed – a sixth-form leaver and a university student on vacation. There were then thirty-four paid-up students. Plate 60 shows the management committee, teaching staff and students of the school in July 1974.

The chief was considering organizing a second Harambee Day for that year to which the Provincial Commissioner would be invited, but this plan fell through. Further promises were made by the MP to buy ceilings for the classrooms, a school sign and paint. A further collection of money throughout the location was planned for October, after the harvest. There were further building problems but these were gradually resolved, and

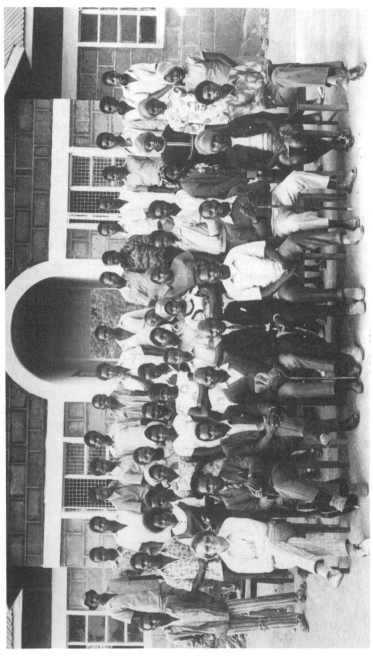

Plate 60   Nzambani Harambee School, 1974 – committee, teachers and students

when I left Kitui in September 1974, the school seemed set to continue.

As regards the students in the school, they were mostly older than the average, between about seventeen and twenty-five years old, most having started primary school as late as ten years old or more, and others having repeated classes to improve their grades. In the English-language classes which I taught, students were mostly of a reasonable secondary school standard. From a questionnaire about their opinions on the school, they evidently understood that they should expect some shortcomings in a new Harambee school, but they showed no serious discontent. In response to an open-ended question about their wishes for the school, they mentioned boarding facilities, lunch to be cooked for them on the premises, a school uniform to wear, improvements to the compound (with which they were willing to assist) and the completion of the buildings, including latrines. They supported the idea of doing agriculture, but not woodwork. The Catholic Mission wanted to introduce 'industrial arts' as well as domestic science in the future.

Parliamentary general elections were held in October 1974, shortly after I had finished fieldwork and left the country. The MP, for all his contributions to Nzambani Harambee School and other Harambee projects in his constituency, lost his seat to his main opponent. A conclusion to be drawn was that a politician could not simply make large Harambee contributions and expect that to outweigh all other factors in whether or not people would vote for him.

7 Analysis and Conclusion

This concluding chapter draws together the empirical data described in previous chapters about workparties, self-help groups and the Harambee movement, and analyses the relation between these forms of traditional and modern community co-operation. It starts with a structural comparison between workparties and self-help groups with regard to their composition, work and sanctions, and moves to an examination of the forms of reciprocity involved. General conclusions are then put forward concerning the continuities and discontinuities between the traditional and the modern organizational forms concerned, and development issues presented by the Harambee movement as a whole.

Structural Comparison of Workparties and Self-Help Groups

SOCIAL COMPOSITION

Both the neighbourhood workparty and the self-help group were based on local community co-residence rather than common descent. No workparty form in Kamale was based on the descent-group. Kamale village had been a geographically distinct social unit since its origins over a century earlier. Throughout the colonial period and since Independence it had also been delineated within approximately the same boundaries as a unit of government administration, for purposes which included communal labour and self-help work. In Kamba cultural terms, villages were essentially (and not accidentally) distinct and separate settlements of people of different descent-groups residing together in a mixed-clan/lineage community. Specific community-wide social institutions cross-cut ties of descent. Community ties of labour co-operation were regarded by the people themselves as being the basis of community co-operation in the field of self-help projects.

Within Kamba society generally and the village community in particular, 'universalistic' ties and values of the local community were maintained alongside 'particularistic' ties of being a member of a specific descent-group. The fundamental right to land was derived principally from membership of a particular local descent-group. The productive resource of labour was inevitably tied at heart to the exploitation of these land rights, but it was also in essence a partially disposable resource. Individual labour was thus available for allocation for other purposes than solely in connection with household needs. The channels along which it was allocated were socially patterned – through recognized extra-descent-group relationships. Allocations were made by the individuals concerned, in terms of socially conditioned choices but with a considerable degree of individual choice too. Some allocations were subject to important obligations and sanctions linked to the maintenance of the village or neighbourhood unit. Other allocations were a matter of personal choice in the area of socially peripheral but affectively important social relationships.

The types of workparty described in Chapter 4 highlighted the differences between these options in respect of the main labour tasks, as well as the benefits of labour co-operation relating to each – the neighbourhood workparty, the small rotating work-team, and the small friendship group, each with its own social basis, sanctions, and form of reciprocity. What they had in common was the fact that they were all based on extra-descent-group ties – that is to say, ties focusing on socially recognized or permitted relationships within the residential community which were not based on descent. It would, however, be wrong to be misled by metaphorical descriptions of these labour allocations as 'following' or 'patterned on' such ties or relationships, because they were an integral part of these relationships themselves. They formed part of the important material infrastructural base for the superstructure of ideas or values associated with them. Because of the structural fragility of such extra-descent-group ties in comparison with the strength of descent-group ties, the importance of neighbourhood labour co-operation in cementing neighbourhood ties was obviously considerable.

The Kamale self-help *mwethya* group was not, however, identical or coterminous with the traditional *mwethya* workparty. Kamale was a relatively large village and the self-help group combined five neighbourhood *myethya*, none of which was regarded as being capable on its own of functioning as a self-help group. The self-help group in 1973 had 306 members, while the three central neighbourhood *myethya* had total adult membership numbers of 61, 47 and 42, although any actual *mwethya* workparty in 1973–4 mobilized only an average of 40–50 per cent of its members, rarely more than thirty people altogether.[1] In contrast, for the labour tasks required of the self-help group – for example, carrying building materials, clearing bush or making bricks – no single neighbourhood *mwethya* in Kamale could have mobilized from its own members the number of workers required – often 50–100 or more – except by imposing very hard and prolonged tasks on them. Even more important, they could not have raised the amounts of money required for self-help projects in the village or outside it.

When the self-help *mwethya* temporarily divided into two competing segments in 1971, this was not regarded as a permanent division but as a temporary solution to the problem that internal 'political' divisions in the village were holding back the general wish of the village to have its own school, based on the numbers of school-age children there. It is possible that the large size of the combined village self-help *mwethya* was a partial factor in the growth of these tensions, but after the temporary division ended, people did not refer to this being the root of any subsequent organizational problems relating to the self-help *mwethya*. The division into two self-help groups competing with each other in work and fund-raising did in fact accelerate the work and lead to the opening of the school in 1973. However, it was clear that no single neighbourhood on its own could have proceeded to form itself into an independent self-help group – neither Itheo in the south nor a combination of the other neighbourhoods – in terms of having the manpower and financial resources needed for the tasks required. Before the temporary division of the Kamale self-help group in 1971 (the first such division in its history going back about fifteen years) none of the Kamale neighbourhoods, singly or in combination, had had any experience of independently organizing its members for any such functions. Self-help activities also required a modern organizational form distinct from the ways in which neighbourhood workparties were organized. This was located at village level. In Kamale there was already a firm sense of the village as a single community of residence distinct from its internal segments. It was on this basis, supported by other social ties and values rather than on the basis of the neighbourhood (a subdivision of the village), that a new organizational form was developed for modern self-help activities. The involvement of the village community in common tasks – particularly those which entailed allocating labour and scarce financial resources to projects which were undertaken as capital investments for the whole community – strengthened and perpetuated the social structural meaning of the village.

The village self-help *mwethya* group thus differed in form, scale and purpose from the traditional neighbourhood *mwethya*, while at the same time utilizing some of its underlying principles.

ORGANIZATION OF WORK

In respect of tasks and how these were organized, the neighbourhood workparty and the self-help group differed considerably. The neighbourhood *mwethya* workparty undertook a range of tasks requiring sudden or regular large inputs of labour. It did not collect money for any of these or other tasks. Each single workparty was organized on behalf of an individual for his or own private task. From the individual's point of view, the workparty performed one of a series of tasks comprising a lengthy work project (for example a season's agricultural work or building a house where other stages of the project were organized in different ways, notably involving family labour and family cash inputs). From an overall perspective, each workparty was one phase in a lengthy series of reciprocal exchanges between different people, most of whom were members of the same neighbourhood. Each workparty was completed quite quickly and workers received an immediate reward of a meal or drinks.

The self-help *mwethya*, in contrast, undertook work which was of a different nature and was usually continuous over a long period, involving a variety of tasks as well as inputs of skilled labour paid for by the group. Financial contributions were required in addition to labour. The contribution of those in employment was solely financial. The self-help group worked approximately twice a week during the dry season, when there was little regular agricultural work, and ended when the rains drew near and the pressure of agricultural work increased. Its main projects were never really finished – building a school, for example, required continual new phases of repair as the school expanded; adding a new class each year up to the full seven-year school complement; taking an extra stream of pupils; building a new teacher's house or a school store-room; upgrading or repairing buildings; clearing ground for a playing field; or providing a water supply.

The continuity and complexity of self-help group work necessitated a different structure of organization and decision-making than was appropriate to the organization of workparties. Where workparties had no specialized leadership roles or decision-making body – except in a limited sense in relation to proper performance of tasks and attendance – self-help groups required differentiated leadership skills for the purpose of planning and co-ordinating the work, mobilizing people and liaising with government officials managing financial matters. There were often conflicting ideas about these leadership roles and the qualities required of the personnel filling them. Leaders received no training for these new roles, and there was little positive monitoring from the government agencies overseeing them. Some of the uncertainties of leadership revolved around the question of the rewards of office in terms not only of local influence and prestige but also of material financial rewards, thus opening the way to possible corruption and embezzlement of funds.

SANCTIONS

The neighbourhood workparty had a series of sanctions which were not often employed. The economic necessity of long-term involvement in reciprocal work co-operation and the linking of this to important social ties ensured that the strongest sanction – ostracism from the neighbourhood – was very rarely applied. Lesser sanctions were applied fairly rigorously, but even they were rarely needed as defaulting was not frequent.

The self-help group, on the other hand, had frequent difficulties in mobilizing labour or collecting cash from members. It was very noticeable from the frequent resort to the sanction of attachment [*kithendu*] that this sanction was critical to the momentum of self-help work. 'Without *kithendu*, nothing will get done' was a frequent comment. *Kithendu* was a second-stage sanction for failure to work – the first being a cash fine – but it was the only sanction for failure to pay the cash fine. Social ostracism from the village would not have been a viable option, as the immediate objective was to obtain the money for the self-help fund. This sanction was backed up by the threat or use of physical force by the *kithendu askaris*, which was supported ultimately by the administrative officials and the law. The question of social ostracism or expulsion from the community did not therefore arise.

A further difference from the traditional jural sanction of attachment to secure payment of a fine was that the proceeds were paid in monetary form to the community self-help fund, with a small supplementary fee to the agents collecting it (the *askaris*). Fines were not 'consumed' by the elders or organizing committee in the form of beer or a feast. The proceeds were simply what the individual owed to the community.

The sanction employed by the self-help group thus represented a refusal to let a person opt out of duties of membership of the community as entailed by residence in it. The community, being a social unit without solidary institutional support, contained no inherent social sanction based simply on rights and duties deriving from other social obligations. It could not, through other means, impose such demands on its members and ensure compliance. In terms, too, of increasing socioeconomic differentiation among community members, the necessity for a defined sanction derived from the lack of strong social cohesion in the self-help community. The only solution had been to impose a universalistic flat-rate payment system for every member, in money terms, to be enforced by an equally universalistic sanction. This resembled the poll tax levied on all non-employed people, which President Moi abolished in 1974. This method of raising revenue for the self-help group had been simple and cheap to administer, the main criticism being that it took no account of individual income levels, which varied substantially in poor communities. However, it would have been impossible to establish a fairer or more graduated system of collecting self-help dues.

In special new situations where even the flat-rate *mwethya* payment seemed to be in danger of being evaded – for example where a person was long absent from the village while leaving dependants there who would have rights to use the self-help facility – the levying of a special admission fee for the facility closed off the loophole created by the self-help enforcers being unable to penalize or catch up with the individual responsible for evading his duties. This was particularly effective with educational projects, where the perceived value of education was so high.

The frequent resort to the threat of *kithendu* in Kamale – although it was actually applied to only a few evaders who tried to hold out to the and – did not itself necessarily indicate lack of commitment to the self-help group or lack of interest in the projects it had undertaken. Kamale was reputedly a development-orientated and progressive village. The function of *kithendu* was, as with sanctions in general, not only to punish anyone who evaded their duties, but also to guarantee to everyone that anyone who sought to evade their duties would not get away with it. This pre-empted evasion by someone with more political or economic weight or personal deviousness. There was evidently a distrust in the efficacy of the social cement of the community as well as a desire, evident in other Kamba institutions, to equalize everybody in this respect too. Yet if there was no idealized community solidarity in the village producing automatic adherence to community values, this does not mean there was no voluntarism about self-help work. 'Voluntarism' in community development philosophy refers not to a new theory of social institutions without social sanctions, but to a contrast from the opposite pole of straight coercion.

In self-help projects which brought together a wider range of people than one self-help group – for example for a Harambee secondary school built on the basis of a combination of *myethya* demarcated in most cases by administrative boundaries – the question of specific sanctions for collection of money or raising of labour became of greater salience than in connection with the local self-help group's projects. In these cases, the self-help community was not a face-to-face community – indeed, contributors might not in many cases even know each other well and might not even feel that there should be any further social relationship among them. The supra-local project relied on an association of local groupings between whom there was no particular social solidarity. The sanction of *kithendu* was crucial to such projects and was applied and carried out under the control of local government officials. This reflected the greater degree of social distance between the self-help participants and the project organizers, as well as the more distant relationship between the contributors and the eventual users of the project. The data collected in Kitui in 1973–4 on fund-raising for larger projects did not indicate any systematic evasion of Harambee dues by wealthier or more powerful individuals in the local area. Promises or cheques from politicians on Harambee Days were by 1973 greatly distrusted, but even there the Harambee committees appeared to have some social or political leverage to pursue broken promises or bounced cheques, although I had no details on this.

It would be reasonable to conclude that the use of externally derived, externally imposed and externally backed sanctions increased in proportion to the remoteness of the project from the local self-help community. The weaker the links between local self-help planning, decision-making and use, the greater the need for strong means to control all stages of the project.

Conversely, where the community had sufficient commitment to its self-help projects, external sanctions and control were not so necessary. This was the case generally with the village self-help groups, where elected committees decided on projects and had to have general support for them, in the sense of people feeling that the projects were directly beneficial to them. In Kamale even the poorest families were not excluded from benefiting from the village projects, as there was no charge for using the facilities. However, cattle-dips and Harambee secondary schools, and any other large-scale projects, were a different matter. Not only were there use and service charges for the facility, but the projects were not likely to be of direct and equal benefit to all members of the community, and certainly not to the poorest. Yet they all had to contribute to the same degree, except that those with definable income-generating activities paid proportionally more.

Methods of collection of assessed dues for such supra-local and large-scale projects were inevitably more coercive, and it was in this area that complaints were most vocal and the voluntaristic ideal of the Harambee movement was most threatened. The available evidence suggests that coercion in this respect had increased substantially after my fieldwork and during the 1980s, though probably with more impact on people in the urban areas than in the villages.

Types of Reciprocity

Frequent reference has been made to the fact that different types of reciprocity were associated with different types of workparties and other labour-assistance arrangements. The choice of different forms of labour-assistance is represented in Table 23, where the terms 'generalized' and 'balanced' reciprocity are used. These terms are taken from Sahlins's analysis of primitive exchange.[2] They indicate contrasting forms of reciprocity, one based on 'centricity' and representing 'generalized reciprocity', where a member of the community had the right to community assistance under certain conditions and was obliged to join in community assistance to other members as appropriate; the other based on 'sidedness' and representing 'balanced reciprocity', where there was a direct and equal exchange.

The *mwethya* workparty system exhibited 'generalized reciprocity', being based on a community relationship where the obligation to participate in the community workparty was fully operative, even if the right to the workparty's assistancee was not being exercised. The *mwilaso* system and the system of friendship help, on the other hand, exhibited 'balanced reciprocity', succinctly defined by Sahlins:

> The pragmatic test of balanced reciprocity becomes an inability to tolerate one-way flows: the relations are disrupted by a failure to reciprocate within limited time and equivalence leeways.[3]

Table 23   *Choice of Forms of Labour-Assistance*

Labour need	Labour-assistance	Immediate reward	Labour reciprocity
large	*mwethya*	meal/drinks	generalized
	friends	feast	balanced
small	*mwilaso* team	nothing	
	hired labour	cash payment	none

The nature of the respective sanctions on the three main workparty institutions further set the stamp on the nature of the social relationships involved. Community-based sanctions were associated with *myethya*, with a range of penalties culminating in expulsion of persistent defaulters from the workparty system. At the same time, there was no strict accounting of reciprocity or what people were owed in terms of labour-assistance for the purpose of ensuring that they all received back what they gave. Reciprocity was delayed, in any case, rather than immediate. With *mwilaso*, on the other hand, the sanctions on non-return of labour were only interpersonal and as such were confined to the break-up of the socially peripheral relationships involved. Because these relationships were so structurally fragile, *mwilaso* was the scene for careful accounting of labour-assistance debts and credits. The *mwilaso* exchange had to be reciprocated at the earliest opportunity.

'Friendship help' also had a similar basis of theoretically equal exchange, but with a somewhat longer cycle of return or delay in reciprocity. It had to be reciprocated not immediately but within a reasonable period – for example, the same season. In *myethya*, by contrast, there was an ideological opposition to such accounting of debts and credits, except where accounting became necessary to protect the institution (and hence the community too) from being exploited by any opportunistic individual member. Under-use of its benefits was not an issue. Neither in expressed ideological terms, nor in any observable practical way, was the generalized reciprocity of the one system regarded as merely a long-term version of the balanced reciprocity of the other two systems. They differed on moral valuation as well as time-cycle,[4] in line with the qualitatively different strengths of social relationship involved. The difference was not simply that of delayed as opposed to immediate balanced reciprocity, which would have meant a quantitative difference measured over time, but one of contrasted forms of reciprocity. Generalized reciprocity was not regarded as collapsible through time into balanced reciprocity. The differentiating factor was the social structural strength or weakness of the social relationship as determining the appropriate form of reciprocity – which was immediate or allowing of only slightly delayed return where the relationship was weak.

In applying the same frame of analysis of reciprocity to self-help group organization, it was immediately evident that the situation was more complex and required a different approach. Workparties involved labour-assistance, which was patterned on a variety of institutional forms which have already been described. These are represented in Table 24 as different 'spheres of exchange'.[5] Self-help activities, however, involved money as well as labour, and the objectives were different too.

Reciprocity in self-help activities involved both a material transaction (or exchange) and a social relationship which contained a giving and a return. In workparties the transaction was the work done in exchange for a future return of work, or for payment of money or a feast. The immediate reward of the meal in the former case symbolized and confirmed the social relationship but did not represent a conclusion of the transaction. The social relationship in the most direct form was between the 'owner' of the workparty, for whom the work was done, and the individual member of that particular workparty. In the self-help group, on the other hand, the transaction was the contribution of labour or money for a particular community project in exchange for the eventual use of or benefit from that project. The social relationship was between all members of the self-help group and those who would use or benefit from the project. This conferred rights of use and benefit, which were notionally to be held in perpetuity. Thus a person's dependants and descendants were included in those who would hold and possibly exercise the rights obtained by the fulfilment of the relevant duties.

Table 24   *Spheres of Labour-Assistance in Workparties*

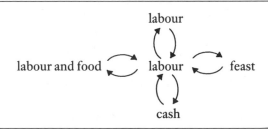

Two aspects of reciprocity involved in self-help activities – the transaction and the social relationship – are now examined in order to elicit the nature of the reciprocity underlying the social organization of self-help.[6]

THE TRANSACTION

This consisted of people's efforts to realize a particular self-help project. It is examined first in terms of their contributions to the project, and secondly what they expected to gain from it – the targeted return.

As regards contributions to the project, a differentiation was made between working and paying members – the latter being required to make greater contributions in acknowledgement of their earnings from wage-employment. Despite significant small socioeconomic differentiation among working members, their contributions of work and money were equalized and not assessed according to individual economic status. (On Harambee Days, however, local notables were expected to give more, and this applied also to any village member known to be better off than others.) Since the basis of the project was the potential equal benefit to all members, all were required to contribute equally. The implicit condition was that use of and benefit from the project were exclusive to those who had participated in it and contributed to it. Others would have to make a special payment or admission fee for such access in lieu of not having had such long-term participation in it.

The equalization of contributions within the working self-help group was linked to the obligatory nature of participation in it. This sanctioned obligation ensured that everyone working on the project was assured that no member could opt out of it or evade it, which would have imperilled everyone's motivation to fulfil their obligations to it.

Beyond this basic level of universal local contribution, which lay at the heart of the self-help movement, further contributions to the project were sought from all those who had anything to do with the community, whether in a contributory or extractive manner, including politicians, traders, churches, government officials and all organizations whose work impinged on the community. All were regarded as having a moral obligation to it deriving from their social relationship with it, whether or not they as individuals would use or benefit from the project or anything to do with it. The self-help group directed their contributions to the project by assessing what these should amount to, as well as inviting them to a Harambee Day where they could make an appropriate additional public contribution.

Behind the contributions of labour or money lay the sanctions which the self-help group, through its representatives, had at its disposal. For its survival, as well as the success of the project, the self-help group tried to ensure the equalization and safe collection of contributions. Work was accounted by time or piecework, with a record kept of defaulters who were pursued and fined. For non-working members, there were similar sanctions against non-contribution. People outside the self-help group, such as politicians and traders, were vulnerable to loss of custom or support. Government officials could also be subject to loss of co-operation, or even of the political support sometimes necessary to keep them in office. The fulfilment of their administrative functions required more than nominal compliance by those subject to them. It was difficult to assess the weight of popular disapproval if any official neglected obligations to self-help groups, but the texts of the *mwethya* songs in Chapter 5 indicate that self-help groups clearly believed they had the capacity and right to involve them in their projects.

As for the targeted returns for these contributions from participation in the project – that is, people's use of the project and benefit from it – the nature of the project obviously determined how it would benefit the self-help group and what its members would gain individually. Everyone would immediately use a village well or road, though possibly not to an exactly equal extent. Most projects were schools, the users of which were the contributors' children. People in Kamale said, 'Self-help is for us and our children', and this was literally true. Members of the self-help group acquired, in exchange for their contributions, rights to use of the project, which they held for themselves and their descendants. The projects became part of the property and stock of the community, and were regarded as being held in perpetuity by the community for its members.

The self-help group was thus regarded as a corporation whose members had rights of access to its corporate property. This was administered at any given time by elected representatives of the community on its behalf. The corporation's existence was not limited to the individuals or to the generation of those active in it at any given time but was regarded as extending into the future, just as other property-holding corporations – for example local descent-groups – had no finite duration. In both cases the corporation's property was perceived as available for the descendants of the actual contributors or users within a generally fixed and stable community.

The actual benefits of the completed project to the outsiders who were asked to contribute to the project were different. Most of this category of contributors would not use the project directly, but they would all indirectly derive some benefit or return from their contribution to it. Their contribution was thus part of a transaction linked to their social relationship to the community. Votes for politicians, custom for traders, and friendly co-operation with administrative officials were some of the spurs to their contribution. Local notables were also given the opportunity to seek or affirm their social prestige and influence in orderly competitive giving at Harambee Days. The stimulus to such giving was often provided by the *mwethya* song-group.

Projects organized on a social basis wider than the local self-group and involving a much wider range of people offered different potential benefits to contributors. In some projects, such as secondary schools, use of the facility would be limited and selective. Relatively few of the children of any particular village would enter the school. Benefit from the project was thus by no means automatic to the contributor. Contributions merely conferred eligibility for benefit. Those who actually used the school would then pay additional contributions – school fees – for their use of it. Such projects were at a greater distance from the basic self-help community and were necessarily organized with much more extensive external administrative support. As for the 'outsiders' asked to contribute to such supra-local projects, their opportunities of seeking influence and prestige through their contributions at publicly reported Harambee Days were correspondingly much greater. Actual and prospective Members of Parliament avidly utilized this infrequent but openly permitted opportunity for political display.

The transaction relating to the individual's work for the self-help project was thus one of balanced exchange. The work was target-orientated, usually over a long period of time rather than in the short term, and the reward was use of the completed project.

THE SOCIAL RELATIONSHIP

In the traditional *mwethya* workparty, the most direct aspect of the transaction was the work done by one person (a member of the workparty) for another (the 'owner'). Indirectly he or she was at the same time fulfilling a general obligation to the community (the neighbourhood) and not just to one individual, who might or might not be a member of that community. In the self-help group, on the other hand, the transaction was not from one individual to another but took the form of the individual fulfilling a general obligation to the community (the self-help group). The social relationship involved was thus the relationship between the individual and the self-help group.

The stress on the equalization of contributions and the theoretically strict application of sanctions to every default of obligation presented a marked contrast to the generalized rights and duties of the *mwethya* workparty system. This in fact reflected the contrast in the material conditions of the respective systems. The *mwethya* workparty, on the one hand, catered to flexible labour demands by ensuring that the workparty was available to anyone needing it, but it did not have to be used if this would be disadvantageous. The self-help group, on the other hand, depended on the total mobilization of the group on each and every occasion. It fitted into the needs of the farming economy by suspending work during the heavy farming season, and even during the slack season it left enough time for other farm or household tasks. The equalization of contributions also fitted into the ideology of equality in Kamba culture, over and above socioeconomic differentials beween individuals or inequalities in certain relations of kinship, generation or gender.

As mentioned above, contributors to some self-help projects would not themselves directly use or benefit from them. In those cases, contributions were considered as conveying rights of access for future generations. This implied a basic commitment to settled residence, through land inherited and vested in permanent jural corporations, which was the prime means of reproduction of the material existence of the society. It was expected that a person's agnatic descendants would live in the same locality and seek their basic livelihood there, or at least have the right to do so, irrespective of temporary residence or education or employment elsewhere. The bonds of patrilineal descent and membership of a land-holding corporation were expected to remain strong and to be permanent. The self-help group thus made a contribution to the resources or stock of the whole community and provided facilities which were perceived as integral to the future of the society and its individual members. If the worth of the project or its practicality were in doubt, reaction would be expected to set in. But with education providing a fundamental potential of individual socioeconomic mobility, it is not surprising that communities all over Kenya had invested their resources and labour in educational projects. The benefits were expected to accrue not just to the individual beneficiaries of the school in respect of the contributors' children improving their chances of wage-employment, but also to their parents later in life, when their (educated) children might be expected to support them.

The social relationship underlying the obligatory commitment of the individual to the self-help group and its projects, which were intitiated and implemented by the group and its elected representatives, was one of generalized exchange. The self-help group was an integral part of the social activities and values of the community: the individual was not an *ad hoc* member of it through choice or voluntary association but was involved with all other members of the community in a multiplicity of role-relationships covering all areas of social life. Target-orientated projects and swift quasi-legal sanctions might suggest that the self-help group's members worked for self-help projects as they might trade their labour for wages. In reality, however, they worked for each other at the same time, fulfilling reciprocal obligations and strengthening the social duties behind them.

Reciprocity in the Harambee Movement

In the Harambee movement in general, running through the equalized contributions of self-help group members and the equality of their relationship *vis-à-vis* the group, there was also the concept of targeted returns on the basis of balanced reciprocity. The balance was effectively simultaneous in self-help contributions: membership of the group required equally matched contributions at every stage. The expectations of the group possessed a similar character in the demands that were made of others – individuals, organizations and the government – arising out of their self-help work. A return was expected out of each social relationship with the community. Each person's work or financial contribution was expected to lead to some future return of benefit to all, when the project was completed.

In traditional workparties, balanced reciprocity was found in *mwilaso*, the small alternating work-team, which was associated with socially peripheral relationships possessing no institutional sanction to support them. This quasi-contractural relationship had no social base of any structural importance. It was a short-cycle exchange involving a temporary team convened for that purpose only and having no further perpetuity. Attempts to develop the principle of alternation or team rotation in agricultural projects in Nzambani in the 1930s (cotton planting) were not successful, and progressive farmers in the 1970s did not even discuss the idea.

The elements of balanced reciprocity found in the self-help groups, in contrast, had a strong social base and a momentum towards the completion of the project in the near or distant future. In other circumstances of exchange, work was exchanged only for money. In self-help activity, work was contributed without payment precisely because it was targeted on a future specific return – the completion of the community project. In addition, contributions from the self-help group elicited contributions from others – the 'outsiders' already mentioned, local government funds, and even foreign charitable organizations. Individual contributions were equalized so that no one benefited or lost more or less than anyone else – the group's sanctions existed to prevent any default of contribution. Self-help thus had strong contractual elements for its individual workers. It was based on a premiss of obtaining a specific return in the long run, where the benefit would be lasting and equally shared.

The other prime component of self-help was collection of money. It might be thought that co-operative labour would be associated with generalized reciprocity and money with balanced reciprocity – the latter being the model of monetary exchange in a market economy. Such a dichotomy, however, would be false. Both work and money were clearly dealt with by the self-help group on the same basis and not on different bases: the sanctions on the two were the same, and failure to work was penalized by a monetary fine.

At the same time, it was obvious that commitment to Harambee projects was not situational or unstructured. People worked for projects in community groups to which they belonged. The social relationship underlying these groups elicited their investment in their self-help projects. The combination of generalized and balanced reciprocity which was found in the self-help group had some parallels with a similar situation found in the *mwethya* workparty. The latter was characterized by generalized reciprocity in view of the strong moral tone associated with the long-term nature of the relationships on which it was based. However, the particular transaction – namely the single workparty – which involved a highly disposable factor of production (labour) carried an immediate reward (a meal or drinks for the workers) which balanced that particular exchange in terms not so much of a kind of payment but of a social return.

The self-help group offered no immediate return or reward for work. Instead, it held out the promise of a greater and more permanent return in the future. The question of immediate return was not relevant. First, the performance of one phase of the long cycle of tasks required for the project was insufficient to demand an immediate reward. Secondly, the group had no resources itself, other than the funds it was collecting, from which any reward would have had to be drawn – for example, by buying food and drink for a special meal to be cooked by the group: such expenditure would have been a severe drain on the group's resources which were being built up with great difficulty to meet the monetary requirements of the project.

What was important was that the strict equalization of contributions was maintained. A prime responsibility of the *mwethya* committee was to ensure that this equalization did not fail, and it sought to achieve this through regular application of sanctions to defaulters. Disturbance of this equilibrium would have struck at the heart of the system of balanced reciprocity in the self-help group and would have risked weakening the commitment of individuals' 'contract' to the group. As Mutinda wa Ndinga, a progressive farmer in Kamale, pointed out: 'If anybody is allowed to escape without paying, everybody will refuse to pay. I am not going to pay if some people will escape paying. If *kithendu* isn't done to everybody, nobody will do anything.'

Discussion of balanced reciprocity so far, in Sahlins's terms, has focused on its short-term benefits and long-term disadvantages. It had elements akin to monetary exchanges of the market economy which might betoken distrust and non-moral ties. In identifying balanced reciprocity in the self-help group, it is not proposed to link it with these features of less firm social relationships. The balanced reciprocity which was present in the activities and ambitions of the self-help group was not associated with the instability or lack of permanence in the balanced reciprocity of the *mwilaso* rotating work-team. People in Kamale did not perceive self-help as originating from or linked to *mwilaso*, nor did they feel that *mwilaso* was a useful or interesting model for self-help structures. Balanced reciprocity in self-help was thus of a different order to balanced reciprocity in *mwilaso*.

In Sahlins's terms, generalized and balanced reciprocity are opposed, mutually exclusive and not reducible one to the other. The apparent contradiction of their coexistence in the Harambee movement is resolved by seeing generalized reciprocity as the principle of the social relationships of the participants, and balanced reciprocity as the principle of the activity or transaction. The two forms of reciprocity existed at different levels of analysis.

In terms of work, collection of money and imposition of sanctions, the principle of the exchange or transaction regulated by the self-help organizing committee was balanced reciprocity. Obligations were clear, specific and universally applicable there and then. Sanctions were instituted and employed to ensure that obligations were met. These were considered as resembling an economic relationship of a contractual kind, similar to other economic relationships characteristic of the market or monetary economy but also found in the pre-colonial Kamba economy too.

At the same time, self-help activity was only one strand of the multi-stranded relationship obtaining among self-help group members as members of a social community whose basis and range of activities was much wider. Self-help work did not conflict with other activities in other social spheres; it was largely autonomous of these. In an important sense, it did not seek to take over other institutional areas – economic, political or symbolic – or to encroach on areas of sociocultural division in the community, whether related to traditional cleavages of descent or differing belief-systems. The type of reciprocity associated with such ties was generalized reciprocity, where the long-term moral commitment was more diffuse, less specifically sanctioned, and less tied up with particular activities.

Generalized and balanced reciprocity were woven together in self-help communities to produce a dense texture of rights and duties, which was given strong support through the ideological patterning of the Harambee movement. It was no coincidence that the term *mwethya* had been and continued to be used for village self-help groups, since it was *mwethya* workparties that provided the relevant model of reciprocity – generalized reciprocity. Generalized reciprocity provided the dominant moral tone of self-help activity that was reflected in the ideology of the Harambee movement as a whole. This also stressed the traditional social basis of self-help and its modern political association with nationalism and Independence.

The interplay between generalized and balanced reciprocity also provided a bridge between traditional and modern social institutions and values, and thus required organizational innovations to operationalize the felt needs and aspirations represented in the self-help movement. Long-term involvement in a community project which was intended to bring lasting value to the whole community required a base of high social value and also a regular operational commitment. These jointly imbued the self-help group with values linked to the commitments of shared residence and general mutual aid. Traditionally these commitments had their expression in a wide range of intermittently regular or occasional social activities. The traditional activities most closely linked to modern self-help were those involving co-operation in work, and it was no accident that the ideology of self-help, where labour was a prime component, so often referred to this connection. At the same time, the operational requirements of the self-help movement entailed commitments and skills related to modern economic relationships and values. These were reflected in the modern organizational forms of the self-help groups, which had no equivalent in traditional workparties.

Tradition and Change

An important finding which was drawn from the analysis of self-help groups was the precise way in which the traditional workparty had lent itself to a modern development institution which did not simply replicate its tasks, social forms, organizational methods or values. The use of the term *mwethya* in colonial community development and the description of communal labour as 'self-help' were somewhat of an obfuscation and concealment of the forced labour laws hidden behind it. The ideology of self-help after Independence did not assert that self-help was simply a tradition unchanged; it pointed out its contrast to colonial communal labour and its revival in new form.

There is no reason to suppose that at the time of Independence those propagating Harambee delved deeply into its sociological structure, but it was implicit in the public formulations of Harambee, as well as the perceptions of the participants, that self-help was not simply traditional mutual aid as it always had been. This would in any case have been immediately obvious to any development administrator, whether colonial or post-colonial, who turned up at a traditional workparty and suggested that instead of weeding someone's field they build a dam. The only way the colonial administrators got people to build a dam was by forced labour. This is not to suggest that that was the only way, for as we have seen above, in Machakos and Kitui at any rate, dams were built through a mixture of force and consent.

After Independence, political reasons dictated that forced labour could not be used for self-help projects, since the basis of the desired relationship between government and the people in Harambee was antithetical to such a prominent and hated aspect of colonial rule. In Kitui, the rural water supply was such a key and apparently intractable issue in development that there was serious consideration of using coercion to build dams, simply because of the amount of labour needed for them. However, in the early 1970s, in discussions about rural water development in Kitui, it was discovered that the options were more complex than whether or not, or how, to utilize some form of coerced labour. As described above in Chapter 5, many of the earth dams built by communal labour in the 1950s had become silted up and broken two decades later. The questions which were raised, both by ordinary people and by district development committee members who were likely to be better informed of the issues, were the following:

- Is unskilled manual labour the best way to build a dam?
- What is the best design for a dam?
- How long will it last before it needs repairing or completely rebuilding?
- Will the enormous amount of labour needed be the best way of utilizing such labour, or would this damage other projects or farm schedules?
- Should not the government, instead, be building dams with heavy digging equipment?

The answers to these questions were not clear, and did not point unequivocally to the necessity to press self-help groups to take on dam-building as a priority. Such questions, which are beyond the scope of the discussion here, drew attention to the complex considerations involved and displayed the thinking in the decision-making structures available, which included the self-help groups themselves.

The context of the changed form of community co-operation that had developed in Kitui was the enormous demand for education and other modern needs, as well as the new organizational forms needed to realize projects designed to meet these demands. The decision-making institutions and processes of the self-help group as described above (in Chapter 5) were radically different to the comparable institutions and processes in neighbourhood workparties. The differentiated managerial roles, the integration (or sometimes malintegration) with governmental development institutions, and the political background, have been described in some detail. The first factor – role-differentiation – was an organizational change, though that is not to say that having arrived at a useful organizational form there were no problems of implementation – indeed there were, and some have been described above. The second and third factors – administrative and political inputs – were historically specific, although some general conclusions may be drawn for the sake of studying similar situations elsewhere and seeking answers to questions relating to community development generally in Africa and the Third World.

The synthesis in the self-help group of traditional and modern institutional forms and values provided an area where new ideas and activities could flourish. In the description of the self-help group officials in Chapter 5, it was seen that most of them had considerable knowledge and experience of more developed and urban areas outside Kitui, while also being familiar with traditional values. In Kamba culture, leadership was an 'achieved' status, constantly imperilled by Kamba reluctance to assign permanent dominance to any individual except in narrow areas of their special expertise and skills. Self-help leaders had to be good at their work or they were discarded and voted out – perhaps by being accused of embezzlement, which might or might not be true or provable. Leaders who could not communicate effectively with the whole range of villagers were not successful. The progressive and Christian farmer, however interested in the self-help projects, could not expect to have the automatic support of traditional farmers and non-Christians. Effective leadership was exercised by 'role hybrids'[7] – those able to operate in opposed traditional and modern value-systems and to maximize the benefits of both. The secretary and treasurer had to have specific modern skills, but the crucial task of the *mwethya* chairman was to mobilize the whole community. This task was difficult at the best of times, and if the chairman was not in tune with opinion in the *mwethya* assembly, nothing was achieved. Assemblies in fact often had a curious inconclusiveness about them which reflected the problem of how to get people to do something without feeling forced into it against their will. Kamba political values regarding leadership and prestige dominated this situation.

The arena in which the 'role hybrid' operated was that area of ambiguous or juxtaposed values where tradition met change. There too, in terms of social and economic exchange in the self-help group, balanced reciprocity – a monetary model of exchange – met generalized reciprocity – a general social exchange. The values to which the 'role hybrid' could refer at any time could be one or the other: specific concern for the project and task at issue (for example the primary school classroom) or general concern about the social relationships involved (for example social solidarity in the village, support for the government, or even opposition to a government official's plan, as happened with one issue in Kamale, as described in Chapter 5). The floating and changing field of values could be manipulated by someone conversant with similar social fields in multi-ethnic urban and employment situations, where symbols and signs were markers of change and modernization for those who were able to transcend the limits of tradition but were at the same time wise and experienced enough to avoid the pitfalls and snares of the new.

Some leaders maintained this tricky balance; others failed. The Nzambani Chief, a Christian and a small businessman, became embroiled in a dispute with Kamale village in 1973–4 because he sought to impose on them a rotating primary school development plan of which Kamale people were intensely suspicious, not having been properly consulted about it. On the other hand, his efforts to force through the opening of Nzambani Harambee School, which had not been achieved in the late 1960s, were successful in the early 1970s through his manipulation of Christian denominational competition and electoral political conflict. In this, he operated solely in the modern political sphere, selecting a favourable school management committee, approaching political candidates for money, and working closely with the Roman Catholic Mission managers to sponsor the school. He obtained the services of an American graduate living in the location to be headmaster, and of an anthropologist living there (myself) to teach part-time free of charge, both in exchange for the social relationships we each desired with the people among whom we were living.

The historical basis of the Harambee movement in traditional co-operative institutions has already been described, but an important question – little touched upon in the literature of the Harambee movement, or of self-help in general – is the extent to which traditional institutions of community co-operation are essential preconditions for the development of successful self-help community development institutions. Without a pre-existing traditional community workparty structure, would the

Harambee notion in Kenya have taken off at all?

The two origins of the Harambee movement in Kitui (and also most of the rest of Kenya) have been traced through the preceding chapters: (i) the social structural factor of the continuity of the neighbourhood workparty system in a patrilineal stateless farming society, which was a matter of pride; and (ii) the historical factor of adaptive reaction against colonial forced labour, which was a matter of discontinuity and hostility. It would be difficult to posit criteria for assessing any precedence between these closely interrelated synchronic and diachronic factors in Kitui, or Kenya in general.

Examples might be found elsewhere of self-help structures which were based on traditional community institutions without any history of state-level forced labour, or of self-help structures which were state-created, or at least brought within state-level organization, without any basis of traditional community mutual aid institutions. Self-help structures have been created elsewhere at state level – for example on the basis of a socialist ideology officially sanctioning the use of state force; and self-help projects have been financed elsewhere by religious, political, commercial or ethnic associations, or by contributory associations comprising – in the case of education in particular – former students, students' parents or individual philanthropists.[8] Many of these structures and projects would not, however, qualify for description as 'community development', or even 'self-help', either because they are too coercive and politically controlled, or because they do not involve the whole local community and rely primarily on local community resources.

Self-help structures are common in other parts of Africa, but they have been little documented. This may be because, like workparties, they tend to be largely invisible to sociologists, political scientists, economists and development planners working at the level of the state political economy.[9] It is not the purpose of this book to engage in a wider comparative study of self-help organization, where there is relatively little sociological or social anthropological research in the literature. It is, however, striking that in the relevant literature the Kenyan Harambee movement stands out as the most-studied and best-known example of a relatively successful self-help movement, although it has its critics, as discussed in the next section.

The Kenyan case shows that in developing countries the adaptation of traditional community co-operative labour institutions can provide a strong base and impetus for a modern rural community self-help movement. This was envisaged by the social anthropologist Philip Mayer when he was working within the colonial situation in Kenya in 1949,[10] and it is implicit in other anthropological writing on colonial societies in the 1940s and 1950s. The point was not, however, pressed particularly strongly by social anthropologists (or others, for that matter), even though anthropologists might have been expected to be especially interested in the issues of modernization through tradition, and continuity in change and development.

In this study from Kitui, which ranges from the level of the traditional workparty to the formal and informal political institutions of the modern state, the Harambee movement is seen to have its roots in an interwoven net of relationships of reciprocity derived from local community structures in a stateless political system based on patrilineal descent. In societies organized on different principles – for example on matrilineal or bilineal descent – and in societies with a different economic base – for example with a pastoral or other non-agricultural base, or with a different political structure, such as societies with chiefs and centralized and hierarchical political institutions – there may be no parallel labour-assistance relationships similar to the workparty institutions found among the Kamba. In those cases, self-help organization would be different and would require a different ideology and model.

In Kenya, the Harambee ideology arose out of the material basis of the community workparty structures found in the majority of Kenyan societies. It was specifically articulated by political leaders in this way. The main intention was to create a rural-based self-help structure and a unifying nationalist commitment. In that sense, the traditional workparty basis and the persistence of traditional institutions and values in the modern state were the essential preconditions of the national self-help movement. Coupled to the post-Independence impetus to development and built on strong feelings of having suffered exploitation and deprivation of development under colonial rule, the Harambee movement had a social structural basis which more than any other factor guaranteed that it too became an important social reality at all levels of the new nation.

Harambee and Development

The sociological literature on the Harambee movement displays a preoccupation, understandably enough, with the question whether this enormous output of social and political energy and the use of the economic resources which it mobilized has been actually 'developmental' or a waste of valuable resources and a threat to genuine and equitable socioeconomic development.[11] The aim of this study was more restricted – to analyse how the Harambee movement came about and why it evoked such commitment and activity. However, the Kitui material does point to certain conclusions about general questions relating to the national Harambee movement as a whole. These conclusions are put forward in so far as they arise out of the understanding of the Harambee movement as observed in Kitui rather than from a wider or more systematic state-level political or economic study, which would be a different research project requiring other information and statistical data not currently available.

The criteria for assessing the Harambee movement as 'developmental' or otherwise depend on how development is defined. Here development is taken to mean, in the broadest sense, the creation of sustained and equitable economic growth for the people of Kenya as a whole, with due regard to their social, economic, cultural, civil and political rights.[12]

In assessing the significance of the Harambee movement, it must be recognized that year by year self-help has occupied only a small niche within the overall government development programme, which has related to the policies of the government in power and has been affected by the international economic and political situation – the international terms of trade and the government's external relations, in particular, which are not the subject of this study.[13] In this respect, the Harambee movement may be characterized as a socially important 'dependent' institution, adjustments to which would be expected to have relatively little impact on the overall political economy. However, it has had major and immediate impact on the lives of millions of people in Kenya, particularly the majority rural population which had least influence on central political and economic decision-making and trends. Furthermore, the effects of the Harambee movement, now approaching its fourth decade, may well be far greater than was envisaged in its first decade and may already constitute a major constraining factor on central government planning. For example, one writer has estimated that with one-third of the rural infrastructure being of Harambee origin, half of recurrent government expenditure has been allocated to maintaining Harambee-built facilities.[14] If this is indeed the case, although the evidence is not clear, the place of self-help in development planning would require major reconsideration.

The issues being considered here derive from the Kitui research and the published literature on the Harambee movement. They are as follows:

– How genuine is the self-help movement in terms of accepted Community Development principles?
– To what extent is it primarily a political phenomenon?
– In what way does it relate to social stratification?
– How does it fit into development planning, and how cost-effective is it?

These issues have already been raised at various points of the description, in earlier chapters, of the situation in Kitui up to 1974. In the following discussion, comments are made in the light of analysis of this data and in relation to positions that have been taken by those contributing to the literature on the Harambee movement.

COMMUNITY DEVELOPMENT PRINCIPLES

The model of successful community development that is relevant here is the 'non-directive' approach set out by Hodge.[15] In this model, goals are determined by the community itself, planned with its participation, and achieved through local autonomous groups with largely untrained local leaders. The technique of the professional community development worker is non-directive and 'enabling', using a variety of skills in the manipulation of group dynamics and knowledge of the means available to realize the chosen ends within the overall objective of creating self-sustaining local improvements. Community development is thus an alternative to, or addition to, other types of directed change achieved through the training of individuals in new techniques ('government extension') or through 'rural animation' at community level – interventionist stimulation of development that is administration-controlled and makes little use of community initiative, resources, ideas or leadership in the planning and implementation process.[16]

The 'Mass Education' or Community Development concept propagated throughout the British Empire by Secretary of State for the Colonies Creech Jones in 1948 related to social and political problems of the time which were governed by the colonial situation. This view of community development was essentially 'directive' and government-organized, with the backing of forced labour laws. In the late 1950s some could assent to giving the approbation of the title 'community development' to projects and organizational structures involving participation which was not at all voluntary,[17] but by the 1960s it was more obvious that colonial community development was in many respects 'a contradiction in terms'.[18] There can be little doubt that the 'self-help' so glowingly written about in colonial District Commissioners' reports for Kitui in the 1950s contained relatively little 'voluntarism' or 'client-centred decision-making', which were at least by the 1960s regarded both by community development workers in the field and by those teaching the subject as the very heart of community development. Indeed, the absence of these features was regarded as highly likely to be detrimental in the long term to the success of the community project or programme.

The reforms in the 1950s of the 'communal labour' system in colonial Kanya were both politically preferable to the coercive nature of the previous system and more successful in achieving developmental objectives. There was 'more self-help' in them than in the previous system, and the Machakos evidence shows that they were embarked upon with considerable enthusiasm, Nevertheless, the fact that location councils approved communal labour resolutions can hardly be regarded as evidence of the fully 'voluntary' or 'self-help' nature of this work, as was often proclaimed by colonial officials in their reports.

Independence and the consequent revaluation of self-help led to new ideas about its relationships and structure. There were still areas of conflict between the official position that the 'spirit of Harambee' (its non-directive, client-centred nature) had to be protected as much as possible, and the equally official efforts to get the Harambee movement going and keep it under close central control. Administrative involvement in the larger Harambee projects precluded much local decision-making – or even actively repressed criticism or dissent. But it is arguable that without such administrative involvement, larger-scale or supra-local projects could not even have been initiated, let alone implemented. The sanctions on which local communities relied did not exist at the supra-local level, nor was there any obvious alternative managerial structure for the projects. Administrative involvement also ensured that projects were more likely to meet the requisite standards of quality and accountability, as well as central development planning criteria. A point worth making in this connection is that Community Development principles do not include complete *laissez-faire* local development. Integration with central planning principles and avoidance of duplication of projects are part of an essential planning process that embraces community projects as well as government extension projects. In that sense, the fact of administrative involvement is not in itself anthithetical to Community Development ideology.[19] In Kenya, consultative bodies, such as district and location development committees, were established to inject a non-governmental input into the planning process, even if their actual influence was relatively small.

Particularly at the local village level, the structure of the new self-help movement, which was grounded on traditional structures of community co-operation and decision-making, found genuine reflection in the community development ideology propagated in the national news media and in the work of community development officials.[20] The latter officials were part of one of the least powerful government departments – a division of the Social Services Department of the Ministry of Housing and Social Services – and their financial and staff resources were meagre, although these had been expanded after Independence. Yet they provided a counterbalance to the authoritarian nature of the Kenyan district administration and did manage to preserve much of the 'spirit of Harambee'. Most important, however, to the preservation of the reality of self-help was the fact that its organization was not simply the creation of an administrative bureaucracy.

Harambee projects have been described as a form of 'community taxation', particularly in respect of compulsory monetary contributions. Taxation is defined as 'a compulsory contribution to the support of government, levied on persons, property, income, commodities, transactions, etcetera'.[21] Some scholars do not find it objectionable that a community 'tax' should be levied by local groups for local projects, at a basic flat-rate contribution for most people but graduated for employed or wealthier people – as was the case in Kitui.[22] In this sense the 'tax' used 'surplus' cash or labour for capital investment and for productive rather than consumptive purposes. Its critics complain not so much about this intention but about the degree of coercion sometimes used to extract this 'tax'. Yet in terms of people's perceptions, Harambee was quite different from taxation, and no one would have used the language of voluntarism to describe their payment of any government tax.

Criticism of the ultimate use of coercion (that is, physical force) in order to ensure collection of funds or provision of labour has often been unrealistic: social institutions are generally sanctioned in various ways, as has been demonstrated in Kamba society. However, harsh and undemocratic methods have undoubtedly sometimes been used to enforce payment, particularly in supra-local projects, for example by requiring Harambee payment receipts to be shown for entry to markets or access to government services. Such methods have been much criticized in the Kenyan news media. In Kitui in 1973, collection of funds for the Ukamba Agricultural Institute (UKAI) was achieved only by the District Commissioner ruling that a receipt had to be shown by anyone wanting any government service. The amounts of money involved were small, but even so this form of extraction of funds for a remote supra-local project was onerous and incompatible with the objective of the community development idea.

Since 1974 the use of coercion in supra-local projects appears to have increased. Despite media criticism, the practice has continued. In 1990 a Presidential Bursary Fund was created to establish scholarships for poorer pupils, but press reports indicated that contributions were deducted from civil servants' salaries without their consent. The following is a strong statement on 'Forced Harambees' in an important and highly critical pastoral letter from the Catholic Bishops of Kenya on 'the present situation in our country'.

> Another area of concern to us at this time is that of forced Harambees. Harambee is a system that many Kenyans embrace and appreciate. It is the system that has proved to be a very effective method of our nation-building. However, sadly now, this concept, whose original inspiration was one of a voluntary giving and doing, has been transformed by some misguided leaders into an obligation and a forced exercise. We know of cases where government officials have issued circulars demanding a certain amount of money from each family, i.e. cases where through department offices, workers got their salaries slashed, chiefs and their assistants wait for people at the cereal boards, parents are compelled to pay money at a time when such funds are being raised, e.g. the Presidential Bursary Fund and many more such cases. And as absurd as it may sound, those who are unable to raise the required amount have suffered the confiscation of their properties which are auctioned in order to raise money. Harambee means people giving what they can afford freely without any pressure whatsoever. How genuine shall it be, for example, if we should succeed in raising a huge sum of money in the name of a bursary fund to help those brighter children who come from poor families while in fact we have created another million cases who will need bursary fund? In this matter, we support the action of the President in making it clear that the recent Harambee for the Presidential Bursary Fund, as well as all Harambees, are free and that nobody should

be in any way coerced into making contributions against his will. (*Daily Nation*, 22 June 1990)

Some form of coercion was present in all self-help activity, as the Kitui material on self-help sanctions shows. 'Voluntarism' in the self-help movement was discussed above, and while the ideology of Harambee prescribed that people should see their actions and contributions as free and voluntary, these derived in reality from a framework of reciprocity and were not in essence purely altruistic in the sense of being motivated solely by an individual's chosen dedication to an ideal. On the other hand, the degree of non-voluntarism or coercion could be assessed quite easily. A critical point of the Harambee movement had evidently been reached when such widespread criticism was being articulated, and the community development basis of the Harambee movement was clearly at risk.

THE POLITICAL PHENOMENON

All social action has its political aspects, but the Harambee movement as it developed after Independence constituted an important and dramatic political phenomenon.[23] It was clearly a key expression of nationalist commitment to development, which was not created by the government or any particular politician. It also tied in with other more formal political processes in the modern Kenya.

The academic discussion of the politics of Harambee has tended to concentrate on the opportunism of some politicians and the distortion of central development planning which resulted when powerful politicians forced through their own Harambee projects in defiance of accepted planning procedures or blatantly utilized self-help groups for their own political purposes.[24] In Kitui as elsewhere in Kenya, it was notable that all politicians had to involve themselves with as many Harambee projects as possible. They had to 'jump on the Harambee bandwagon', as some described it, and to collect considerable financial backing to meet the enormous obligations that were inevitably incurred. An important part of campaigning for election to Parliament and local district councils was forced into the area of Harambee. Politicians campaigned for election partly on the basis of their contributions to Harambee projects. The Kitui material shows how this alone did not guarantee the eventual political outcome, which was influenced by political factors and voters' assessment of the candidates.

One point must be stressed here, arising out of the fortuitous opportunity provided by fieldwork taking place as election fever was getting started in 1973: that the extreme politicization of Harambee was confined to certain points in the electoral cycle, notably when parliamentary elections were due, approximately every five years (see Table 20). Election fever affected Harambee by increasing political support and funds for Harambee projects. More Harambee projects were activated and completed as a result. The boost to Harambee was dramatic and contrasted with the 'normal' situation in that an additional pool of funds became available to supplement the ongoing collections people made for their own projects. Without politicians' contributions, the success of many Harambee projects could not have been guaranteed – this was particularly the case with Nzambani Harambee School, for example. A negative consequence was that politicians approached Harambee competitively and political motivations were in danger of becoming paramount as, where politicians set their targets, for example, on larger and more prestigious projects, with lesser degrees of community input.

The way in which the Harambee movement was thus politicized derived in part from the universally approved involvement in it of every citizen. Harambee, as mass mobilization for development, took on the nature of a political ideology which the government and the sole permitted political party, which had little distinct ideology of its own and was not a mass democratic movement, attempted to appropriate. There was at the same time a deliberate government policy to exercise maximum political control over politicians, not only to prevent political disputes endangering Harambee projects but also to limit political activity that could be critical of the government. Making politicians compete in Harambee contributions also had the effect – perhaps initially unintended but strikingly useful to the government – of favouring politicians with substantial financial backing and making it very difficult for 'grass-roots radicals' or opposition politicians who lacked extensive financial resources to be politically successful.

In that sense, Harambee was harnessed to central political processes and control mechanisms, although it could hardly be asserted to have been created specifically to serve those purposes. 'Harambee' became a powerful symbolic tool in the hands of the government. That is not to say that it became an instrument of political repression itself, or linked inevitably to one political direction or ideology. Indeed, it would be expected that any political tendency, including that of a radical opposition movement, would have wanted to utilize the symbol of Harambee for its own objectives, so powerfully was it rooted in social reality at village level no less than at national level. Interestingly, radical dissidents in the 1980s did not pick out the Harambee movement as a central item in their critique of the government. What was most criticized from all quarters – but without much reaction from the government or district administration – was the growing extent of coercion which threatened to turn what was presented as a genuine community development movement into 'rural animation' supervised by the administration.

A particularly interesting political analysis of the Harambee movement – advanced by Mutiso and shared by Holmquist[25] – is that, contrary to any view that the government or national bourgeoisie were simply exploiting peasant participation in Harambee as a means of avoiding any genuine devolution of development from the urban/industrial/commercial centres to the rural peripheries, the Harambee movement had succeeded in forcing the political centre to transfer resources to the rural areas in order to strengthen and maintain Harambee-initiated projects. The motivation for this was seen as deriving from the use by the Harambee movement of social and political links between the small urban and rural political elites and the majority rural population.

The Kitui material on politics of self-help indicated considerable conformism in people's attitudes to the administration's propaganda on self-help. There was universal support for Harambee in principle, although there were also examples where people's views were put forward quite forcefully when they felt that these were being neglected or overridden by administrative officials, or if they believed that their real needs were being ignored. Examples of such criticisms were the Kamale *mwethya's* dispute with the chief in 1974 and some of the *mwethya* songs quoted above.

As regards the issue of the Harambee movement being a vehicle for turning development towards the rural areas, urban migrants from Kitui were pressed to contribute extensively to rural self-help projects. Their main route to prestige or political influence in their rural home areas appeared to be through participation in Harambee projects. However, more research would be needed to assess how far these social and political pressures actually worked.

SOCIAL STRATIFICATION

Several scholars have expressed concern that the Harambee movement appears to have become a dynamic instrument of social division.[26] It has been argued that nationally the Harambee movement increased socioeconomic divisions between richer and poorer districts of the country, which in political terms meant richer and poorer ethnic groups; and that locally it exacerbated similar increasing divisions between wealthier and poorer rural-dwellers.

There can be little dispute that the mobilizing force of the Harambee movement, coupled with greater financial resources, organizational ability, infrastructure services and the more intensive 'development orientation' derived from fuller in-volvement with social change processes linked with urban and industrial development, inevitably brought new development projects within the range of wealthier regions. Pre-existing regional development inequalities, which were due to a variety of historical and environmental factors, were almost certainly exacerbated, although precise details would be difficult to obtain. Tables 25 and 26, detailing official statistics on self-help contributions in the different provinces up to 1972, give an impression of provincial development differentials, although official Harambee statistics must be treated with considerable reserve and explanation of the differentials would be difficult.

Similar differentials were present within each district too, as well as between provinces and districts. In Kitui in 1973, for example, the target of one Harambee school in each location in Kitui was still being proposed, but some wealthier central locations in the district, such as Changwithya and Mutonguni, already had two or three schools in their location and were planning their fourth or fifth. In 1974 two new Harambee schools opened in Mutonguni and none in most of the other locations in Kitui. In parts of central Kenya, Harambee schools were so numerous that the stage of universal secondary education had almost been reached. Some more developed areas in Kenya were planning multi-million-shilling Harambee projects – for example, to provide piped water to every home in the area – that would have been inconceivable for poorer regions like Kitui.[27] Poorer areas were also disadvantaged because of the frequently inferior quality of their completed projects. In the flooding of the employment market with Harambee school leavers, poorer districts were already beginning to lose out even more, not only because of the smaller number of their Harambee graduates but also because of the poorer quality of many of their Harambee schools.

It might be supposed that the answer to that problem would be one of 'positive discrimination' in favour of poorer districts, either through 'directed development' by means of special inputs of central government resources, or through greater central control over which Harambee projects would be permitted to proceed. The former was politically and economically out of the question, except to a limited degree in respect of the nomadic areas, where in fact the intended measures of this kind did not appear to have succeeded;[28] and the latter was difficult in practical terms. No government in Kenya could stop Harambee. Harambee was the ideology of Independence and had a momentum of its own, generated by its own social dynamic, developed independently of government control.

In one respect, the Harambee movement had a positive effect on existing social divisions. Harambee schools appear to have increased proportionally the number of secondary school places for girls.[29] In Kitui and probably elsewhere this was due to a deliberate planning policy decision in the district development committees, which was in line with the Ministry of Education's national objectives. This may have a significant impact in the future on the position of women in development, especially in a poor district like Kitui where many of the girls in secondary school were the first educated females in their families.

Table 25 *Provincial Self-Help Contributions, 1967–72*

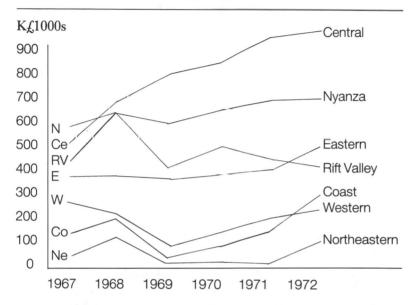

Source: Department of Community Development, Self-Help Statistics, 1967–1972 (Nairobi, 1973)

That the Harambee factor has increased social stratification in Kenya is impossible to deny, but the precise extent of this is difficult to assess. There are major problems in the use of self-help statistics, as the collection and presentation of the data cannot be regarded as reliable and comprehensive. Clearly, though, the Harambee movement has been used to better effect in wealthier districts than in poorer districts, through proportionally greater contributions to self-help projects. Wealthier individuals have also probably used the Harambee projects for their own ends to a greater degree than poorer people could, although not without making proportionally greater contributions to the projects as well as paying for their use of them. In many of the bigger projects, poorer contributors (who of course gave less than wealthier people) probably benefited very little from the projects in practical terms and might not even have been able to afford them.

Table 26   *Provincial Self-Help Contributions per head, 1972*

Province	Population (millions)	Self-Help Contributions (K£ millions)	Per head (K£)
Central	1.85	1.00	0.53
Coast	1.03	0.24	0.23
Eastern	1.91	0.48	0.25
Northeastern	0.28	0.06	0.24
Nyanza	2.33	0.46	0.20
Rift Valley	2.43	0.64	0.26
Western	1.46	0.23	0.16

Source: 1969 population census and 1972 Department of Community Development figures

At village level, the same processes operated. There was a partial 'levelling mechanism' in village *mwethya* organization which obliged everyone to participate in the self-help group and drew larger contributions from employed people than from ordinary farmers. This was also part of the 'balanced reciprocity' aspect of self-help organization. Wealthier villagers could neither evade their contributions nor turn the self-help group or its projects to their sole advantage.

DEVELOPMENT PLANNING AND COST EFFECTIVENESS

It should not be a matter for surprise that all the main problems of the Harambee movement – those arising from over-enthusiastic proliferation of self-help projects, political factors and socially divisive tendencies – coalesced in the area of development planning. In 1974 central government and district planning procedures had been established, with five-year district development plans published and discussed at length in each district through district and location development committees, but there was still much room for improvement in implementing local consultation and creating a responsible realism about the Harambee movement. Nevertheless, the concept of equitable and rational development planning had considerable political support, despite other tendencies to the contrary.

The principal problem of the Harambee movement, for both political scientists and development planners, was whether its apparent practical gains and political success were worth what some saw as its long-term economic disadvantages. The problem was particularly perceived in terms of cost effectiveness and the extent of wastage of energy and resources through project failures or inappropriate completed projects. It was indisputable that the people had a 'right to development'.[30] It was explicit and obvious that 'development' was both a national goal and also an inherent right of individuals and communities. The mass of the people lived in rural areas, where the rate of development was slow or even declining. Self-help development for a developing country with a low Gross National Product presented the only possible form of mobilization of manpower and finance resources that could respond to the felt needs and aspirations of the mass of the people. Kenya's economy was geared to central planning that aimed to make the best use of the country's limited resources for present and future generations, but it accepted a role for 'unplanned' self-help development, provided this did not conflict with central economic objectives.

In the field of educational development, some planners around the time of Independence believed that educational growth should be restricted to match economic growth – in other words, that the needs of the economy should dictate what educational provision was available to the people. Political decisions inevitably quickly overrode this – mainly because of awareness of the major repression of educational progress by the colonial government and the new economic needs and opportunities created by Independence, but also because the view came to be accepted that rapid acceleration of education and training was needed to stimulate economic growth. The expansion of education became the main political goal that had to be fulfilled. Where government fell short in the expansion of mass education, it was not the private sector (commercially run private schools which few could have afforded) nor the religious schools (most of which were gradually being absorbed into the national educational system) but the rural public self-help sector, which by itself soon began to fill the gap between expectation and provision and was then given that exclusive function.

It rapidly became politically impossible to impose severe restrictions on the Harambee movement, because there was probably little or nothing else the government could otherwise offer to meet the felt and expressed needs which Harambee represented throughout Kenya. The opposition that would have been created if the government had sought to deal heavy-handedly with the Harambee movement would have been considerable and would have vastly compounded the government's problems in its handling of criticism and dissent. In 1974 the government was heavily engaged in the propagation of Harambee and had accommodated many of its demands. Rather than restricting Harambee projects it continually encouraged them: calling for more and more contributions, publicizing Harambee Days, providing administrative support for collecting money for big projects – sometimes in highly coercive ways – and allocating an increasing proportion of the budget to assisting and maintaining Harambee-created public facilities. There had also at the same time been attempts to create a counterbalance to this 'runaway' situation by means of some administrative checks on the quality of Harambee projects and also by establishing local development planning procedures, which represented some of the interventions that the central development planners wanted.

The goal of achieving universal primary education as soon as possible was not disputed, but planners were concerned about increasing problems deriving from a combination of rapid expansion of low-quality educational facilities with slow economic growth. This disjunction in terms of increasing unemployment of secondary as well as primary school leavers was compounded by Kenya's high population growth of over 3 per cent per annum. Politicians and government officials had responded to or even deliberately increased popular demand by forcing the pace on educational expansion, putting quantity before quality. The main problem area was the Harambee secondary schools, where failures of projects were largely unrecorded in the official statistics – though perhaps exaggerated by some critics. Planners tended to a pessimistic view of Harambee schools. The view was that money extracted for a proliferation of Harambee schools could have been better used in other developmental areas, for example in agriculture or technical training. Year by year, planners bemoaned the problem of 'waste' in relation to the Harambee schools in particular. Educationalists were also becoming concerned about the quality of Harambee schools in terms of examination results, although in 1974 it was perhaps too soon to assess this fairly.

At the time of writing (in 1990) it was still fair to say that insufficient research had been done to allow any comprehensive assessment of the cost effectiveness of the Harambee movement. Reliable statistics were not yet available, and assessments were consequently fairly impressionistic. Even the criteria for such assessment were not clear. (The same might be said of many government-funded or non-governmental-organization-funded projects too, where the literature on cost effectiveness was also thin.)

Some useful pointers to assessing the end-products can be derived from the Kitui material. In the first place, the distinction between local and supra-local projects is important in assessing project efficiency. Some self-help work may have been fairly desultory and unenthusiastic, as in Kamale at one time, but over a longer period, the aims of the Kamale self-help group were largely achieved. Shortcomings may have persisted in the quality of the education provided in its primary school, but this was not the responsibility of the self-help group but a consequence of aiming at and achieving universal primary education with scanty resources. The meagre resources available could be said to have been reasonably well utilized.

Nzambani Harambee School, a supra-local project, took nearly ten years to reach fruition, though in fact it took only a little over one year of determined activity, starting in 1973, to get it opened in 1974. It kept going and during the 1980s was taken over by the government, thus guaranteeing that it would continue.[31] The general record of Harambee schools in Kitui up to 1974 was fairly good: only two out of seven schools which had been taken over by the government had been aided as a 'rescue' operation, and only one of the twelve Harambee schools not receiving government aid was in serious trouble (see Table 21 above). Some of the problems encountered by Harambee schools in Kitui have been described above, and it would be unwise to ignore them, but the existence of the problem was perhaps less striking than the fact that they were mostly overcome in the end. On this assessment, Kitui's Harambee schools in 1974 seemed to be in a fairly healthy state, to which Roman Catholic managerial and financial assistance no doubt contributed considerably. A decade and a half later, there had been considerable further expansion of schools. Although some were said to be in a poor state, insufficient information on the post-1974 situation was available to make a more recent assessment.

Information was not collected on the success or otherwise by 1974 of Harambee cattle-dips or water projects, such as earth dams, other than what was observed of the beginning of a cattle-dip project and the problems of an earth dam near Kamale, which are described above. It is probable that these two kinds of project were particularly beset by problems.

The biggest supra-local project in 1974, the Ukamba Agricultural Institute, seemed at the time to be unrealistic and its fund-raising highly coercive. It did become operational some years later, although it did not match up to some other ethnic-based institutes of technology which received extensive overseas funding. No detailed information about it was available at the time of writing.

As to the question whether the same amounts of money collected in self-help projects in Nzambani in 1973–4 could have been put to better productive use, given the poor agricultural potential of most of the district and its overall low state of development, it is difficult to see what alternative use these relatively small amounts could have been put to. In Kamale, people often found it difficult to pay their self-help dues as against other demands on their extremely meagre financial resources, but it was not at all clear how any different expenditure of the amounts being demanded – 10 or 50 shillings per head per year, for example – could have produced a more directly productive development investment.

With regard to the Harambee schools, the equality of opportunity of access to them, if not the equality of the means to seize the opportunity, was regarded as a democratic right. Debts may have been incurred by some poorer people to send their children to a Harambee school, but these debts were treated as investments where the return was potentially greater than in any other field. If a Harambee school leaver was unemployed for one or two years, at least he or she might be lucky enough to get a job in the end – and would be better equipped for that purpose than otherwise. As the average age of leaving primary school was getting lower, because children were starting school at an earlier age (at seven or even five), parents became more concerned about what a twelve- or thirteen-year-old primary school leaver could usefully do if he or she failed to get a place in any other area of secondary education. From an individual perspective in Kitui, where farm development opportunities were very limited and labour-migration was the established avenue to individual progress, there seemed to be nothing else on which the investment in building the Harambee school, or paying school fees for a child to be educated at a Harambee school before entering the job market, could be better spent.

In the first decade of the Harambee movement, considerable interventionist efforts had been made to improve the quality of Harambee development. These included procedures for registering and funding Harambee schools and for planning self-help projects through location and district development committees, as well as the routine work of Community Development officials in monitoring self-help activities. These inputs, however, were not always systematic or effective, and in retrospect much more might have been achieved if the planners had recognized the political and social unstoppability of the Harambee movement and brought the Harambee sector more fully into the planning process at an earlier stage.

One recent study of secondary school attainment concluded that the Harambee schools not only wasted resources that should have been better utilized but also created unrealistic expectations in students and the communities which built the schools.[32] But to expect Harambee schools to perform as well as government schools would be a distorted view. It was not a hidden fact that they were 'second-chance institutions', but it was widely believed that despite a poorer-quality student intake and few resources, there were still benefits held out for students. In Kitui in 1974 there seemed to be a considerable degree of realism among students and communities about Harambee schools and the difficult employment prospects for Harambee school leavers, but the momentum for expanding the numbers of Harambee schools continued, and the schools found their pupils. If, however, the situation arose that Harambee students' examination results became so poor that parents and communities felt that their investment was being completely wasted, this would precipitate political pressure on the government's educational policy.

In some quarters, particularly where politicians had an influence, there was marked unrealism – for example when the Kitui District Development Plan in 1979 proposed forty more Harambee Schools in the next five years, almost double the number opened in Kitui in the previous fifteen years and nearly four times the number opened in the previous five years.[33] There was an obvious need for more interventionism by development planners, but in the direction of regulating the Harambee process rather than trying to stop it.

The importance of assessing the Harambee movement in terms of its end-products and rectifying deficiencies as early as possible is obvious. But to take a strongly critical view of the movement and aspire to replace it with controlled or directed development of the 'rural animation' type would be to ignore its social significance and undervalue its social and political roots. As already mentioned, the literature on the Harambee movement has been relatively short on explanations of this extensive mobilization of human and financial resources. The Kitui study points to the positive features of this movement at village level in particular, where a genuine reflection of community development philosophy was found, despite the problems that had arisen. Though this situation may have been affected by the danger of increasing use of coercion in major

Harambee projects, it is nevertheless reasonable to suppose that these could never have been developed except on the foundation of village self-help organization.

What could make the Harambee movement more effective? Detailed research over nearly three decades would be needed to assess the extent of the problem and thus obtain a clear overall view of how to avoid the same mistakes in the future. Towards the end of fieldwork in Kitui in 1973–4, the most obvious improvements that could be discerned for village self-help groups lay in providing leadership training for their leaders, particularly in accounting and financial matters; better planning and monitoring of projects by district officials in consultation with local politicians, churches, traders, self-help groups and other concerned local people; and constant attention to 'preserve the spirit of Harambee' and avoid coercion.[34] These were obvious recommendations to make at the time, and they derived from the lack of support for self-help groups from the Community Development Department, which did not have the necessary manpower or financial resources, or sufficient administrative or political support. Further attention to the quality of Harambee education was also an obvious need, for example by establishing minimum standards of teacher quality and educational resources in schools. It is worth repeating the observation that the government had put very few resources into the Harambee movement in proportion to its national importance and its achievements.

Although the main research in 1973–4 was confined to Kitui district, much self-help work in more developed districts in Kenya was being done through women's *mabati* groups, which did not exist at the time in Nzambani location. The official record of *mabati* group work in the nearby wealthier Murang'a district was impressive: 594 groups with over 34,000 members were earning money through farming and other work to provide better housing and roofing for their members, installing water-tanks in houses and buying improved cattle stock ('grade cows'). These examples had lessons for those concerned with self-help in less developed areas, where a similar process of change in co-operative farm labour could have been linked to similar developments in the self-help movement.[35]

An obvious point to emerge from the Kitui material on Harambee schools is that many schools benefited enormously from the assistance of the Catholic Church – in management, provision of teachers and other financial assistance, and co-ordination of such assistance on a district-wide basis and in consultation with governmental and other bodies. There were some examples of assistance to the Harambee movement from other agencies outside the government. Yet there was scope for much more assistance to Harambee schools and other Harambee projects, for example through non-governmental development relief agencies working in a partnership in development with existing community bodies. The Kenya-side structures for such partnership existed, and without detracting from the community development philosphy of self-reliance, organizations with a commitment to basic needs provision to poor communities could provide valuable supplementary assistance.

Conclusion and Summary

The Harambee movement has been seen to have its origins in two sources: traditional community workparty institutions and reforms of colonial forced labour. The former source was constantly stressed, the latter less so. The continuity between the Kamba *mwethya* workparty system and village self-help groups in Kitui was striking, although organizational forms in self-help groups were different and adapted to the new needs of communities and their projects. As colonial forced labour came to an end, the post-Independence revival of village community development work was expressed in nationalist and voluntaristic terms.

In the first decade of Harambee, communities moved through different levels of projects according to their resources. As some districts struggled towards universal primary education, others approached universal secondary education. Ambitious projects to provide piped water to all homes and build tertiary educational institutions, some to university level, required massive resources which were within the capacities of some communities, impossible for others. The village workparties of peasant farmers survived in less developed districts like Kitui, while in more developed areas hired labour was replacing reciprocal labour in most economic activities. Self-help was increasing the development gap between better-off and poorer communities, and the community development ideal was giving way to the highly organized large-scale project backed by strong and direct sanctions. The voluntaristic ethic of Harambee – although in fact always backed by sanctions of one kind or another which were on occasion applied quite forcefully – was clearly in some jeopardy, especially in bigger projects involving urban people, long before the Catholic Bishops' pastoral letter in 1990 criticizing 'forced Harambees'.

Research was done in a fairly marginal part of Kenya. This was in some respects an advantage in that the Harambee movement could be seen in higher profile than in an area which was developing at a faster rate in terms of both government and private-sector activity. How typical Kitui was in 1974 in relation to other rural societies in Kenya is difficult to say. There was no attempt to replicate this fieldwork in any other area, although I briefly visited different parts of Machakos district in 1973. There is insufficient published ethnographic material on similar workparty institutions or self-help structures in other Kenyan societies to clarify whether the Kamba *mwethya* model described here is found more generally. Similarities of political institutions – for example in the lack of centralized political institutions such as kings or chiefs, the dominance of patrilineal descent in the society – do not necessarily make for similarities in other areas, for example in economic organization or beliefs and ritual, even in adjacent societies of similar culture or language grouping. Yet some kind of village self-help organization and similar involvement in the overall Harambee system are found throughout Kenya. The structural analysis here of the Kitui Kamba *mwethya* system should still be relevant to self-help organization in other parts of Kenya even if some of the factors of reciprocity are differently arranged.

The actuality of self-help in other areas and other societies may also present different faces, with more or less self-help activity, more or less coercion, more or less politicization, more or less domination or exploitation by wealthier individuals, or more or less administrative control. Yet it is probable that such localized differences do not mean that the Harambee movement in other parts of Kenya is fundamentally different in its social and historical origins and present-day reality.

The present study was based on research conducted in 1973–4, and I had no opportunity to undertake any further study of Harambee in Kenya or in Kitui. Some events and trends in the country since 1974 may have had substantial effects on the Harambee movement. President Jomo Kenyatta died in 1978 and was succeeded by his Vice-President, Daniel arap Moi, who promised continuity of policies with his new slogan '*Nyayo*' (Footsteps).[36] Under the Moi government there has been an intensification of political opposition and repression,[37] which has also affected academic activities in Kenya and research into some of the issues addressed here. The educational structure was drastically altered in 1983, although it is not known how this has affected the Harambee schools movement.[38]

However, judging from more recent published material cited above, one feature of modern Kenya appeared to be relatively unchanged at the time of writing – the Harambee movement. In Kitui the Harambee schools had continued to increase in number, with only a few said to be in a very poor state, and it would be surprising if the *mwethya* self-help group structure had substantially changed.

This sociohistorical study of the Harambee movement, with its focus on one particular place and time, has sought to present the first decade of the movement in its full social reality to counter partial or distorted views of it. On close inspection, the Harambee movement, which had taken firm root in Kenya and was highly praised internationally, turned out to be relatively under-researched. It is hoped that this study has also set out the basis for further studies of the self-help phenomenon in Kenya and elsewhere.

Notes

List of Abbreviations

ASA	Association of Social Anthropologists (UK)
BER	Bureau of Educational Research, University of Nairobi
CJAS	*Canadian Journal of African Studies*
CUP	Cambridge University Press
EAJ	*East African Journal*
EALB	East African Literature Bureau
EAPH	East African Publishing House
HMSO	His/Her Majesty's Stationery Office, London
IAI	International African Institute
IDS	Institute of Development Studies (University of Nairobi)
JAA	*Journal of African Administration*
JAH	*Journal of African History*
JMAS	*Journal of Modern African Studies*
KLB	Kenya Literature Bureau
KNA	Kenya National Archives
MUP	Manchester University Press
OUP	Oxford University Press
RAI	Royal Anthropological Institute
ROAPE	*Review of African Political Economy*
SIAS	Scandinavian Institute of African Studies
SWJA	*Southwest Journal of Anthropology*
TPH	Tanzania Publishing House

1: Introduction

1. The literature on the Harambee movement includes particularly the following: Anderson, 1977; Bray and Lillis, 1988; Colebatch, nd; Feldman, 1984; Godfrey and Mutiso, 1974; Hill, 1974, 1975, 1990; Holmquist, 1984; Keller, 1974, 1975; Mbithi, 1972; Mbithi and Rasmussen, 1977; Mutiso, 1975, 1977a; Mwaniki, 1986; Stamp, 1986; B.P. Thomas, 1985, 1987, 1988.

2. This is the case particularly with Mbithi and Rasmussen, 1977, but it applies to most of the other studies too. This is not to dispute the value

of such studies or their conclusions, but it does point to a limitation on them.
3. Lindblom, 1969, originally published in 1920.
4. Brokensha, 1966; Brokensha and Hodge, 1969; Brokensha and Pearsall, 1969; Cochrane, 1971; Long, 1977; Wallman, 1977. The term 'anthropology of development' is discussed in Grillo and Rew, 1985.
5. See note 1 above.
6. For example Holmquist, 1984; B.P.Thomas, 1985, 1987, 1988; Bray and Lillis, 1988.
7. Lindblom, 1969. His full name was Karl Gerhard Lindblom, but he was known as and published under the name of Gerhard Lindblom. He was born in 1887 and died in about 1970. His study of the Kamba, in the revised edition published in 1920, was remarkable in its wealth of detailed ethnography and his advanced knowledge of Kikamba, in the infancy of participant-observation ethnography and social anthropology. His data were collected in fourteen months of fieldwork during 1911 and 1912, mainly near the towns of Machakos, Kibwezi, Kitui and Ikutha (in southern Kitui). This was some years before Malinowski started fieldwork (1915) and his monograph was published before Malinowski's first study of the Trobriand Islands (1922). Apart from this 607-page monograph in English, which was a revised version of his PhD thesis accepted and published by the University of Uppsala in 1916, he also wrote two booklets on Kikamba grammar and published three collections of texts of Kamba folk stories. He became Professor of Comparative Ethnology at the University of Stockholm and Curator of the Ethnographical Museum of Sweden in Stockholm. He later visited other parts of Kenya and wrote short general books about his travels and some comparative articles, mostly in Swedish or English but also in French and German, from a diffusionist point of view. The subjects were particular material artefacts, such as initiation sticks, hammocks, stilts, 'the spiked wheel-trap and its distribution', spears, harpoons, razors, wire-drawings, string-figures, pipes, slings and nose ornaments, and he wrote one article on 'the one-leg resting position'. He did not attempt to make any contribution to anthropological theory and remained completely outside the main developments of social anthropology as pioneered by Malinowski and others. His travel books are of little ethnographic interest other than as a record of ideas of the time in Sweden.

I am indebted for much of this information about Lindblom to Wilhelm Ostberg, curator of the research division at the Ethnographical Museum of Sweden, where Lindblom's Kamba collection is deposited and partially on view, including artefacts and photographs published in his monograph. The University of Uppsala Library kindly provided me with a full list of Lindblom's publications.
8. Stanner, 1940, 1969.
9. For example, Lambert, 1947; Carson, 1958; Penwill, 1951; Nottingham,

1959, and publications by early colonial administrators, several of them listed in Middleton and Kershaw, 1972, such as Hobley, Dundas, Beresford-Stook and Blackwood-Murphy, who were interested in Kamba customs.
10. Kavyu, Mbithi, Mutiso and Ndeti (see Bibliography). Kimilu, 1962 is a book on Kamba customs ('The True Mukamba') written in Kikamba.
11. Ambler, 1988; Kimambo, 1970; Jackson, 1970; Munro, 1975; Newman, 1974; O'Leary, 1984; Tignor, 1976; A.Thomas, 1969.
12. Middleton and Kershaw, 1972. This survey, when tested against field data in Kitui, proved to include numerous inaccuracies and gaps due to the extremely uneven nature of the primary source material, very little of it deriving from trained social anthropologists.
13. See Chapters 3 and 4. Mbithi and Rasmussen, 1977 and Mutiso, 1975 are particularly interesting on village self-help structures.
14. Chapter 2. The main historical account of the Kamba is Munro, 1975, which focuses on Machakos. There is additional Machakos material in Kimambo, 1970; Jackson, 1970; Newman, 1974; and further material on Machakos and Kitui in Tignor, 1971, 1976. Ambler, 1988 (for the pre-colonial period in north-central Kitui), Stanner, 1940 and O'Leary, 1984 contain material on Kitui history, but there is no separate published history of Kitui itself.
15. Chapter 5.
16. Chapter 6, p.242.
17. Ibid., p.222.

2: From Forced Labour to Harambee

1. The main source for the historical material presented here is the Kenya National Archives (KNA), principally the Annual Reports from the Kitui District Commissioners. See also references in Chapter 1, note 14. References to money are mostly in United Kingdom sterling equivalents, taking 20 Kenya shillings (20shs) or a Kenya pound (K£) as equivalent to UK£1, as it approximately was in 1973. One shilling contained 100 cents.
2. Akong'a, 1988.
3. Krapf, 1860.
4. Lamphear, 1970.
5. The quotations here and below are from the Kitui District Commissioners' Annual Reports in the KNA.
6. Quoted in Manners, 1962, from a speech reported in the *East African Standard*, 8 February 1913.
7. Savage and Munro, 1966.
8. KNA.
9. Brett, 1973.

10. KNA.

11. Stanner, 1940. This is a rare instance of a sustained contemporary and fieldwork-based anthropological critique of colonial rule. It was unfortunately never published, partly because his fieldwork, begun in Mutito (eastern Kitui) in February 1939, was cut short in August 1939 by the imminent outbreak of war and a feared invasion of eastern Kitui from Italian Somaliland. Stanner also later accepted advice that 'publication of the report as written would reflect on many officials who had been obliged to follow the policies I had criticized' (Stanner, 1969). He visited Kitui in 1952 but did not succeed in obtaining funds to continue his fieldwork there. Apart from a radio talk (Stanner, 1949) and an article on Kitui markets (Stanner, 1969), Stanner did not do any more work or writing on Kitui. His manuscript in the KNA has been frequently consulted and has been of much interest to Kenyan and particularly Kamba scholars. Set against the less political and more personal accounts by anthropologists about their place in the African colonial world (Loizos, 1977; Grillo and Rew, 1985), Stanner's Kitui study occupies a place of its own in the history of the relationship between anthropology and colonialism.

12. This is the term which informants in Kamale in 1973 said they had used for communal labour.

13. Tignor, 1971; for a description of Kamba political structures, see Chapter 3, p.87.

14. On the history of education in Kenya, see Abreu, 1982; Anderson, 1970, 1977; O'Connor, 1974; Ranger, 1965; Tignor, 1976.

15. Chiefs were empowered to require able-bodied male Africans to work for minor communal services for not more than six days per quarter. In addition, on the instructions of the Provincial Commissioner they could instruct Africans to work compulsorily but on the payment of wages for conservation of natural resources or in connection with any emergency resulting from fire, flood, earthquake, epidemic or invasion by insect pests (Kenya Government, 1960).

16. For example, Maher's detailed study of soil erosion in Kitui (1937).

17. The text is published in UK Colonial Office, 1954, Appendix D.

18. Creech Jones, 1949.

19. UK Colonial Office, 1954.

20. Ibid.

21. Ibid.

22. Creech Jones, 1949.

23. Cohen, 1959.

24. Askwith, 1958, 1960.

25. Huxley, 1960.

26. Batten, 1957. Brokensha and Hodge (1969) later pointed to the inherent contradictions in colonial community development.

27. KNA.

28. These quotations are all from District Reports in the KNA.

29. Mutiso, 1977c.

30. Admiration of Kelly's work was expressed to me in 1973 by the Nzambani Chief. Of all the post-World War II District Commissioners in Kitui, he alone seemed to have made a lasting impression through his dedication to development in the district. I am grateful to the historian Dr John Lonsdale for the information that Kelly later retired from colonial service and became an Anglican priest in Britain.

31. KNA.

32. For material on the politically important independent schools movement in colonial Kenya, see Ranger, 1965; Ndungu, 1972; Anderson, 1977.

33. Mayer, 1951.

34. Ibid. There may have been other undocumented or unpublished instances of colonial officials or community workers initiating similar schemes based on traditional workparties: cp. Little, 1949.

35. Interview with Malinda, Nairobi, 1974. He was then a businessman. He is mentioned in Huxley, 1960 and Boninger, 1956. In six months in western Machakos, the achievements were: 177 houses plastered, 310 windows installed, 260 cattle-sheds built, 347 compost-pits dug, 240 latrines dug, 46,000 yards of terracing, 360 acres of bush cleared, and much planting of hedges, trees and flowers (Boninger, 1956).

36. Askwith, 1958, 1960.

37. Huxley, 1960. The account is glowing but cannot be taken as objective because of the colonialist frame of thinking which is so evident throughout her novels. However, the Machakos experiment was undoubtedly a success story in comparison to failed efforts elsewhere which attempted to use coercive means for the same ends, for example in Tanzania (Cliffe, 1970; McHenry, 1973).

38. Tignor, 1971; Newman, 1974; Munro, 1975.

39. Informants in Kitui and Nairobi expressed the general notion that Kamba and Kikuyu were *athoni*, affines, on account of intermarriage, historical relationships and linguistic and cultural similarities.

40. Interview with Mbathi, Nairobi, 1974. He was then a businessman, later a Member of Parliament and government minister. See also Mbathi, 1958.

41. KNA.

42. Ibid.

43. Ibid.

44. Hill, 1974, 1975.

45. Kenyatta, 1964 – the speeches should probably be regarded as the approved work of official speech-writers who were not individually identified.

46. These figures are taken from 'Ten Great Years of Self-Help Movement in Kenya (1963–1973)', Community Development Division, Self-Help Statistics Section, 1975.

310   *The Harambee Movement in Kenya*

47. Godfrey and Mutiso, 1974.
48. The community/government linkage in Kenyan education is discussed in Abreu, 1982; Anderson, 1977 and Bray and Lillis, 1988 in particular.
49. On education in independent Kenya, see Sheffield, 1967; Jolly, 1969; Court and Ghai, 1974.

3: Kamale Village

1. The material presented here is based on fieldwork in and around Kamale. The purpose of this research was to study self-help organization and its sociocultural background, not to correct previous ethnographic details on Kitui culture and society (which differ in important minor respects from Machakos Kamba society, to which much of the published material refers), or to trace the changes since Lindblom's research over sixty years earlier. A recent study by an anthropologist and former Catholic missionary in Kitui focused on economic change from a cultural ecology perspective, based on fieldwork near Nuu in eastern Kitui and near Kitui town in 1975–77 (O'Leary, 1984). Further fieldwork would be needed to undertake a definitive ethnographic study of the Kitui Kamba.
2. The figures provided here are from a village census I carried out in Kamale during fieldwork, mainly in the central neighbourhoods but broadly covering the southern and eastern neighbourhoods too.
3. No attempt was made to conduct fieldwork research into local history, which would have been a separate project. The little material that is included here, supplementing the archival material in Chapter 2, was obtained in the course of fieldwork.
4. Material on Kamba clans is found in Lindblom, 1969; Middleton and Kershaw, 1972; Jackson, 1970; and Ndeti, 1973. It was not within the scope of this study to pursue several of the questions about Kamba clans in Kitui which are not clear in the literature.
5. A more thorough economic study of village settlement and domestic groups is found in O'Leary, 1983, 1984.
6. The former is generally known as 'ghost marriage' but the latter, although found in many societies, has no specific name in the anthropological literature.
7. The survey material obtained during fieldwork was most detailed for Kamale, Kiliku and Utuneeni neighbourhoods. Kamale Itheo – which in geographical and descent-group terms was almost a separate segment of the village – was surveyed only briefly. The fifth neighbourhood, Kamale Number 6, which was a considerable distance away, had only a small population and was only loosely integrated with the village, was surveyed even more briefly.

8. The importance of this workparty is discussed in Chapter 4, p.147.

9. The published ethnographic material on Kamba kinship and marriage is incomplete and unclear. Fjellman (1971) points to some of the problems in collecting the data. The material on kinship here is based on Kamale fieldwork data, but more detailed study is needed.

10. The *mwethya* of affinity probably fitted into this pattern too. It is interesting to speculate from a structuralist perspective whether there might be a symbolic connection between this marital alternation and the reciprocation inherent in the *mwethya* workparty system.

11. Data about Kitui and Nzambani is mainly taken from the Kitui District Development Plan, 1971, covering the period of the 1970–74 National Development Plan and published in mimeographed form by the Eastern Province Planning Team.

12. Data on Kamale here and below are taken from my Kamale household survey data. For further details of the Kitui economy, see Middleton and Kershaw, 1972; Stanner, 1940 and O'Leary, 1984.

13. Stanner, 1969.

14. This was also the conclusion of Oliver, 1965 and Edgerton, 1971, in their psychological anthropology-orientated work.

15. Lamphear, 1970.

16. Krapf, 1860: see reference to Kivoi (or Kivui) in Chapter 2, p.14.

17. This dispute is analysed in detail in Chapter 5, p.211.

18. Further research on the three initiation rituals would expand on the basic details given here – for example on the meanings of symbols and ritual dramas, and on the songs and dances, which were evidently important parts of the rituals. Information on the first *nzaiko* was obtained mainly from the ritual operator who performed the operations mentioned in Kamale. Information on the second *nzaiko* was given by two women who had regularly been ritual guardians up to the 1950s, as well as passing through the rituals themselves. The third ritual was revealed to me by an elder aged about seventy-five, a *mundu mue* himself, who appeared to have taken a liking to me through my assumptive kinship relationship as his grandson (who could therefore make any requests of him) and was willing to accept payment (as traditionally required) for information on this and certain other rituals, some of which he still performed. Many details of the rituals, however, are incomplete, and although the details presented here are consistent in many respects with Lindblom's fuller accounts, some contradictions with his material still exist. Whether this is because of local variations, changes since his account of 1911–12, the reliability or completeness of informants' accounts, is difficult to say, but further research is clearly indicated if a definitive account of Kamba initiation rituals is to be arrived at.

19. I am indebted to Ndilya wa Kavyu of the University of Nairobi for introducing me, before I had started my fieldwork in Kitui, to an anthropologist working in Kyuso in northern Kitui – Hitoshi Ueda of the

University of Osaka, Japan. We both visited him and his wife in Kyuso, and I am grateful to them for enabling me to witness part of the *nzaiko* ritual described here, and on a later occasion to photograph and record traditional 'acrobatic' dances and songs which still survived there (Plates 47–50). I also attended a Harambee Day in Kyuso. Unfortunately I have no further knowledge of publications by Ueda after his early article, Ueda, 1971. Kavyu's work on Kamba songs, including *nzaiko* songs, is found in Kavyu, 1977.

20. Stamp, 1986 states that clitoridectomy was officially banned in Kenya in the early 1980s, though whether this actually ended the ritual in Kitui is not known.

21. Some initiation sticks (called *musai* in Lindblom, 1969) which were collected by Lindblom may be viewed at the Ethnographical Museum of Sweden in Stockholm.

22. Mayer, 1970 summarized the state of interest in socialization among social anthropologists at the time, and called for further studies. This section on socialization is intended to draw attention to some aspects of social change relevant to perceptions of modern education in Kitui society.

23. Cf. O'Neill, 1987.

24. Mutiso, 1977b uses the term *asomi* (literally in Kikamba, 'those who read', i.e. read the Bible – used previously in Kimilu, 1962) and non-*asomi* to express this sociocultural dichotomy.

25. Spencer, 1985 – his analysis of dance could apply also to songs.

26. Lindblom, 1969.

27. Much more research is needed into Kamba beliefs and rituals, where the published material is incomplete and theoretically inadequate. The material presented here, with little attempt at substantial analysis, is based on fieldwork data in Kamale.

28. Odak (1973) refers to the little-known Kavia (or Kathia) cave paintings in Nzambani as unique in Kitui and among the most interesting in Kenya.

29. Lewis (1971) includes reference to spirit possession among the Kamba, citing Lindblom's work.

30. This refers to the definitions based on Evans-Pritchard's study of the Azande in Sudan (Marwick, 1964). Kitui was noted in Kenya as an area of powerful sorcery and oath-fetishes, to which people from other societies sometimes had resort.

31. Lewis, 1971.

32. A. Thomas, 1969.

33. Fieldwork data, supplemented by Kenya National Archive material. See also Penwill, 1951.

34. Glazier (1985) describes a similar judicial oath ritual among the neighbouring Mbeere.

4: Workparties

1. Descriptions of workparties by anthropologists include Abrahams, 1965; Ames, 1959; Barth, 1967; Charsley, 1976; Donham, 1985; Firth, 1965; Gulliver, 1974; Holy, 1970; Leach, 1961; Mayer,1951; O'Neill, 1987; Ortiz, 1965; Riley and Brokensha, 1988. Useful comparative discussions of workparties are found in Erasmus, 1956, 1977; M.P.Moore, 1975; and Swindell, 1985.
2. Gulliver, 1974.
3. Lindblom, 1969; Stanner, 1940. O'Leary, 1984 has useful chapters on agricultural and herding co-operation, with some material on *myethya*.
4. Work songs are mentioned in Kavyu, 1977.
5. Workparties were difficult to observe, and much of the information had to be collected after the event. In retrospect, it might have been useful to examine some workparties in fine detail, analysing the relationships between those who participated and the flow of labour-assistance between them, but whether in the overall context of my research objectives this substantial task would have been worth the possible results is debatable.
6. See Chapter 3, p.88, on age-statuses in Kamba society.
7. This term derives from Gulliver, 1974.
8. M.P. Moore (1975) suggests that the use in some societies of an 'intermediary' for recruiting workparties was due to the time and social skills needed for organizing large workparties. Quite apart from consideration of the alternative that the 'owner' could have done this, it is doubtful that this explanation would be applicable among the Kamba, where the explanation advanced here relates it to Kamba political institutions and values. 'Intermediaries' are noted in the Mbeere *wira* workparty (Riley and Brokensha, 1988).
9. See Chapter 3, p.68 on the 'workparty of affinity'.
10. Chapter 3, p.63.
11. Erasmus (1956) categorized workparties as either 'festive' (non-reciprocal) or exchange-based (reciprocal). M.P. Moore (1975) notes the variety of each type along a continuum, and that both may be found in the same society. Erasmus, Moore and Swindell (1985) all fail to distinguish between meals and feasts, assimilating both to a category of 'festive' workparties, and also make no use of Sahlins's typology of reciprocity. This makes it more difficult to analyse in their terms the differences between workparties and community self-help work.
12. This is the term used in Firth, 1965.
13. The same workparty appears to be called *kitete* in Mutonguni location in central Kitui. There may be other alternative terms for certain workparties in different parts of Ukambani: for example, Mutiso (1975) identifies a form of *mwethya* in Machakos called *vuli*, a term not used in Kamale or perhaps in Kitui as a whole.

14. This term is used in Gulliver, 1974.
15. On women's self-help groups or *mabati* groups, see Feldman, 1984; Mwaniki, 1986; Stamp, 1986; and B.P. Thomas, 1985, 1987, 1988. In areas where they had become firmly established, it was not clear whether they had replaced or merely supplemented the village self-help group system, and, if the latter, how they were integrated into it.

5: The Self-Help Group

1. See Chapter 3, p.64.
2. See Chapter 6, p.249.
3. I was unable to discover conclusively the reason for this, though rumours abounded as to whether it signified a deliberate decision or simply lack of opportunity.
4. See Chapter 3, p.124 for discussion of *nzama* as a traditional mechanism of dispute-settlement.
5. This material was collected when I visited all *myethya* in Nzambani location while accompanying the Chief and the Location Development Committee on a location tour.
6. This is an 'arena council' – Bailey's useful term (1965). See also Richards and Kuper 1971 for discussion of councils and committees.
7. Marwick 1964.
8. S.F.Moore (1972) discusses this in a legal context in different societies.
9. The dances were described as 'acrobatic' because at certain stages they involved dramatic leaps, aerial somersaults, whirls and cartwheels by the men.
10. Kavyu, 1977.
11. The musical analysis is taken from Kavyu, 1977.
12. Mutiso, 1977c.
13. Mutiso (1977a) describes an unusual situation where a prominent politician in Machakos formed a district-wide political organization in 1961 based on 'clans of daughters' (*mbai sya eitu*, i.e. women from the same natal clan). Formed mainly from among women who were not educated (though probably including many Christians), its organization was reinforced by the use of traditional ritual elements. One of its functions was to collect money for self-help projects, but Mutiso estimated that 90 per cent of the money collected was appropriated by the organization officials (who were all women). It was banned in 1970 when the administration decided to act on complaints about the forcible extraction and misuse of Harambee funds and the political tensions it had generated.

6: The Harambee Schools Movement

1. Anderson, 1970, 1977; Keller, 1975.
2. Anderson, 1966.
3. Table 16 gives figures for unaided secondary schools in Kenya – the precise figures of Harambee schools in 1973 and 1974 were not available, but a reasonable estimate was about 470 in 1973 and about 500 in 1974.
4. Information was gained through visiting all the Harambee schools and some of the former Harambee schools in Kitui. On most of these visits I interviewed the school head, some teachers and members of the school committee, and in most cases I talked to a class of students and administered a questionnaire to them.
5. Kitui District Development plan, 1974–8. In fact during 1974–8 the government took over two Harambee schools (Kimangao and Mutomo), nine new Harambee schools were opened (including four in 1974), and six private secondary schools were opened in urban areas. The 1979–83 district development plan proposed a further forty Harambee schools.
6. Anderson, 1970.
7. See Chapter 5.
8. One might distinguish this from money or services demanded or given for personal benefit. However, Harambee contributions were also a political investment and thus contained potential personal benefit as well as being put to good community use.
9. Information was obtained from questionnaires distributed to higher forms in each school government and Harambee school which I visited and completed by students in my presence. A more detailed survey of student attitudes and opinions was conducted in Nzambani Harambee School. For other material on Harambee student attitudes see Keller, 1974; and for comparison to government schools, Prewitt, 1967.
10. See discussion in Kinyanjui and Shepherd, 1972; also Court and Ghai, 1974; Keller, 1975; Sheffield, 1967.
11. The school was five kilometres from the village where I lived, and I visited it regularly. I taught part-time there for some months and also attended Harambee committee meetings and frequently met the chief to discuss the school's progress and problems.

7: Analysis and Conclusion

1. The figures are from Tables 4, 10 and 11.
2. Sahlins, 1965. MacCormack (1976), in a terminological discussion of reciprocity, points out the different and often imprecise ways in which the term reciprocity has been used. It is used here in the restricted sense of

Sahlins's typology, because this was particularly useful and appropriate to the empirical situation at hand.

3. Sahlins, 1965.

4. Cf. Bloch, 1973.

5. This uses a term developed for other purposes by Barth, 1967.

6. This represents the 'transactional analysis' framework developed in social anthropology particularly by Barth (1966).

7. This useful term is found in Wallman, 1974.

8. Bray and Lillis, 1988.

9. This often applies to social anthropologists too. There have been few other pieces of research similar to Mayer's (1951), although O'Brien (1970) is an interesting similar study. Apthorpe (1961) contains little reference to research on adapting traditional community co-operation institutions to modern community development. He points out the problem, which he had come across in Northern Rhodesia (now Zambia), that some societies lack institutions of labour co-operation as a basis for community development work. Grillo and Rew (1985) refer to the role of (established) anthropologists in acting as consultants to development projects, but omit to mention the part they could play in self-help movements.

10. Mayer, 1951.

11. For example Mbithi and Rasmussen, 1977; B.P. Thomas, 1987; Bray and Lillis, 1988.

12. The first part of this definition of development follows Chambers, 1983. The rights referred to in the second part derive from the Universal Declaration of Human Rights and the subsequent international instruments which focused on certain aspects of human rights, in particular the International Covenant of Social, Cultural and Economic Rights and the International Covenant on Civil and Political Rights, both of which the government of Kenya ratified in 1972 and which came into effect in 1977. The 'right to development' is asserted in the UN Declaration on the Right to Development, adopted by the UN General Assembly in 1986. Women's rights are also concerned. One important development question to which no clear answer can be given from this research is the extent to which the Harambee movement has improved the status and development opportunities of women, who comprised the majority of participants in self-help work as a result of male urban labour-migration. The important women's self-help groups found in more developed parts of Kenya had not yet been formed in Nzambani in 1974.

13. The ILO report on Kenya (1972) was intended to provide a development blueprint for Kenya, but it was not expected to be implemented to any great extent because its stress on redistribution from growth, rather than economic growth itself, ran counter to the government's political and economic objectives.

14. B.P. Thomas, 1985.

15. Hodge, 1970. See also Biddle and Biddle, 1965; UK Central Office of Information, 1966; Batten, 1967; Brokensha and Hodge, 1969; Prosser, 1969.

16. It is not intended to assert here that government extension and rural animation are 'inferior' to community development or without value, but it is important to distinguish these forms of 'directive' development from community development, particularly when analysing self-help organization.

17. Batten, 1957.

18. Brokensha and Hodge, 1969.

19. Holmquist (1984) notes the 'half way' nature of the Harambee movement in its political sense, but this is typical of any community development activity which arises from people's felt needs but within an overall governmental framework. Community development theorists do not usually advocate projects being completely client-centred irrespective of any central planning or other considerations.

20. For an interesting study of the work of community development officials in post-Independence Kenya, see Lamb, 1977. Oyugi (1973) and Leonard (1973) discuss rural administration in general, and there are useful studies of rural development in Heyer, Ireri and Moris (1971) and Hyden, Jackson and Okumu (1970).

21. Definition from the *Shorter Oxford English Dictionary*.

22. Bray and Lillis, 1988.

23. Interesting political science analysis of the Harambee movement is found in the work of Mutiso and Holmquist in particular (Mutiso, 1975, 1977a; Holmquist, 1979, 1984). For general political analysis of post-Independence Kenya, see Gertzel, 1970; Leys, 1975; Barkan and Okumu, 1979, which touch briefly on the relation between the Harambee movement and major political trends.

24. Colebatch, nd; Holmquist, 1979, 1984; Mutiso, 1975. Mutiso (1977a) describes an extreme example, probably unique in Kenya, of deliberate political manipulation of Harambee for electoral purposes.

25. Mutiso, 1975; Holmquist, 1984. These are more realistic and empirically based than Frank's (1975) dismissal of applied anthropology as neo-colonialism and of community development as designed to integrate traditional communities more efficiently into the class exploitation system. Stavenhagen (1973) sees community development in general as a 'conservative' policy protecting existing power structures. In the same Marxist framework, Stamp (1986) assesses the achievements of women's self-help groups in central Kenya as a positive 'resistance to exploitation' by the state, the bourgeoisie, and men.

26. B.P. Thomas, 1987, in particular.

27. In Kiambu district in central Kenya in 1974, for example, a piped-water project was being proposed, with each family paying three instalments of 500 shs – a sum far beyond the capacity of Kitui people.

28. Many school places in nomadic areas were reportedly taken up by urban children or children of agricultural settlers.
29. Bray and Lillis, 1988.
30. See note 12 above.
31. I am grateful to Anders Narman of the University of Goteborg, Sweden, for brief information on these later developments regarding Harambee schools in Kitui.
32. Cited in Bray and Lillis, 1988.
33. Kitui District Development Plan, 1979–83.
34. Hill, 1974.
35. Ibid.
36. President Moi launched a new slogan for his rule, *Nyayo* ('Footsteps'), which was evidently intended to mean (i) that he was following in President Kenyatta's footsteps and policies and thus expected to be accorded the legitimacy that this continuity would convey; and (ii) that Kenyans should similarly follow in his footsteps and support him.
37. Amnesty International, 1987.
38. In 1983 the government changed the educational structure from the previous 7-6-3 system (i.e. 7 years' primary, 6 years' secondary and 3 years' tertiary education, as sct out in Table 18) to an 8-4-4 system (8 years' primary, 4 years' secondary, 4 years' tertiary). The change was apparently decided with little forewarning or planning, and entailed major disruptions to educational institutions at all levels, as well as causing some political protest. It initially led to the doubling-up of classes and a huge new building programme for primary schools. Whether it would affect the four-year Harambee schools much in the long term was unclear.

Bibliography

Abrahams, R.G., 1965, 'Neighbourhood organization – a major sub-system amongst the Nyamwezi', *Africa*, 35,1.

Abreu, S., 1982, *The Role of Self-Help in the Development of Education in Kenya, 1900–1973*. Nairobi: KLB.

Akong'a, J., 1988, 'Drought and famine management in Kitui district, Kenya', in Brokensha and Little, 1988.

Ambler, C., 1988, *Kenyan Communities in the Age of Imperialism: The Central Region in the Late Nineteenth Century*. New Haven: Yale University Press.

Ames, D.W., 1959, 'Wolof co-operative work groups', in Bascom and Herskovits, 1959.

Amnesty International, 1987, *Kenya: Torture, Political Detentions and Unfair Trials*. London: Amnesty International.

Anderson, J., 1966, 'Report on the conference of Harambee school headmasters', IDS, Nairobi.

—— 1970, *The Struggle for the School*. London: Longman.

—— 1977, 'Self-help and independency, the political implications of a continuing tradition in African education in Kenya', *African Affairs*.

Apthorpe, R. (ed.), 1961, 'Social research and community development', Rhodes-Livingstone Institute Conference papers, Lusaka.

Askwith, T.G., 1958, *Kenya's Progress* (2nd edn). Nairobi: EALB.

—— 1960, *Progress through Self-Help*. Nairobi: EALB.

Bailey, F.G., 1965, 'Decisions by consensus in councils and committees: with special reference to village and local government in India', in Banton, 1965b.

Banton, M. (ed.), 1965a, *The Relevance of Models for Social Anthropology* (ASA vol. 1). London: Tavistock.

—— 1965b, *Political Systems and the Distribution of Power* (ASA vol. 2). London: Tavistock.

Barkan, J.D. and Okumu, J.J. (eds), 1979, *Politics and Public Policy in Kenya and Tanzania*. New York: Praeger.

Barth, F., 1966, *Models of Social Organization*. London: RAI.

—— 1967, 'Economic spheres in Darfur', in Firth, 1967.

Bascom, W.R. and Herskovits, M.J. (eds), 1959, *Continuity and Change in African Cultures*. Chicago: Chicago University Press.

Batten, T.R., 1957, *Communities and their Development*. London: OUP.

—— 1967, *The Non-Directive Approach to Community Development*. London: OUP.

Bernstein, H.L. (ed.), 1973, *Development and Underdevelopment*. London: Penguin.

Biddle, W.W. and Biddle, L.J., 1965, *The Community Development Process*. New York: Holt, Reinehart & Winston.

Bloch, M., 1973, 'The long-term and the short-term: the economic and political significance of the morality of kinship', in Goody, 1973.

Bohannan, P. and Dalton, G. (eds), 1962, *Markets in Africa*. Evanston: Northwestern University Press.

Bolnick, B.R., 1974, 'Comparative Harambee: history, and theory of voluntary collective behaviour', IDS, Nairobi.

Boninger, J., 1956, 'New ways of living for the Kamba tribesmen', *Community Development Bulletin*, 7, 2.

Bray, M. and Lillis, K. (eds), 1988, *Community Financing of Education: Issues and Policy Implications in Less Developed Countries*. Oxford: Pergamon.

Brett, E.A., 1973, *Colonialism and Underdevelopment in East Africa: The Politics of Economic Change, 1919–1939*. London: Heinemann.

Brokensha, D., 1966, *Applied Anthropology in English-speaking Africa*. Kentucky: University of Kentucky.

Brokensha, D. and Erasmus, C.J., 1969, 'African peasants and community development', in Brokensha and Pearsall, 1969.

Brokensha, D. and Hodge, P. (eds), 1969, *Community Development: An Interpretation*. San Francisco: Chandler.

Brokensha, D. and Little, P. (eds), 1988, *Anthropology of Development and Change in East Africa*. Boulder: Westview.

Brokensha, D. and Nellis, J., 1974, 'Administration in Kenya – a study of the rural division of Mbere, part 1 – the District Officer, the chief and the subchiefs in the 1970s', JAA, 4.

Brokensha, D. and Pearsall, M. (eds), 1969, *The Anthropology of Development in Sub-Saharan Africa*. Lexington: Society of Applied Anthropologists.

Carson, J.B., 1958, *The Life Story of a Kenyan Chief: The Life of Chief Kasina Ndoo*. Nairobi: Evans.

Chambers, R., 1983, *Rural Development: Putting the Last First*. London: Longman.

Charsley, S., 1976, 'The *silika* – a co-operative labour institution', *Africa*, 46, 1.

Cliffe, L., 1970, 'Nationalism and the reaction to enforced agricultural change in colonial Tanzania', *Taamuli*, Dar es Salaam.

Cliffe, L., Coleman, J.S. and Doornbos, M.R. (eds), 1977, *Government and Rural Development in East Africa: Essays on Political Penetration*. The Hague: Nijhoff.

Cochrane, G., 1971, *Development Anthropology*. London: OUP.

Cohen, A., 1959, *British Policy in Changing Africa*. London: Routledge & Kegan Paul.

Colebatch, H., nd, 'Rural services and self-help', IDS, Nairobi.

Court, D. and Ghai, D.P. (eds), 1974, *Education, Society and Development: New Perspectives from Kenya*. Nairobi: OUP.

Creech Jones, A., 1949, 'The place of African local administration in colonial policy', JAA, 1, 1.

Davis, J. (ed.), 1974, *Choice and Change: Essays in Honour of Lucy Mair*. London: Athlone.

Donham, D., 1985, *Work and Power in Maale, Ethiopa*. Ann Arbor: University of Michigan Press.

Edgerton, R.B., 1971, *The Individual in Cultural Adaptation: A Study of Four East African Peoples*. Berkeley: University of California Press.

Erasmus, C.J., 1956, 'Culture, structure and process: the occurrence and disappearance of reciprocal farm labour', SWJA, 12, 4.

—— 1977, *In Search of the Common Good: Utopian Experiments, Past and Future*. New York: Free Press.

Feldman, R., 1984, 'Women's groups and women's subordination: an analysis of policies towards rural women in Kenya', ROAPE, 27.

Firth, R., 1965, *A Primitive Polynesian Economy* (2nd edn). London: Routledge & Kegan Paul.

—— (ed.) 1967. *Themes in economic anthropology* (ASA vol. 6). London: Tavistock.

Fjellman, S.M., 1971, 'The organization of diversity: a study of Akamba kinship', PhD thesis, Stanford.

Frank, A.G., 1975, 'Anthropology = Ideology, Applied Anthropology = Politics', *Race and Class*.

Gertzel, C., 1970, *The Politics of Independent Kenya, 1963–1968*. Nairobi: EAPH.

Glazier, J., 1985, *Land and the Use of Tradition among the Mbeere of Kenya*. Lanham: University of America Press.

Gluckman, M. (ed.), 1972, *The Allocation of Responsibility*. Manchester: Manchester University Press.

Godfrey, E.M. and Mutiso, G.C.M., 1974, 'The political economy of self-help: Kenya's Harambee institutes of technology', in Court and Ghai, 1974.

Goody, J.R. (ed.), 1973, *The Character of Kinship*. Cambridge: CUP.

Gray, R. and Birmingham, D. (eds), 1970, *Precolonial African Trade: Essays on Tradition in Central and Eastern Africa before 1900*. London: OUP.

Grillo, R. and Rew, A. (eds), 1985, *Social Anthropology and Development Policy*. (ASA vol. 23). London: Tavistock.

Gulliver, P.H., 1974, *Neighbours and Networks: The Idiom of Kinship in Social Action among the Ndendeuli of Tanzania*. Berkeley: University of California Press.

Heyer, J., Ireri, D. and Moris, J., 1971, *Rural Development in Kenya*. Nairobi: EAPH.

Hill, M.J.D., 1974, 'Self-help in education and development: a social anthropological study in Kitui, Kenya', BER, Nairobi.

—— 1975, 'The roots of Harambee', *New Society*, 15 December.

—— 1990, 'The Harambee self-help movement in Kenya: a social anthropological study among the Kamba of Kitui district', PhD thesis, University of London.

Hodge, P., 1970, 'The future of community development', in Robson and Crick, 1970.

Holden, M. (ed.), 1975, *Yearbook of Politics and Public Policy*. Beverley Hills: Sage.

Holmquist, F., 1970, 'Implementing rural development projects', in Hyden, Jackson and Okumu, 1970.

—— 1972, 'Towards a political theory of rural self-help development in Africa', *Rural Africana*.

—— 1979, 'Class structure, peasant participation and rural self-help', in Barkan and Okumu, 1979.

—— 1984, 'Self-help: the state and peasant leverage in Kenya', *Africa*, 54, 3.

Holy, L., 1970, *Neighbours and Kinsmen: A Study of the Berti People of Darfur*. London: Hurst.

Huxley, E., 1960, *A New Earth: An Experiment in Colonialism*. London: Chatto & Windus.

Hyden, G., Jackson, R. and Okumu, J. (eds), 1970, *Development Administration: The Kenyan Experience*. Nairobi: OUP.

International Labour Organization, 1972, *Employment, Incomes and Equality in Kenya: A Strategy for Increasing Productive Employment in Kenya*. Geneva: ILO.

Jackson, K., 1970, 'Gerhard Lindblom and the first treatment of the Akamba clans', in Ogot, 1970.

—— 1972, 'An ethno-historical study of the oral traditions of the Akamba of Kenya', PhD thesis, University of California.

Jolly, R. (ed.), 1969, *Education in Africa: Research and Action*. Nairobi: EAPH.

Kavyu, P.N., 1977, *An Introduction to Kamba Music*. Nairobi: EALB.

Keller, E.R., 1974, 'Education as an agent of national development in Kenya: does schooling really make a difference?' Conference of Black Political Scientists, Georgia, USA.

—— 1975, 'The role of self-help schools in education for development: the Harambee movement in Kenya', in Holden, 1975.

Kenya Government, 1960, *The Work of an African Chief in Kenya* (2nd edn). Nairobi: EALB.

—— Various official publications, mostly published by the Government Printer, including:
  – Ministry of Education Annual Reports
  – Kitui District Development Plans (Provincial Planning Office, Eastern

Province)
- Kenya Population Census (Statistical division, Ministry of Finance & Economic Planning)
- Survey of Kenya maps
- Statistical Abstracts
- Self-Help Statistics (Community Development Division, Department of Social Services, Ministry of Housing & Social Services).

Kenya National Archives (KNA): Various government documents and other material, including records of the Kitui District Commissioner (DC/KTI), Annual District Reports, Handing-Over Reports.

Kenyatta, J., 1964, *Harambee! Jomo Kenyatta, the Prime Minister of Kenya, Speaks, 1963–1964*. Nairobi: OUP.

Kimambo, I.N., 1970, 'The economic history of the Kamba, 1850–1950', in Ogot, 1970.

Kimilu, D.N., 1962, *Mukamba wa wo*. Nairobi: EALB.

Kinyanjui, J. and Shepherd, P., 1972, 'Unemployment among secondary school-leavers in Kenya', EAJ, Nairobi.

Krapf, J.L., 1860, *Travels, Researches and Missionary Labours in Eastern Africa*. London: Trubner.

Lamb, G., 1977, *Peasant Politics: Conflict and Development in Murang'a* (2nd edn). London: Friedman.

Lambert, H.E., 1947, 'Land tenure among the Akamba', *African Studies*, 6.

Lamphear, J., 1970, 'The Kamba and the northern Mrima Coast', in Gray and Birmingham, 1970.

Leach, E.R., 1961, *Pul Eliya, a Village in Ceylon*. Cambridge: CUP.

Leonard, D.K., (ed.), 1973, *Rural Administration in Kenya*. Nairobi: EALB.

Lewis, I.M., 1971, *Ecstatic Religion*. London: Penguin.

Leys, C., 1975, *Underdevelopment in Kenya, 1964–1971*. Nairobi: Heinemann.

Lindblom, G., 1969, *The Akamba in British East Africa, an Ethnological Monograph* (2nd edn, enlarged). New York: Negro Universities Press (originally published by Lundell for Archives d'Etudes Orientales, Uppsala, 1920).

Little, K., 1949, 'The organization of communal farms in the Gambia', JAA, 2.

Loizos, P., 1977. 'Anthropological research in British colonies: some personal accounts', *Anthropological Forum*, 4,2, Perth.

Long, N., 1977, *An Introduction to the Sociology of Rural Development*. London: Tavistock.

MacCormack, G., 1976, 'Reciprocity', *Man*, 11,1.

McHenry, D., 1973, 'The utility of compulsion in the implementation of agricultural policies: a case-study from Tanzania', CJAS, 7.2.

McIntosh, B.G. (ed.), 1972, *Ngano: Studies in Traditional and Modern East African History*. Nairobi: EAPH.

Maher, C., 1937, 'Soil erosion and land utilization in the Ukamba (Kitui) Reserve', Kenya Colony and Protectorate, mimeo.

Mair, L., 1936, *Native Policies in Africa*. London: Routledge & Kegan Paul.

Manners, R.A., 1962, 'Land use, labour and the growth of market economy in Kipsigis country', in Bohannan and Dalton, 1962.

Marwick, M. (ed.), 1964, *Witchcraft and Sorcery*. London: Penguin.

Mayer, P., 1951, 'Agricultural co-operation by neighbourhood groups among the Gusii in South Nyanza', in Mayer, P., *Two Studies in Applied Anthropology in Kenya*. London: HMSO.

—— (ed.), 1970, *Socialization: the Approach from Social Anthropology* (ASA vol. 8). London: Tavistock.

Mbathi, T.K.B., 1958, 'The Jeanes school camp', *Community Development Bulletin*, 1, 2.

Mbithi, P.M., 1972, 'Harambee self-help: the Kenyan approach', *African Review*, Nairobi.

Mbithi, P.M. and Rasmussen, R., 1977, *Self-reliance in Kenya: The Case of Harambee*. Uppsala: SIAS.

Middleton, J. and Kershaw, G., 1972, *The Kikuyu and Kamba of Kenya* (2nd edn with supplementary bibliography). London: IAI.

Moore, M.P., 1975, 'Co-operative labour in peasant agriculture', *Journal of Peasant Studies*, 2.

Moore, S.F., 1972, 'Legal liability and evolutionary interpretation: some aspects of strict liability, self-help and collective responsibility', in Gluckman, 1972.

Munro, J.F., 1975, *Colonial Rule and the Kamba: Social Change in the Kenya Highlands, 1889–1939*. London: OUP.

Mutiso, G.C.M., 1975, *Kenya: Politics, Policy and Society*. Nairobi: EALB.

—— 1977a, 'A low-status group in centre–periphery relations: *mbai sya eitu*', in Cliffe, Coleman and Doornbos, 1977.

—— 1977b, 'Creation of the Kitui *asomi*', IDS, Nairobi.

—— 1977c, 'Kanduti: a case study', IDS, Nairobi.

Mwaniki N., 1986, 'Against many odds: the dilemmas of women's self-help groups in Mbeere, Kenya', *Africa*, 56,2.

Ndeti, K., 1973, *Elements of Akamba Life*. Nairobi: EAPH.

Ndungu, J.B., 1972, 'Gituamba and Kikuyu independency in church and school', in McIntosh, 1972.

Newman, J., 1974, *The Ukamba Members' Association*. Dar es Salaam: TPH.

Nottingham, J., 1959, 'Sorcery among the Akamba in Kenya', JAA, 11.

O'Brien, C.C., 1970, 'Co-operators and bureaucrats – Senegalese peasants', *Africa*, 41,4.

O'Connor, E., 1974, 'Contrasts in educational development in Kenya and Tanzania', *African Affairs*, 73.

O'Leary, M., 1983, 'Population, economy and domestic groups: the Kitui case', *Africa*, 53,1.

—— 1984, *The Kitui Akamba: Economic and Social Change in Semi-Arid Kenya*. Nairobi: Heinemann.

O'Neill, B.J., 1987, *Social Inequality in a Portuguese Hamlet*. Cambridge: CUP.

Odak, O., 1973, 'A trip to some archaeological sites in Kitui district', Institute of African Studies, Nairobi.

Ogot, B. (ed.), 1970, *Hadith II*. Nairobi: EAPH.

Oliver, S.C., 1965, 'Individuality, freedom of choice and cultural flexibility of the Kamba', *American Anthropologist*, 67.

Ortiz, S.R. de, 1965, *Uncertainties in Peasant Farming: A Colombian Case*. London: Athlone.

Oyugi, W.O., 1973, 'Participation in rural development planning at local level', in Leonard, 1973.

Penwill, D., 1951, *Kamba Customary Law*. London: Macmillan.

Prewitt, K. (ed.), 1967, *Education and Political Values: An East African Case Study*. Nairobi: EAPH.

Prosser, A., 1969, 'Community development and its relation to development', JAA, 8,3.

Ranger, T.O., 1965, 'African attempts to control education in East and Central Africa 1900–1939', *Past and Present*, 32.

Richards, A. and Kuper, A. (eds), 1971, *Councils in Action*. Cambridge: CUP.

Riley, B. and Brokensha, D., 1988, *The Mbeere in Kenya, vol. 1: Changing Rural Ecology*. Lanham: University of America Press.

Robertson, C. and Berger, I. (eds), 1986, *Women and Class in Africa*. New York: Holmes & Meier.

Robson, W.A. and Crick, B. (eds), 1970, *The Future of the Social Sciences*. London: Penguin.

Sahlins, M., 1965, 'On the sociology of primitive exchange', in Banton, 1965a.

Savage, D.C. and Munro, J.F., 1966, 'Carrier Corps recruitment in the British East African Protectorate, 1914–1918', JAH, 7,2.

Sheffield, J.R. (ed.), 1967, *Education, Employment and Rural Development*. Nairobi: EAPH.

Spencer, P. (ed.), 1985, *Society and the Dance*. Cambridge: CUP.

Stamp, P., 1986, 'Kikuyu women's self-help groups', in Robertson and Berger, 1986.

Stanner, W.E.H., 1940, 'The Kitui Kamba: a critical study of British colonial administration in East Africa', unpublished manuscript, KNA.

—— 1949, 'The colonial dilemma', *The Listener*, 11 August.

—— 1969, 'The Kitui Kamba market, 1938–9, *Ethnology*, 8,2.

Stavenhagen, R., 1973, 'The changing function of community in underdeveloped countries', in Bernstein, 1973.

Swindell, K., 1985, *Farm Labour*. Cambridge: CUP.

Thomas, A., 1969, 'Community adaptation in health services in Machakos', IDS, Nairobi.

Thomas, B.P., 1985, *Politics, Participation and Poverty: Development Through Self-Help in Kenya*. Boulder: Westview.

—— 1987, 'Development through Harambee: who wins and who loses? Rural self-help projects in Kenya', *World Development*, 15,4.

—— 1988, 'Household strategies for adaptation and change: participation in Kenyan rural women's associations', *Africa*, 58,4.

Tignor, R.L., 1971, 'Colonial chiefs in chiefless societies', JMAS.

—— 1976, *The Colonial Transformation of Kenya: The Kamba, Kikuyu and Masai from 1900 to 1939*. Princeton: Princeton University Press.

Ueda, H., 1971, 'Witchcraft and sorcery in Kitui', IDS, Nairobi.

United Kingdom Central Office of Information, 1966, *Community Development, Britain and the Developing Countries*. London: HMSO.

United Kingdom Colonial Office, 1954, *Social Development in the British Colonial Territories: Report of the Ashridge Conference on Social Development*. London: HMSO.

Wallman, S., 1974, 'Status and the innovator', in Davis, 1974.

—— (ed.) 1977, *Perceptions of Development*. Cambridge: CUP.

Wolff, R.D., 1974, *Britain and Kenya, 1870–1930: The Economics of Colonialism*. Dar es Salaam: Transafrican Publishers.

Index